WORLD RAILWAYS

WORLD RAILWAYS

AN ILLUSTRATED HISTORY OF THE IRON HORSE

JOHN WESTWOOD

GRAMERCY BOOKS

NEW YORK

This 2001 edition is published by Gramercy Books™, an imprint of Random House Value Publishing, Inc., 280 Park Avenue, New York, NY 10017, by arrangement with PRC Publishing Ltd, Kiln House, 210 New Kings Road, London, SW6 4NZ.

Gramercy Books™ and design are trademarks of Random House Value Publishing, Inc.

Random House
New York • Toronto • London
• Sydney • Auckland
http://www.randomhouse.com/

Printed and bound in China

A CIP catalogue record for this book is available from the Library of Congress.

ISBN 0-517-16389-6

8 7 6 5 4 3 2 1

Previous page: **US and Canadian locomotives awaiting restoration at the Steamtown railroad museum in Scranton, Pennsylvania.**

Abbreviations

ac	Alternating current
Alco	American Locomotive Co
APT	Advanced Passenger Train
ARTC	Australian Rail Track Corporation
B&O	Baltimore & Ohio Railroad
BEF	British Expeditionary Force
BNSF	Burlington North Santa Fe Railroad
BR	British Railways/British Rail
C&O	Chesapeake & Ohio Railroad
CER	Chinese Eastern Railway
CIE	Coras Iompair Éireann (Ireland)
CNR	Canadian National
CP	Caminhos de Ferro Portugueses (Portugal)
CPR	Canadian Pacific
D&RGWR	Denver & Rio Grande Western Railroad
DB	Deutches (Bundes)Bahn (Germany)
dc	Direct current
DR	Deutches Reichsbahn (Germany)
DSB	Dankse Statsbaner (Denmark)
FEC	Florida East Coast Railroad
FGW	First Great Western
FS	Ente Ferrovie dello Stato (Italy)
IE	Iarnród Éireann (Ireland)
GE	General Electric Co (USA)
GJR	Grand Junction Railway
GM	General Motors
GN	Great Northern
GNER	Great North Eastern Railway
GWR	Great Western Railway
HST	High-Speed Train
ICC	Interstate Commerce Committee
JNR	Japanese National Railways
KNR	Korean National Railroad
KP	Kansas Pacific
L&MR	Liverpool & Manchester Railway
L&YR	Lancashire & Yorkshire Railway
LMSR	London, Midland & Scottish Railway
LNER	London & North Eastern Railway
LNWR	London & North Western Railway
LRC	"Light, Rapid, Comfortable"
LSWR	London & South Western Railway
M&HR	Mohawk & Hudson Railroad
MML	Midland Main Line
MR	Midland Railway
N&W	Northern & Western Railroad
NP	Northern Pacific
NR	National Rail
RDC	Rail Diesel Car
REC	Railway Executive Committee
Res	Rail express systems
S&DR	Stockton & Darlington Railway
SJ	Statens Järnvägar (Sweden)
SMR	South Manchuria Railway
SNCF	Société Nationale des Chemins de Fer Français (France)
SR	Southern Railway
SRA	State Rail Authority
TEE	Trans-Europ Express
TOC	Train Operating Company
TOFC	Trailer on Flat Car
TGV	Train à Grande Vitesse
UP	Union Pacific
USRA	United States Railroad Administration
USTC	United States Transportation Corps

CONTENTS

PART 1 THE EARLY YEARS

1   The First Steam Railways   8
2   Early Intercity Lines   12
3   Private Enterprise Takes Charge 16
4   The Networks Evolve   18
5   The Iron Road   20
6   Forward from the *Rocket*   22
7   The Early Trains   24
8   The Railroad at War   28
9   Locomotive Development
     1850-1875   30

PART 2 THE GOLDEN AGE: 1876-1914

10   Worldwide Expansion   36
11   The Gauge Connection   42
12   Unscrupulous Operators   46
13   Battle of the Brakes   48
14   Luxury on the Line   52
15   Train Services   58
16   The Transcontinentals   62
17   The Narrow-gauge Railway   64
18   Improving the Locomotive   70
19   Railroad Electrification   78

PART 3 FEELING THE STRAIN 1914-1945

20   World War I   82
21   Postwar Upheaval   86

22   The Streamliners   88
23   Train Services   96
24   Steam Locomotive Development   100
25   Unorthodox Steam Power   116
26   The Locomotive Exported   120
27   The Inter-war Electrifications 124
28   The Coming of the Diesel   130
29   The Lines Behind the Lines   136

**PART 4 NEW DIRECTIONS:
1945 TO THE END OF THE CENTURY**

30   Reorganization and
     Modernization   142
31   Triumph of the Diesel   144
32   Postwar Electrification   154
33   Survival of Steam   158
34   The Passenger Train:
     Crisis and Survival   174
35   International and
     High-speed Trains   186
36   Piggyback, Kangaroos and MGR   192
37   Success on Shortlines   196
38   Preserving the Railroad   200

**PART 5 RAILWAYS ENTER THE
21st CENTURY**

39   General   212
40   British Railways:
     Boom and Crash   214
41   Continental Europe   222
42   The Former Soviet Bloc   230
43   The Americas   234
44   Australasia   242
45   Africa and Asia   244

     Index   254

PART ONE

THE EARLY YEARS

Left: A large US passenger depot. This sketch shows departure time at Chicago, which by the 1860s was becoming America's biggest railroad interchange.

1
THE FIRST STEAM RAILWAYS

It would be wrong to describe northeastern England as the birthplace of the railroad, for its two essential components — the railed way and the mechanical traction running over it — first appeared elsewhere. Wooden railroads were used for horse traction in European mines at least as early as the 16th century. In North America an early railroad appeared in the 18th century; a short cable-operated line was built by British troops at Lewistown, New York, to move supplies uphill from the Niagara River to their base. Early in the next century, the three-mile Granite Railway was built at Charlestown in Massachusetts, and this had an iron strip that formed a running surface on top of the rails made of wood.

The first successful steam railroad locomotive was the Cornishman Richard Trevithick's 1804 creation, which ran on an iron plateway in South Wales. It was also in South Wales that the first regular movement of railway passengers took place; over the horse-operated line between Swansea and Mumbles in 1807.

All the same, if northeastern England cannot claim to be the birthplace of railways, it can be described as their cradle. For it was here that lines built variously of wood

and of iron, of rails or L-shaped plates, linking mine with wharf, gradually progressed to a point where steam traction became not only practical, but also greatly preferred.

At the Middleton Colliery Railway, near Leeds in Yorkshire, John Blenkinsop introduced two steam locomotives in 1811 whose cylinders drove pinion wheels that engaged in projections cast on the side of one rail. They could pull 150 tons at 3mph, and among the many mechanics who came to view them was George Stephenson, who was an enginewright at Killingworth Colliery near Newcastle-upon-Tyne in northeast England.

Not far from Killingworth, at Wylam, William Hedley proved that iron wheels could grip iron rails without resorting to cogs and pinions. Hedley's locomotive was also scrutinised by Stephenson, who built his own steam locomotive in 1814, which was very similar to Blenkinsop's but without the cogs. It could pull 50 tons at 3mph, replaced 20 horses, and was soon joined by other engines of similar type.

The Hetton Colliery Railway, opened in 1822, was not only powered by Stephenson's locomotives but was also surveyed and constructed by him. When it was decided to build a far more ambitious 25-mile railway from the river at Stockton to the collieries around Darlington, Stephenson's reputation gained him appointment as the new railway's engineer. The Stockton & Darlington Railway (S&DR), although essentially a long colliery line, also carried miscellaneous freight and passenger traffic in scheduled services, making it the genuine precursor of the modern public, or common-carrier, railway.

The S&DR was laid with two types of track because the directors had been unable to choose between cast iron and wrought iron. All the rails were of the fish-bellied type,

Below: **One of the later designs by the Norris Brothers of Philadelphia, a 4-4-0 supplied to the Syracuse & Utica RR in 1851.**

Left: **The first locomotive to run in New York State was the *De Witt Clinton* of the Mohawk & Hudson RR, in 1831. This is a working replica, built for the Chicago World Exposition of 1893.**

deeper in the middle than at the ends, and were seated in cast-iron chairs. The chairs were pinned to wooden blocks cut from the oak timbers of warships made redundant by the ending of the Napoleonic Wars, although, at the Darlington end, blocks made of stone were used.

Stationary engines drew the trains by cable up two inclines, but steam locomotives were used for freight trains on the long level section. These were built at a new locomotive works which Stephenson and his son Robert had established at Newcastle. The first of the initial four, *Locomotion No 1*, hauled the long inaugural train on 27 September 1825. Carrying over 500 passengers instead of the expected 300, and incurring only two brief breakdowns and the amputation of a brakeman's leg en route, *Locomotion No 1* reached 15mph on two downhill stretches.

The Stephenson firm, Robert Stephenson & Co, soon developed a healthy locomotive-building business, founded on its success with the S&DR. Among its early exports was *America*, a four-wheel locomotive built for the Delaware & Hudson Canal Co, which needed steam railroads for its

coal mines in Pennsylvania. Together with *Stourbridge Lion*, built by another British company, *America* arrived in the USA in January 1829 but seems to have remained unused. *Stourbridge Lion*, on the other hand, made a spectacular trial trip but was too heavy for the flimsy track and saw no further service. Although a small steam locomotive built by John Stevens had already circulated on an oval trial track at Hoboken, New Jersey, *Stourbridge Lion* was the first full-scale locomotive to run on a US railroad.

Whereas *Stourbridge Lion* slightly improved upon Hedley's second colliery engine, *Puffing Billy*, *America* was a development of the more modern *Locomotion No 1*. Locomotive design progressed rapidly in the late 1820s. Timothy Hackworth, superintendent of the S&DR locomotive stock, developed the blastpipe, which passed exhaust steam up the chimney in such a way as to provide a draught for the fire. The Stephensons introduced the six-wheel locomotive with their *Experiment*, built for S&DR freight service, and with their *Lancashire Witch* they brought the cylinders down, inclining them at 45°; this reduced the

Left: ***Pioneer*, built in 1836, became in 1848 the first locomotive to steam out of Chicago. It is the oldest surviving Baldwin-built locomotive.**

Above: **The B&O's *Andrew Jackson* of 1836, rebuilt to look like the *Atlantic* of 1832, is shown hauling the distinctive B&O "Imlay" passenger carriages.**

Right: **An early (1830) Stephenson locomotive, the *Invicta* of the Canterbury & Whitstable Railway.**

Right: **A 16th century mine tramway wagon from Central Europe.**

Below: **A scene on the Mohawk & Hudson Railroad. The passenger carriages resemble highway coaches on flanged wheels.**

damaging up-and-down thrust experienced by the previous vertical-cylinder designs, and also made springing of both axles into a practical proposition.

Meanwhile George Stephenson had been appointed consulting engineer to the Liverpool & Manchester Railway (L&MR), whose directors could not decide whether to use locomotive or cable traction. To help them reach a decision, the pro-locomotive faction suggested a locomotive competition over a portion of completed track at Rainhill. This took place with the enormous publicity that the British traditionally accord any unusual sporting event. There were three serious competitors. Stephenson entered his famous *Rocket*, which was a "Lancashire Witch" type with its connecting rods removed (that is, it was a 2-2-0 rather than an 0-4-0). It was also noteworthy for its multi-tubular boiler; instead of passing the smoke and hot gas from the fire through a wide flue and up the chimney, Stephenson provided 25 three-inch copper tubes leading from the firebox, through the water space of the boiler and

from there up the chimney. This was a borrowed idea, but the execution was novel in its precision, and the innovation raised more steam for the same expenditure of coke. Another competitor, *Novelty*, designed largely by the same John Ericsson who would design the ironclad *Monitor* in the American Civil War, was ingenious but lacked robustness; during the competition it disappeared in a cloud of sparks and smoke when its leather bellows caught fire. A more serious rival was Timothy Hackworth's *Sanspareil*, based on his powerful *Royal George*, built for the S&DR. This performed fairly well until several manufacturing defects put it out of the running, so the *Rocket* won. The real prize was not the monetary award, but the subsequent flow of locomotive orders, not only from the L&MR, but from a host of other new companies which were appearing both in Britain and overseas. During the Rainhill trials the *Rocket*, weighing little more than four tons, hauled 13 tons and reached the unprecedented speed of 29mph. This was bad news for coach proprietors.

2
EARLY INTERCITY LINES

Being the first intercity railway, the L&MR proceeded on a basis of trial and error, evolving methods and techniques that subsequently became standard on British railways and, to a large degree, on overseas railways too. For example, the L&MR's refusal to guarantee arrival times was perpetuated on all subsequent railways of the world. On the other hand, the total ban on smoking was soon changed, as was the regulation that policemen pursuing a criminal could travel free but were required to pay the correct fare if they caught him.

As with subsequent railways, the L&MR, although initially aimed at freight traffic, soon gave priority to passengers. Freight trains had to wait in a loop or siding to allow passenger trains to overtake them, and they had no fixed schedules. At first, fires caused by locomotive sparks were a hazard on freight trains, and so open cars were covered with tarpaulins; a practice which continued on British railways for more than a century afterwards.

Early passenger services followed the traditions of highway coaches. Lineside coaching inns sometimes became railway booking offices, and buying a ticket was a long process in which details like dates, times and seat numbers, as well as names and addresses of passengers, were laboriously hand-written on the paper ticket. As highway coaches had "outside" as well as "inside" passengers, it is unsurprising that some preferred to travel on the sides and roofs of rail vehicles, and many passengers fell or collided with bridges until the practice was totally banned.

The L&MR was officially opened in the presence of the then Prime Minister, the Duke of Wellington, on 15 September 1830. During the festivities *Rocket* ran down and fatally injured the then President of the Board of Trade, William Huskisson, but, despite this, the day was considered a success. Although freight traffic developed more slowly than had been hoped, passenger traffic was unexpectedly large. After just six months the Company was able to announce a dividend, and, by the summer of 1836, 12 passenger trains were running in each direction, of which two were first class, making the 31-mile trip in one hour 20min.

Even before it was opened, the L&MR received delegations and engineers from railway committees of other cities. They typically visited the L&M and the S&D

Below: **Germany's first railway was from Nurnberg to Furth in 1835. A decade later it built this solid, somewhat ecclesiastical, terminal at Nurnberg.**

Left: **The B&O** *John Hancock* **of 1836, renamed** *Thomas Jefferson,* **is another survivor of that railroad's "Grasshopper" type.**

Below left: **Isambard Kingdom Brunel, photographed toward the end of his life.**

Below right: **The Englishman William Wilson, Germany's first locomotive driver.**

railways and then returned home to write up their recommendations. In 1828 two engineers came from Baltimore, where promoters were planning to lay a railroad to the Ohio River to win back traffic lost to other American ports. The men took back encouraging ideas, as well as a conviction that the British gauge of 4ft 8in (later stretched by half an inch making standard gauge [1,435mm]) should also be adopted for American railroads.

Nevertheless, the Baltimore & Ohio (B&O) directors still believed in the merits of horse traction, and, when the first 13 miles to Elicott's Mills were opened in May 1830, only horses were employed. It was the enthusiasm of Peter Cooper, a New Yorker, who persuaded the directors to allow him to try out his small vertical-boilered locomotive, that changed this situation: *Tom Thumb* may have lost that famous race against a horse. However, this was only because of a slipped belt, and its demonstration of convenience and speed caused the directors to think again. Horses had been rented from local coach companies and were changed every six or seven miles; this was workable over a 13-mile line but began to seem uninviting to a railroad determined to stretch as far as the Ohio.

Left: **Brunel's viaduct at Maidenhead, with its daringly flat arches.**

Below: **Replica coaches of the Liverpool & Manchester Railway, on exhibition at the National Railway Museum, York.**

Right: **The original Dutch 6ft gauge, on show at the Utrecht Railway Museum.**

Consequently, the B&O held a locomotive competition in 1831. Phineas Davis, whose 3.5-ton *York* managed to pull 50 tons at 30mph, sold his engine to the Railroad and was appointed chief locomotive engineer. By 1835 horse traction had disappeared, being replaced by just seven locomotives.

Unlike the L&MR, which suffered many casualties in its first years, there were no deaths on the early B&O passenger trains. Even when the first fatality occurred in 1833, it was to a man who had fallen asleep on the track because, it was said, he had been drinking excessively. By 1834 the railroad had reached Harpers Ferry, and, in the following year, opened its Washington branch, graced by the granite Thomas Viaduct. It had not yet reached the Ohio, but was regarded as the most experienced line in America, and an example to be followed by the several newer railroads that were being sponsored up and down the seaboard.

3

PRIVATE ENTERPRISE TAKES CHARGE

Although the B&O was the first US public railroad offering a regular service, it was not the first to provide a regular steam train. That distinction was won by the South Carolina Canal & Railroad Co, which used steam right from the start of operations on Christmas Day 1830. The South Carolina, for a while, was the world's longest railway after it reached the Savannah River near Augusta in Georgia. It was then 136 miles long, more than any of the British railways.

The South Carolina Railroad started from Savannah and its initial aim was to secure cotton traffic for the port. In this it succeeded. It also ran a passenger service, which covered the first 90 miles from the coast in 10.5hr; passengers then spent the night in rudimentary accommodation before continuing their trip the next morning. Night operations soon became feasible, however, through the introduction of loco-

motive headlamps; the first experiment was simply a flat-car, supporting a shaded bonfire, pushed ahead of the locomotive, but soon a true locomotive headlamp was developed.

In England, trunk lines were beginning to take shape. The success of the L&MR encouraged a new company, the Grand Junction Railway (GJR) to extend the track down to the industrial Midlands. The GJR connected at Birmingham with the London & Birmingham Railway, which had been laboriously laid northward from London by Robert Stephenson. Like others, the Stephensons could turn readily from mechanical to civil engineering although, as time went on, it was found better to employ specialised civil engineers. Already, in the L&MR surveys, George Stephenson had displayed incompetence that would not have been tolerated by the directors of later railways.

By 1838 it was possible to travel by train from London to Liverpool and Manchester. Elsewhere, the civic luminaries of ports like Bristol and Southampton had also sponsored railways. The London & Southampton (later the London & South Western [LSWR]) Railway, linked Southampton to the capital in 1840, while the Great Western Railway (GWR) reached Bristol in 1841. Engineered by the idiosyncratic engineer, Isambard Kingdom Brunel, the GWR adopted the broad gauge of 7ft 0¼in (2,140mm); this was not to cause an immediate problem, but once the concept of a national network developed the impracticalities of this change of gauge became apparent. Brunel, among his other innovations, built a viaduct over the Thames at Maidenhead with unprecedentedly shallow arches; people prophesied its imminent collapse, but it is still in use today. Of the several other lines, the short London & Greenwich was distinctive in that it was built on a brick viaduct, while the Newcastle & Carlisle was the first coast-to-coast line in Britain.

In America, although railroads had enthusiastic sponsors, capital was less readily available than in Britain, so after the B&O's first line was built, there was a tendency to construct low-cost lines. On the other hand, the British lines were solid and carefully engineered. Many were so lavishly built that, for the most part, their infrastructure still remains in use, carrying the heavier and faster trains of today. On both sides of the Atlantic there were periods of great optimism, when investors avidly sought railway shares; in Britain there was a "Railway Mania" when, for a time, any railway share found a ready buyer. This was followed by a crash in 1847 that ruined many families. In the USA, the crash of 1857 included among its victims many small Midwestern farmers, who had mortgaged their farms to buy shares in the Milwaukee & Mississippi Railroad. This was one of several occurrences that over the years turned initial Midwestern enthusiasm for railroad companies into deep-seated suspicion.

The first steam locomotive appeared in Chicago as early as 1848, when *Pioneer* first performed on the new track of the short Galena & Chicago Union Railroad. By 1850, railroads were still rare outside the eastern states, but America could already claim 9,000 miles of railroad. Pennsylvania,

American passenger comfort improved. During the 1840s double-bogie eight-wheelers began to replace the smaller four-wheel passenger cars. These new cars had a central aisle leading to open platforms at each end, but their couplings were still of the loose link-and-pin type. This looseness helped small locomotives to start heavy trains by, as it were, adding the weight of each car successively as the train moved from rest. But this was at the price of considerable jolting that could prove lethal to train-men and passengers moving between the end platforms. Gradually, stoves and washrooms became common on this new breed of eight-wheel carriages, and some railroads, especially in the south, began to provide cars for ladies that were secure from the over-friendly, over-noisy, tobacco-spitting males who could so readily become unwanted traveling companions.

The typical American passenger train averaged about 15mph in the early 1840s. For most, this seemed commendably fast. Accidents were frequent, but relatively harmless because of the low speeds. In both Britain and the USA, people often complained about the increasing speeds on precisely this ground. But as signaling and train control improved this argument lost its force until, after the mid-century, high speed became a selling point.

In Britain, with its more expensive track, speeds reached by the new passenger trains were even higher. By the mid-1840s 60mph was quite frequently attained for short distances, while train schedules demanded average running speeds of about 30mph for first-class trains. Despite these high speeds, there were relatively few fatalities. In 1842 about 24 million passengers were carried in the United Kingdom but only five were killed "from causes beyond their own control."

New York and Massachusetts had more than 1,000 miles each, and, in 1851, the 483-mile New York & Erie Railroad would link the Atlantic with Lake Erie. This was not the first line across New York State; after the opening of the Mohawk & Hudson Railroad (M&HR) in 1831, a series of connecting short lines had been created to make a route between Albany and Buffalo which would eventually form the main line of the New York Central System.

It was said that the M&HR's inaugural passenger train covered the 17 miles in 38min. This may have been true as the New York-built *De Witt Clinton*, which hauled it, threw out enough sparks to ruin the clothing of the somewhat exposed passengers. In the following two decades

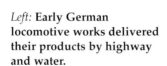

Left: **Early German locomotive works delivered their products by highway and water.**

Above: **A mid-century railroad magnate; John Ross, founder of the Grand Trunk Railway.**

Right: **Crampton's patent locomotives had the driving axle behind the firebox, permitting large driving wheels. They were popular in continental Europe, but few were purchased by American or British companies.**

4
THE NETWORKS EVOLVE

British and US railways were laid in the absence of any national railway policy, but elsewhere in the world governments, profiting from this experience, exercised greater control to avoid capital being wasted building unnecessary lines. Belgium was remarkable in that its initial rail network, consisting of one north-south and one east-west trunk route, was owned and planned by the state. In France, private companies were encouraged but were subjected to searching government supervision; as befitted a highly centralized state, the main lines converged on Paris. In Germany (which was then not a single country but a number of independent states), the individual states organized their own railways, and it was King Ludwig of Bavaria who built the first, five-mile, line in 1835. Friedrich List, after viewing the pioneer US railroads, managed to persuade the Saxony government to back his proposal for the first. intercity line, from Leipzig to Dresden, which was finished in 1839.

In colonial territories the first lines, usually running from ports into the interior, appeared around mid-century, although the very first was built by the Spanish in Cuba as early as 1837. The latter was a remarkable case of a colony gaining a railway before its home country; William Norris of Philadelphia supplied the locomotive power. In Australia (not united as a single Commonwealth until 1901), the states of Victoria, New South Wales and South Australia had each opened a short line in the 1850s, followed by New Zealand in 1862. In South Africa, although a two-mile line at Durban was opened in 1862, the first substantial line was that from Cape Town to Wellington in 1863, followed the next year by the Cape Town-Wynberg line. Both these railways had difficulty recruiting construction workers and both were opposed by local interests led, quite often, by the clergy. Canada saw its first short railway at Montreal in 1836, and, after the 1854 opening of the 9,155ft bridge across the St Lawrence, the Grand Trunk Railway linked Montreal and Toronto with Portland, Maine.

By 1875, some of the western trunk routes still remained to be built in the USA but in Britain the network was more or less complete, with the principal companies well established. In many respects the London & North Western Railway (LNWR) was the biggest; it combined the earlier L&MR, GJR and L&BR and ran from London to its main junction at Crewe, and from there to Carlisle, Holyhead, Liverpool and Manchester. It liked to style itself the "Premier Line" and, in co-operation with the Caledonian Railway in Scotland, operated the Anglo-Scottish West Coast service in competition with a route along the East Coast run by a consortium of three other railways: the Great Northern from London to Yorkshire; the North Eastern up

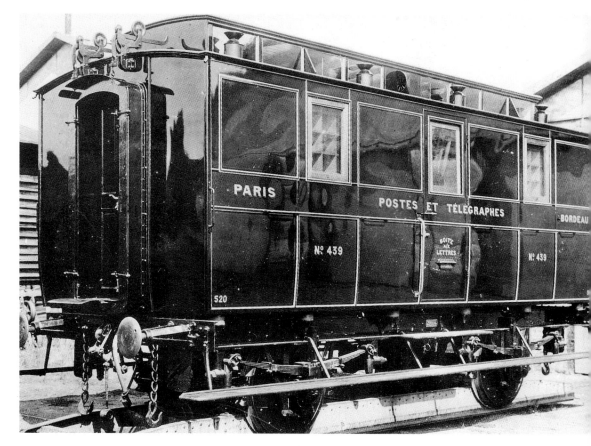

Right: **A traveling post office of France's Paris-Orleans Railway. Mail cars were attached to the faster passenger trains and sometimes, as in this case, late letters could be posted through a flap in the side.**

18

Above: **Celebrating the first locomotive in California, sent by ship around Cape Horn for the Sacramento Valley Railroad in 1855.**

to the border at Berwick; and the North British Railway on to Edinburgh. Lying between these two routes was the Midland Railway, which did eventually run its own London-Scotland service by a circuitous route, but its spine was from Yorkshire, through Birmingham, down to Bristol. The west of England was served mainly by the GWR, which faced competition from the LSWR between London and Devon, and from the LNWR between London and Birmingham, but which had a monopoly from London to Bristol and South Wales. The competition that the GWR fought on two of its main lines resulted in a very high standard of service and equipment, which also benefited its Bristol and Welsh services. This competitive stimulus was less rewarding in the southeast of England, where the cut-throat rivalry of the South Eastern and London, Chatham & Dover railways resulted in extremely high standards in some services, but abysmal standards in many others. South of the capital the London, Brighton & South Coast Railway served Brighton and helped to increase land values in the outer suburban areas, while in the agricultural expanses of East Anglia, the Great Eastern Railway had a monopoly, though this was not very remunerative. Other regional monopolies, just managing to pay a dividend most years, could be found in Ireland and also in Scotland, where the Highlands were shared by the Great North of Scotland and Highland railways.

In this period from 1850 to 1875, railway building continued in the eastern states of America but also spread to the Midwest and eventually to the Pacific. In the 1850s four main routes were laid from the east, across the mountains to Lake Erie or the Ohio. These included the New York & Erie and the newly-formed New York Central. The B&O reached the Ohio in 1852, and the Pennsylvania Railroad, following an earlier route which had combined canals, railways and cable-operated inclines, reached Pittsburgh from Philadelphia in 1852 and then linked up with the associated Pittsburgh, Fort Wayne & Chicago Railroad to provide a through service from Philadelphia to Chicago in 1858.

In the USA the railroad offered a short-cut to the economic development of the wide open spaces in the west that the federal government wished to develop and populate. So from the 1850s subsidies were granted to railroad companies in the form of land grants. Companies were offered federal land along the routes of their projected railroads; these blocks of land, together with the intervening blocks retained by the government, could be expected to rise in value in line with the service provided by the new railroad and so helped to attract investors to the railroad and buyers for the land,

The total length of American railroads had begun to exceed Britain's in the 1830s, and, by the mid-1850s, the US owned about 50% of the world's mileage. By 1870 US mileage was 93,000, and still growing. In the prairies, four land-grant lines — the Chicago & North Western, the Milwaukee, the Rock Island and the Burlington railroads — were dominant and, farther west, new lines had been encouraged by the completion of the first transcontinental railroad.

The latter, divided between the Union Pacific Railroad laid westward from Omaha and the Central Pacific (later Southern Pacific) laid eastward from the Pacific, was the fruit of the Pacific Railway Bill, signed by President Lincoln in 1862. Despite financial mismanagement, and thanks largely to hard work by Chinese and Irish construction gangs, the two lines, totalling 1,780 miles, linked up in Utah in 1869. The telegraph laid alongside the line conveyed the news that the last, golden, spike had been driven in, and this event of 10 May 1869 was recognized then, as later, as a landmark in the US's progression from a bundle of states to a nation.

5
THE IRON ROAD

By 1830, the cast-iron rail laid on stone blocks was already obsolete. Instead, wrought-iron rails fixed to sleepers (crossties) were preferred. These ties provided a cushion for the rails and also prevented them spreading apart. Flat-bottom rail, spiked directly to the ties, was usual in North America and some colonial lines, whereas bullhead rail, seated in cast-iron chairs which themselves were bolted to the ties, was usual in Britain and parts of Europe. It was only after more than a century that British engineers changed to flat-bottom rail, and it is still possible to see sections of bullhead track in Britain today, although this is most common in sidings where old track has been reused.

There were occasional variations, as engineers sought better alternatives. Brunel of the GWR laid his broad-gauge rails along timber beams, or balks, which themselves were supported by timber piles. He also used bridge rail, whose cross-section was an inverted "V," but neither of these innovations survived. President Lord of the Erie Railroad, also a broad-gauge enthusiast, attempted with scant success to lay his track on deep oak piling. Another innovation was strap rail, in which the rails were made of wood but had a thin strip of iron to provide a. running surface. This brought considerable economy of iron, but not of blood, for the iron strip tended to be dislodged by passing trains, to form a "snakehead," which sometimes burst through the floor.

In North America the underlying philosophy was that railroads should be built cheaply and improved later. For this reason curves were often sharp, with grades tending to follow rather than oppose the lie of the land. While in Britain most main line railways were double-track, in America the single-track line was standard in the early decades. When serious water obstacles were encountered, it was common for the railroad to terminate at the waterside, and a train ferry provided a connection with the other bank. Accordingly the South Carolina Railroad terminated at Hamburg, opposite Augusta, Georgia, and the Central Pacific ended at Oakland, rather than San Francisco.

Although in the early decades it was clear to many promoters and engineers that sooner or later individual railways would be linked to form complete national networks, this likelihood was not enough to persuade companies to adopt a uniform rail gauge. George Stephenson, by perpetuating the gauge of his colliery line in subsequent railways, founded the standard gauge of 4ft 8½in (1,435mm), and this spread with Stephenson locomotives to the USA and elsewhere. But some American lines chose 4ft 10in (1,473mm), while many railroads of the American South preferred 5ft (1,520mm). Between New York and Washington, trains of compromise cars were run. These had wide-tread wheels which could run on standard and 4ft 10in gauge tracks.

Most of continental Europe adopted standard gauge, but Portugal, Spain and Russia preferred a wider gauge. Russia's decision to adopt the broad gauge, although attributed by the British press to nefarious strategic aims, was actually taken on the advice of the American Col Whistler, who had engineered several lines in the southern states of America and naturally recommended the same 5ft (1,520mm) gauge.

Below: **British bullhead rail. One of the wedges ("keys") has worked free, a frequent occurrence which required daily monitoring of the track.**

Above: **British bullhead trackwork in the 1950s, just before the switch to flatbottom rail.**

In Britain the 7ft 0¼in (2,140mm) gauge of the GWR enabled it to provide the fastest and most comfortable trains in the land, but the inability to exchange rolling stock with other railways was a great inconvenience. So the narrow-gauge interest evolved, intent on persuading Parliament to end the GWR gauge, but the campaign was handicapped by the apparent technical superiority of the broad gauge. Eventually, following a parliamentary Commission, the Gauge Act was passed in 1846, specifying that 4ft 8½in (1,435mm) was to be the maximum gauge in England, Wales and Scotland (but not in Ireland, where a considerable mileage of 5ft 3in [1,600mm] track had already been laid). However, it would not be until the early 1890s that the final sections of Brunel's broad gauge were converted to standard gauge.

In the end Britain, with the exception of lines built by the GWR in broad-gauge times, had the most restrictive height and width limitations of all standard-gauge railways (known technically as the "loading gauge"). Whereas GWR rolling stock could be almost 11ft (3.35m) wide and 15ft (4.57m) high, the present-day standard maximum loading gauge for British stock is 9ft (2.74m) wide and less than 13ft (3.96m) high. Even the South African Railways, with their 3ft 6in (1,065mm) gauge, can use 10ft (3.05m)-wide vehicles. The continental European loading gauge is a few inches greater in width and considerably higher than the British, while US rolling stock can be somewhat bigger than European, over 16ft (4.88m) being available vertically and nearly 11ft (3.35m) horizontally. But the 5ft (1,520mm) gauge Russian railways were, and remain, the best placed, with a height restriction of more than 17ft (5.18m) and a maximum width of over 11ft (3.35m).

6

FORWARD FROM THE ROCKET

Innovation did not end with Stephenson's *Rocket*. For the L&MR contract, the Stephensons at first built enlarged versions of *Rocket*,. They followed these with *Northumbrian*, in which for the first time the firebox was not hung onto the back of the boiler, but was part of it. This machine also had a smokebox leading to the chimney, and, instead of a water barrel, its tender carried an iron tank. Then, still in 1830, came *Planet*, in which the cylinders were placed beneath the smokebox, between the frames, with their connecting rods driving cranks on the rear axle. From *Planet* the Stephensons derived *Patentee*, similar but bigger, with a carrying axle leading and trailing, and a driving axle in the middle (making it a 2-2-2).

Edward Bury, engineer of the L&BR, designed small four-wheel (0-4-0) locomotives in which bar frames were used, instead of the plate frames preferred by the Stephensons. Bury's locomotives also had the "haystack" firebox, which was a vertical cylinder terminating in a dome (the predecessor of the steam dome), whose height above the water level enabled fairly dry steam to be drawn off to the cylinders. Bury's locomotives, with their bar frames, were more suited to the rough American track than the Stephensons', and formed the basis for the Norris line of American-built locomotives. Norris retained the bar frames and the haystack firebox, but also provided a leading truck (or bogie) to help the locomotive negotiate sharp curves. The result was an effective outside-cylinder 4-2-0 which sold well not only in the USA, but also abroad; even the British Birmingham & Gloucester Railway bought a batch. During the 1840s the 4-2-0 layout acquired an extra driving axle, thereby becoming a 4-4-0. It was the 4-4-0 which from then on was the dominant wheel arrangement on North American railroads until, toward the end of the century, it was superseded by larger types.

The leading four-wheel bogie had been devised by John Jervis of the M&HR, who realized that British-style locomotives were not designed for the sharp curves of American track and with his locomotive *Experiment* he showed that a leading, swiveling, truck could solve this problem. Another American innovator was Joseph Harrison, who made the 4-4-0 a viable proposition at the higher speeds with his equaliser, which enabled all four driving wheels to absorb bumps in the track. His 4-4-0 *Gowan and Marx* of 1840 weighed 11 tons and pulled a 432-ton Philadelphia & Reading Railroad freight train at an average speed of 10mph.

Far left, above: **A Stephenson Patentee locomotive.**

Far left, below: **A "Camel" of the B&O Railroad.**

Below Left: **The large oil lamp and capacious spark arrestor of a US woodburner.**

Above Right: **A B&O RR eight-wheeler, developed from the "Mud diggers" and built in 1848.**

Right: **A later example of the "American" 4-4-0 type.**

Below: **The Englishman William Buddicom's locomotives had outside cylinders, unlike Stephenson's, and were preferred by some European railways. This is a French example, built in 1843.**

For the B&O, Ross Winans built his 0-8-0 "Mud diggers" from 1844. With their eight-coupled wheels, these could start heavy loads without wheel-slip, and were soon followed by the "Camels," in which he placed the driver's cab above the boiler. These had plate frames, and burned coal instead of coke.

The last major contribution by Robert Stephenson was the "long-boiler" configuration in which, by accepting overhang fore and aft, long boiler tubes could be accommodated, thereby extracting more heat from the hot fire gases on their way to the chimney. Meanwhile, Thomas Crampton, in order to accommodate the big driving wheels

that were required for high speeds, placed them behind the firebox and so created a very distinctive type, which became popular in Germany and France, but was only tried in small numbers in Britain and the USA.

On the broad-gauge GWR, Daniel Gooch introduced the "Iron Duke" series in the 1840s. These were large engines with a high boiler pressure of 100 pounds per square inch (psi) and they remained in service for decades. One of these 4-2-2 engines took a 100-ton train 53 miles along the GWR's superb track in just 47min. This was a record no other railway of the world could equal in 1848.

23

7

THE EARLY TRAINS

On Western European railways the highway coach tradition lasted longer than in America, and the rigid-wheelbase four- or six-wheel coach became the standard railway passenger vehicle for decades. Originally this was virtually three or more coach bodies joined together and placed on railway wheels; the compartment style of accommodation, with facing seats, was a coaching configuration that would last to the present day on some railways of the world.

With their eight-wheel, center-aisle, washroom-equipped coaches, the American railroads were well ahead of Europe at an early stage, and eventually several American ideas were adopted in Europe. In Britain the four- and six-wheeler survived for many years, with examples of the latter remaining well into the 20th century, but lavatories were soon necessary as long non-stop runs became more common. There were several ingenious attempts to introduce these without providing central aisles or side corridors, but eventually the British long-

distance train was provided with corridors. Corridors implied non-revenue space, and so, to compensate for this, both trains and passenger carriages tended to become longer, and the long, fast-running, passenger carriage required an American-style chassis on swiveling trucks (called "bogies" in Britain).

The long distances run by American trains led to the development of sleeping cars. This was not purely an American idea, for the L&BR had provided rudimentary convertible bed carriages in the early 1840s. In the 1850s several American inventors sold their sleeping car ideas to individual railroads, which faced the problem that sleeping cars accommodated far fewer revenue passengers. Various methods of converting seats into narrow berths were patented to overcome this difficulty, and, in the 1850s, George Pullman produced a coach incorporating several of these ideas. Pullman was not particularly inventive, but he had marketing skills and was attracted by the idea of the "hotel on wheels." His company slowly overcame its competitors and operated Pullman cars on an increasing number of US long-distance services.

Pullman also operated parlor cars and dining cars, and soon the basic class distinction on US railroads was between those who paid extra to travel Pullman, and those who did not, traveling "coach." In Britain and Europe, class distinctions were more refined. From 1844 British lines were required to run at least one daily train — known as "Parliamentaries" as the legal requirement had been laid down in statute — for third-class passengers at a low fare

Below: **A pastoral, if not idyllic, US railroad scene soon after mid-century. End-platform cars with clerestory roofs were becoming standard equipment.**

Above: **A French combined First and Second class passenger car, dating from the 1850s. The oil lights were tended from roof level.**

Left: **An 1857 announcement of the Sacramento Valley RR. At that period, and for long afterward, scheduled connections with stage coaches were all-important.**

SACRAMENTO VALLEY RAILROAD.

SUMMER ARRANGEMENT.

On and after the 15th of March, the Trains of the Sacramento Valley Railroad will leave as follows, viz:

PASSENGER TRAINS WILL LEAVE

Sacramento daily........at 7½, A. M., and 3½, P. M.
Folsom daily......at 7¾, A. M., 12 M., and 5, P. M.

On Sunday, besides the above, there will be from Sacramento a 10, A. M., train

FREIGHT TRAINS WILL LEAVE

Sacramento........................at 7½, A. M., and 2, P. M.
Folsom..................................at 7¾ A. M.

☞ The 7½ A. M. train will take through freight only.
☞ No freight transported on Sundays.

STAGES

Connect with the 7½ A. M. trains out for

GRASS VALLEY,   AUBURN,
FOREST CITY,   DOWNIEVILLE,
NEVADA,   OPHIR,   GOLD HILL,
IOWA HILL,   YANKEE JIM'S,   GREENWOOD VALL'Y
ORLEANS FLAT,   MORMON ISLAND,   COLOMA,
ILLINOISTOWN,   DIAMOND SPRINGS,   PLACERVILLE.
GEORGETOWN,   MICHIGAN BAR,   COOK'S BAR,
EL DORADO,   LIVE OAK CITY,   ARKANSAS DIGGINGS
PRAIRIE CITY,   DRYTOWN,   AMADOR,
WALL'S DIGGINGS,   JACKSON,   FIDDLETOWN,
WILLOW SPRINGS,
SUTTER,   And all the Intermediate Places.

RETURNING—the Stages will connect with the 12 M. train in arriving Sacramento, in time for the San Francisco boats.

☞ For freight or passage apply at the Railroad Stations.

J. P. ROBINSON, Superintendent.

and reasonable speed. Many railways responded by providing the most Spartan accommodation possible, but, as the years passed, the number of third-class passengers increased and they became highly profitable; so some small improvements were made. Nevertheless, for those unable to endure third-class travel, and unable to afford first, second-class accommodation was provided.

The rigidity of the British-class distinctions was eroded when the Midland Railway, in a bid to attract first-class passengers from rival lines, imported American Pullman cars in 1874. It became evident that even on British track the US-style suspension provided a more comfortable ride, and so the Midland Railway (MR) began to build bogie vehicles (with four-wheel bogies) for its other services. Having taken one step, it was easy to take another — passengers traveling third-class were allowed to travel on all trains. This change was achieved by withdrawing third-class vehicles, eliminating second class, and reclassifying second-class carriages as third class. Curiously, this resulted in the MR providing just two classes — first and third. With these improvements the MR duly attracted passengers from rival lines and the other British companies began to follow suit.

The Pullman concept, however, did not dominate in Britain, where journeys were short and first-class travel provided all the amenities required by the wealthy. But, in continental Europe, the Belgian Nagelmackers introduced a

service very similar to that of George Pullman. Nagelmackers' carriages were a little more luxurious than Pullman's, and were intended to run on international services. He had to face competition from the American William Mann, but, in 1876, the two rivals merged to form the International Sleeping Car Co (Wagons-Lits).

In the early 1870s the fastest New York-Chicago train averaged 30mph. In Britain speeds were also creeping upward. Long station meal breaks — where trains halted at stations like Swindon to allow passengers to take refreshments — were being eliminated, and running speeds often exceeded 50mph. The "Flying Scotsman" was scheduled to run the 392 miles from London to Edinburgh in 9½hr, averaging 48mph for the first 76 miles.

Although it was passenger services that aroused greatest public interest and which made or unmade a railway's reputation, the majority of the world's railways obtained most of their revenue from freight operations. In the late 1840s the LNWR was despatching daily from London six night and four day freight trains. These consisted, typically, of some 40 tarpaulin-shrouded cars, most of which weighed 3 tons when empty and 6 tons loaded.

While the early impetus for many railway schemes, such as the S&DR and the L&MR, had been to reduce the cost of freight, either, in the case of the S&DR, coal to the ports on the River Tees, or, for the L&MR, the shipment of raw cotton to the booming cotton industry of Manchester, much of the freight carried in both Britain and the USA over long distances tended to be of relatively high value. But bulk freight was always likely to predominate. Coal was the most important in this category, and companies like the rich North Eastern Railway and the small Taff Vale Railway in Wales made their living by hauling coal in block trains at low rates but correspondingly low costs. These two railways, like

Above: **A passenger car of the Virginia & Truckee RR, a company that boomed and declined with the Nevada gold rush.**

Right: **"32 men; 6 horses" was a common inscription on French freightcars, and could be significant in wartime troop movements.**

Above: **An early example of "catch and deliver" mailbag pick-up on the Lakeshore & Michigan Southern RR, later part of the New York Central RR.**

others, were also in the docks business, building their own wharves so as to provide an integrated export service. By the early 1880s the Cardiff docks, essentially a railway creation, were exporting 8,000,000 tons of Welsh coal annually. There was a similar situation in the US, where railroads in Pennsylvania were already handling heavy coal tonnages in the 1860s, while those in the Midwest were beginning to handle grain. In the 1860s fast freight links were set up by freight agencies, which would load their own cars and despatch them over routes consisting of several adjacent railroads. This eliminated the costly transhipments suffered by most freight, because the railroads were still not passing railroad-owned cars through from one company to another. In Britain, the problems associated by the complex network of lines and with the inter-company use of rolling stock was solved by the creation of the Railway Clearing House, which distributed payments between companies based on the mileage undertaken and the rolling stock used.

In the 1840s eight-wheel freight wagons were in common use in the USA. As early as the 1850s, the B&O was using all-metal 20-ton coal hoppers, although this was not typical of American railroads at that time. Wooden boxcars were predominant, although flatcars and gondolas were also popular. Stock cars for moving cattle were the most common type of specialized vehicle and the first successful refrigerator car would appear in 1877.

Crew cars (cabooses), required by the numerous train staff (conductor, trainman, and brake-men) were attached to the tail of US freight trains from the early years, and, in the 1860s, they began to be fitted with observation cupolas, from which the train could be watched; for example, hot axle boxes, unless spotted early, could set trains on fire. With heavy trains and steep grades, braking American freight trains demanded a complement of brakemen who, responding to locomotive whistle signals, would mount the roofs of the cars to tighten the brake wheels. In Britain, freight trains were stopped at the tops of inclines so that a proportion of the wagon brakes could be pinned down; at this stage each individual wagon was fitted with its own brakes and the concept of through braking — using either air or vacuum — from the locomotive or brakevan had not yet been developed. At other times, on level track, the guard, traveling in his heavily ballasted brakevan at the rear, could screw down its brakes and this, together with the locomotive brakes, would slow the train.

8

THE RAILROAD AT WAR

As early as the 1830s the British army had used the L&MR to speed the despatch of troops to Ireland, but, in the American Civil War, the whole campaign was dominated by the ease with which the opposing sides could shift masses of troops and supplies.

The Confederate States, which had most need of good transportation, were handicapped because, having taken up arms on the principle that outside interference was intolerable, they were reluctant to impose much-needed central control over the 113 different railroad companies in their territory. Thus companies that had long resisted the linking of their lines with adjacent railroads continued to do so, and, when soldiers laid lines along city streets to effect just such connections, they were abused by the companies and the local populace.

In the absence of central control, it was the Confederate army officers who began to direct railroad operations. This added yet another obstacle to the efficient functioning of the southern network, as the officers, overriding the advice of railroad managers, hindered operations by hoarding empty freight cars for their own possible use, sending off trains in one direction without making provision for the return of locomotives and stock, and threatening any of the railroaders who dared to dissent with courts-martial.

The Federal government did much better than the Confederates, setting a pattern for other governments in future wars. It did not impose army officers as managers. Instead, it gave railroad managers military rank, so that they could not be intimidated by regular officers and were more or less free to balance war needs against railroad necessities. The US Military Railroads Administration was also formed to operate those lines built or, as with the vital Philadelphia, Wilmington & Baltimore, directly taken over by the government.

For the Confederacy, the cheap structural standards of the US railroads proved to be especially damaging. With practically no heavy industry in its territory, it was unable to replace worn-out rails and rolling stock. One northern general, viewing a train proceeding along recently

Below: **The US Military Railroad terminus at City Point, Virginia, at the mouth of the Appomattox River. The City Point RR ran from there to Petersburg, to the southwest.**

captured southern track, compared the scene to a fly crawling over a corrugated washboard. Both sides soon made raids to wreck their enemy's railroads, and it was the South which had most difficulty in repairing the acute damage caused.

The tactical importance of the railroads was recognized early, for the very first major battle, Bull Run, was won by the South after it had successfully brought up reinforcements by trains which ejected their complements virtually on the battlefield. The South, too, was initially most successful in raiding enemy railroads. Stonewall Jackson once managed to surround 56 of the B&O's locomotives. He carried off about 12 of these as trophies, hauled over the highway by horse teams, and wrecked the rest, thereby closing down the B&O main line for several months.

As the war progressed, the northerners became more skilled in railroad destruction. Their Andrews Raid, which became famous as the "Great Locomotive Chase," was foiled through the tenacity of a southern railroader, the resulting chase ending when the locomotive commandeered by the raiders ran out of fuel. At first, to destroy railroads, raiders simply removed and bent the rails round nearby trees, but it was easy to correct that kind of damage. A northern officer was soon telling his men that rails should be rolled up like doughnuts, and, by the time Sherman began his march through Georgia, he had been equipped with a machine that heated rails and then twisted them like corkscrews.

Another Federal innovation was the Railroad Construction Corps, an army organisation which had the responsibility to construct and maintain military railroads. This idea was noticed in Prussia, which in imitation introduced railway operating regiments. When the Franco-Prussian War broke out in 1870 the German railways were well prepared and had some success in the first few weeks. However, later, when the battles moved onto French territory, supplies were slow in coming up, with transit times so long that meat was often foul-smelling by the time it was delivered. German locomotives and rolling stock were used inside occupied France, but as French bridges were lower than German, a number of locomotive chimneys were knocked off; from then on, Prussian locomotives were designed with two-piece chimneys, the cap being detachable.

Where the German railways excelled was in the mobilization period, troop movements and schedules having been planned meticulously in advance. The Prussian conscription system, which entailed army service for all young men and the creation of a citizens' army of ex-conscript reservists, depended on the railways to carry reservists to their army depots and then, with their regiments, to the front. Other continental European governments soon followed the Prussian example, thereby taking a long step toward total war, a concept that would not have been possible before the Railway Age.

Below: **A United States Military Railroad train passes a guarded bridge on the Orange and Alexandria Railroad.**

9
LOCOMOTIVE DEVELOPMENT 1850-1875

Locomotives developed steadily during the 25 years between 1850 and 1875. Change was directed more to improvement and enlargement than to radical redesign. New wheel arrangements were introduced to permit bigger locomotives, cabs began to be provided on most engines, and better manufacture, including a growing use of steel, made locomotives safer and more reliable.

John Ramsbottom in Britain and William Mason in the USA are good examples of engineers who improved on tradition and produced superb locomotives. The Mason 4-4-0 gave classic form to that wheel arrangement and, both aesthetically and technically, surpassed its predecessors. Mason used components that were carefully machined so that they would fit snugly, without caulking, his holes were bored so that bolts would fit tightly, and he avoided open seams. By placing his cylinders horizontally, alongside a four-wheel leading truck of extended wheelbase, he enhanced both appearance and stability.

The so-called "Mason bogies" were less handsome. Mason initially built these for narrow-gauge lines, considering that the 4-4-0, with its firebox constrained by the driving wheels flanking it, was unsuitable for such lines. They were an Americanized version of the locomotive design patented by the Scotsman, Robert Fairlie, in 1864. Fairlie was also trying to solve the problem of providing

Main picture: **A 4-4-0 of the Hartford and Connecticut Western RR, which became part of the New Haven RR in 1882.**

Left: **Another 4-4-0, this one built by Baldwin for the Missouri RR. Highly decorative paintwork was a feature of US locomotives for much of the 19th century.**

Above: **Austrian railways, which were lightly laid, very curved and hilly, developed their own particular design concepts. This six-wheeler has outside frames and dates from 1860. Its maximum permitted speed was 28mph.**

Left: **A six-wheeler class designed in Britain for the New South Wales Government Railways in the 1870s. Here it is seen still going strong in the 1970s.**

Below left: **A Reading RR "Camelback" four-wheel type with wide firebox for burning anthracite. It was driven from the cab, and the fireman worked alone. Built as late as 1903, it was intended for slow work over sharply-curved city tracks.**

powerful motive power for sharply curved narrow-gauge lines. The Fairlie locomotive was articulated (jointed) and had two pivoting bogie-and-cylinder units, each carrying a boiler, placed back-to-back with the cab in the middle. His *Little Wonder*, working on the narrow-gauge and mountainous Ffestiniog Railway in Wales from 1870, attracted visitors from all over the world and many of them placed orders for the type. Mason's variant, beginning with *Onward* of 1872, had a single boiler supported by a truck, which accommodated the four driving wheels and the cylinders, with the rear section, bolted to the firebox, consisting of the tender mounted on another four-wheel truck. Despite the steam leaks inevitable with jointed steampipes, these locomotives were successful, and about 150 were built. These were not all of identical design, although Mason was one of the first American locomotive engineers to standardize components.

Locomotive standardization was more advanced in Britain, and Ramsbottom's "DX" class 0-6-0 freight locomotive, a very simple and reliable design, was built for the LNWR in unprecedented numbers, totalling no fewer than 943 units when production ceased. Ramsbottom was the inventor of water troughs in the center of the track for replenishing locomotives at speed with water; these were widely used in Britain, and also by the Pennsylvania

Railroad in the USA. He also designed a speedometer, and a sight-feed lubricator; the latter enabled enginemen to check oil levels at a glance. His safety valve, based on two vertical tubes, hummed loudly just as blowing-off pressure was reached.

Coke, or wood, had been the usual locomotive fuel in the first decades, but in the 1850s ways were found to burn coal efficiently. In America, the locomotive builder Matthias Baldwin experimented with a deflector plate inside the firebox; this tended to burn up, but a firebrick structure proved suitable and was used on the Pennsylvania Railroad in 1854. The aim was to lengthen the path of the hot gases passing through the firebox so as to provide a greater opportunity for coal particles to be burned-up, rather than wasted through the chimney. The final solution came from Matthew Kirtley of Britain's Midland Railway; this was a brick arch which forced the gases to pass back over the fire before entering the boiler tubes.

In order to burn small coal, which was plentiful in his home country, Belgium, Alfred Belpaire replaced the high, narrow, firebox with one of his own design. When fully developed, the Belpaire boiler had a square firebox, which provided an increased grate area. It was more costly to build than a round-top firebox, but produced better results.

Left: **A Fairlie double-ender type locomotive, still at work on the Ffestiniog Railway in Wales.**

Below: **The late-developing Japanese railways used mainly British locomotives at first. This 4-4-0 type with inclined cylinders was a classic British export to, among others, Australia.**

Throughout the rest of the steam era some engineers preferred the round-top, and some the Belpaire.

Kirtley's progression from the "Single" (engines with a single pair of large-diameter driving wheels) to the 2-4-0 for passenger work typified many British engineers' work of this period. At first, they continued to use double frames, with the driving wheels sandwiched between them to avoid disaster, should a driving axle fracture. Eventually, however, axle manufacturing techniques improved so much that single frames could be used, so saving considerable weight and expense.

By this time, the American and British styles of locomotive were very different, although good ideas crossed the Atlantic in both directions. British railway companies tended to establish their own locomotive design and construction facilities, where locomotives that were both obviously British and yet characteristic of a particular railway were produced. Independent British locomotive-building companies — such as the Glasgow-based North British — had to rely increasingly on exports. In the USA there were also railroads, for example the Pennsylvania, which built their own locomotives, but outside locomotive builders provided the bulk of requirements. Some of these companies, like Baldwin in Philadelphia and the American Locomotive Co (Alco) which developed at Schenectady from the Brooks and other works, were destined to grow into huge corporations which would survive well into the next century.

PART TWO

THE GOLDEN AGE:
1876-1914

Left: **A grand station of the British Empire; Victoria Terminus in Bombay.**

10
WORLDWIDE EXPANSION

Well before 1875 railways had shown that they were destined to be the principal feature of the 19th century's economic landscape, and it was not long before it became evident that their dominance would also be social and military; there was hardly an aspect of human existence that in one way or another had been unaffected by the coming of the railway.

In the small, densely peopled countries of Europe, including Britain, the population had almost daily contact with the railways. They made it possible to live a healthy distance from the place of work, they enabled production of commodities to be concentrated in those areas where conditions were most suitable for production, rather than be scattered in areas close to the consumers. They enabled families to go away for their annual holidays, and for new towns to be used as leisure resorts. They also enabled the newspapers of the capital to be read the same day in the most distant corners of the country. In the USA, the same picture could be seen in the regions of the larger cities, but elsewhere the railroad, while bringing communities closer, did not bring them into the same kind of new intimacy as in Europe; the distances and the differences were too great.

In the newer colonial countries, there were areas, such as the hinterlands of Melbourne, Sydney, Cape Town and Toronto, where the railway seemed to be everywhere and all-powerful; however, there were also vast areas not far away where the railway had not penetrated, and, indeed, would never penetrate. Meanwhile, along the few long-distance routes, communities would develop around the railway stations; some of them were destined to blossom and become townships, while others would remain undistinguished.

In America the feeling of national unity, which flared briefly when the Union Pacific and Central Pacific linked up as the first transcontinental railroad, was short-lived. But in other countries, and internationally, the moral and binding force of a railway route would be acknowledged openly when other transcontinentals, like the Canadian Pacific, Trans-Australian and Trans-Siberian railways were undertaken. Moreover, it was not always a question of binding nations, but sometimes of binding empires. The Cape to Cairo Railway, which was never completed, was to cement British control from the north to the south of Africa and reflected British control over much of the eastern half of the African continent, from Egypt in the north to the Cape Colony in the south. The British Empire, although principally reliant upon shipping routes for its communication — hence the importance of colonial possessions such as Gibraltar, Malta, Cyprus and Aden as well as the strategically important Suez Canal — was to develop significant railway networks in its many colonial possessions for internal communication. Even in countries like Argentina,

Below: **An American locomotive hauls the inaugural train from Spain's second city, Barcelona, into Vilanova in 1881.**

officially outside the Empire but strongly within the British sphere of influence, British finance was essential to the development of railway communication.

In Britain, although railways were owned by shareholders and run by managers whose first duty was to provide a dividend, people did believe that the companies were sympathetic to the national (or local) interest. In the USA, for good reason, the average citizen felt that the railroad companies were only interested in making a profit. What was worse was that they were controlled by men intent on a quick profit and fast getaway; men ready to milk the area the company served by extracting high charges from their clients and by running down the capital value of the lines they controlled and on which the whole community ultimately depended.

The Granger movement, which united farmers of the Midwest and gained great political momentum, was fired by resentment felt by farmers against railroad freight rates. They alleged these were so monstrously high as to keep their produce out of the eastern markets unless they sold it at a ridiculously cheap price to the wholesalers.

By the end of the century, this movement and other organisations were succeeding in obtaining federal controls over the railroads, limiting their freedom to fix freight rates, to offer rebates to favored clients, and to make inter-railroad pricing agreements. In Britain during the same period, there was similarly a tightening of central control, but for different reasons. In the 1840s and 1850s, just when the British railways were in their most formative period, the party system in Parliament was weak. This meant that

Above: **Laid to 3ft gauge, the North Pacific Coast RR was built to exploit the giant redwoods of California. Built in 1876, it was abandoned in 1930.**

Left: **The terminal of the Nord Railway in Paris.**

WORLD RAILWAYS

Main picture: **The Austro-Hungarian Empire built some grandiose stations. This is the Keleti Terminus in Budapest.**

Below: **The "Neo-Slavic" facade of the Riga Terminal in Moscow.**

Right: **A South African Railways train passes a long girder bridge over the Souritz River in Cape Province.**

just a few members representing the railway interest could cripple legislative attempts to impose greater control over the companies. With the consolidation of the party system in the 1860s, the railway companies lost this advantage and over the next decades the government's Board of Trade was able to exercise greater control. This control resulted in better railway safety when, for example, the railways were compelled to install automatic brakes or block signaling and to limit railwaymen's working hours. However, attempts to regulate freight rates were less successful and culminated in a situation where the railways found it difficult either to raise or lower their rates.

Growing interest and understanding of railway transport shown in Congress and Parliament was echoed in the public at large, which began to concern itself not only in how railway policy might affect its own particular interests, but also in the details of railway operation and engineering. This was a period when the railways were seeking to impress the populace with big schemes like the Forth Bridge and Severn Tunnel in Britain, the new terminals in Manhattan, and the well-publicized operation of fast trains. There was now a section of the public wanting even more detailed knowledge, and railway publications appeared, which provided comprehensive information but were intended neither for railway employees nor for investors. What was later known as the Golden Age of railways also witnessed the emergence of the railway enthusiast.

In the USA, total railroad mileage reached an all-time peak in 1916 of 254,000 miles. Much of the mileage built over the previous decades had not been really needed, and was destined for a short life. Traffic had been increasing, but profits had not, and a sixth of the mileage was already in the hands of receivers and trustees. In that year there was an intervention by the federal government that forced the railroads to grant a reduced working day (in effect, and intention, an increase of the average railroader's pay). Other costs, like coal, had also gone up, but railroads were not allowed to adjust their rates to cover these. In 1916 almost 500,000 motor trucks were already registered in the

USA, and the first regular air service (New York-Washington) was only two years away. Clearly, the railroads faced a tough future.

The situation facing Britain's railways was similar. For them, the last year of the so-called Golden Age was 1914, not 1916, but they also had been deprived of the freedom to set rates at a time when their costs were rising. They did not yet face highway competition, still less air competition, but the alternative competing technology was visible. They, also, faced a tough future, aggravated by the four years of hard use and deferred maintenance that World War I would bring.

Main picture: **Ribblehead Viaduct in the Yorkshire Dales. This formed part of the Midland Railway's bid to capture London–Scotland traffic.**

Above left: **Girder bridges in the Feather River Valley in California.**

Below left: **The Bear River Bridge of the Nevada County Narrow Gauge RR. Built in 1908, this elegant structure survived until 1963.**

Above: **Williams, a Grand Trunk Railway station in Ontario.**

11
THE GAUGE CONNECTION

When the first railways were built they were short and isolated, and although a few engineers visualized a time when they would link up to form nationwide networks, there was no pressing need for companies to agree on a standard width between the rails so that rolling stock could run from one railway to another. Moreover, there were some managers who found the idea of through running very distasteful, arousing nightmare visions of a railway finding itself denuded of rolling stock in a peak traffic period because adjoining railways were receiving, but not returning, its freight wagons. Also, towns at the break of gauge points between railways did well out of the situation, because the transhipment of freight and its cartage through the streets to another terminal represented valuable employment and income.

Added to all this was technical uncertainty over the best gauge for a railway. It was generally thought that a narrow gauge was cheaper to build, especially in hilly areas where its short radius curves cheapened construction markedly, whereas the broader gauges accommodated trains of greater capacity traveling safely at higher speeds.

The coexistence in some parts of the USA of 4ft 8½in (1,435mm), 4ft 10in (1,473mm) and 5ft (1,520mm) gauges was just as much an obstacle to low-cost long-distance transportation as the coexistence in Britain of the standard 4ft 8½in (1,435mm) with the GWR's 7ft 0¼in (2,140mm). It is quite likely that, left to themselves, the British and American companies would have never agreed on a standard gauge. This was something that required political intervention. In Britain the intervention came very early, with Parliament establishing a Gauge Commission to decide whether the 4ft 8½in (1,435mm) or the 7ft (2,140mm) gauge should be standardized. This Commission held comparative trials in which the Stephenson interest (standard gauge) put up a markedly inferior performance to that of the GWR (broad gauge). Nevertheless, because there was so much more standard gauge than broad gauge in Britain, the Commissioners decided that the broad gauge should not be extended. For a few more decades the GWR kept its broad-gauge track to the west and laid mixed-gauge (three-rail) tracks on most of its mileage. Finally, in 1892, over a

meticulously planned weekend, the final sections of the broad gauge were converted to standard gauge.

In the USA, a final decision on gauge came later, and standardisation resulted not from governmental coercion, but from the federal choice of 4ft 8½in (1,435mm) for the first transcontinental railroad. This gave the standard gauge a valuable seal of approval at a time when it was used on barely 50% of US mileage.

Until the American gauge was standardized, various expedients were used to handle long-distance through traffic. Transhipment, although costly and time-consuming, was the most common method of handling long-distance freight. For passengers, a change of train, and usually of station, was the familiar and much-resented procedure. Just as in Britain, where critics as well as cartoonists liked to exaggerate the hardships of the break of gauge at Gloucester, so in America these enforced tramps along station tracks built up a powerful public opinion in support of gauge standardisation.

The Illinois Central Railroad, which interchanged traffic with 5ft (1,520mm) gauge lines at Cairo on the Mississippi, had car-lifting equipment, which transferred car bodies

Above: **Mixed-gauge trackage in Merida, Mexico. Both locomotives are standard gauge.**

from one set of trucks to another. Elsewhere in the USA it became common to lay a third rail so that mixed-gauge track was created.

When it was decided to build the transcontinental at 4ft 8½in (1,435mm) instead of the original 5ft (recommended because most Californian lines were 5ft [1,520mm]), existing Mid-Western companies with non-standard gauges began to conform. In 1880 the main line of the Erie Railroad across New York was converted from 6ft (1,828mm) to 4ft 8½in (1,435mm) in the course of a day. Nevertheless, even after this major conversion a fifth of US mileage was non-standard. Most of this was in the south, where much 5ft (1,520mm) gauge survived. But in 1881 the Illinois Central, which was standard gauge in its northern reaches, converted its southern main line to standard gauge. This was a line of almost 550 miles, and the conversion was achieved on a Friday, using about 3,000 carefully instructed workers who were required to move one of the two rails 3½in (90mm) closer to the other.

Other southern companies then agreed among themselves to standardise in the spring of 1886. In preparation, just as the British GWR had built locomotives easily con-

vertible from broad to standard gauge, the Baldwin Locomotive Works built a series of convertible engines for these southern lines. The conversion was not to 4ft 8½in (1,435mm), but to 4ft 9in (1,448mm), which was the gauge of the nearby Pennsylvania Railroad. However, over the years this half-inch (13mm) difference, which was negligible in practice, disappeared.

Gauge differences were a characteristic of the British Empire, and the consequences are still apparent. Some territories, such as South Africa, had the good fortune to standardise early but in others, notably India and Australia, a multi-gauge network became permanent. What happened in South Africa was that the first railway was built to the 4ft 8½in (1,435mm) gauge, probably because the British locomotive builders recommended and preferred to supply engines of that gauge. But when the need came to push the railway from Cape Town northward from Wellington to Worcester, the surveyor said it was only possible to break through the mountain range with a 2ft 6in (762mm) gauge, because of the need for sharp curves. Once through the mountains, however, it was clear that a narrow gauge would be disadvantageous. In the end, the 3ft 6in (1,065mm) gauge was chosen by the Cape parliament as a compromise, and thereby became the South African standard. When the line through the Hex River Pass was completed, the existing Cape Town-Wellington line became mixed gauge for a few years.

Australia was less fortunate. The British government, bearing in mind the trouble experienced with the Great Western broad gauge at home, was anxious that each of the colonies in Australia should have the same gauge. However, Australia's first railway, from Melbourne to Port Melbourne, was of 5ft 3in, whereas the second, from Sydney to Parramatta, was 4ft 8½in (1,435mm). The New South Wales administration — each state was separately governed at this time — was persuaded to change to 5ft 3in (1,600mm), but, before doing so, it reduced the salary of its chief engineer, who resigned. His successor, from England, was a strong supporter of the 4ft 8½in (1,435mm) gauge, and persuaded the New South Wales government to continue with that gauge. Any hope of a standard gauge for Australia was thereby lost. Later, Western Australia and

Queensland chose 3ft 6in, South Australia stayed with adjacent Victoria on the 5ft 3in gauge while Tasmania, starting with 5ft 3in (1,520mm) for its Launceston-Deloraine line in 1871, soon changed its mind and adopted 3ft 6in (1,065mm). It was not until the 1960s that major constructions alleviated much of the Australian gauge problem. A standard-gauge line was laid from Albury in New South Wales to Melbourne. Another standard-gauge line in Western Australia connected Perth with the 4ft 8½in (1,435mm) gauge Trans-Australian Railway, while the latter, at its eastern end, connected with a standard-gauge line from Port Pirie in South Australia to Broken Hill in New South Wales, making it possible to run 4ft 8½in (1,435mm)

Below: **3ft gauge (left) and standard gauge (right) locomotives on the Mexican mixed gauge.**

Above right: **Metre-gauge in India; a British-built locomotive hauls a passenger train out of Ahmedabad.**

Below right: **Another view of the Mexican mixed gauge at Merida, in Yucatan. Both locomotives are US-built; the Ten-wheeler on the right was built by Baldwin in 1888.**

gauge trains from Sydney to Perth. Another state capital, Brisbane, had been connected to the New South Wales gauge by a 95-mile line in 1930.

In India, where a multi-gauge system has become almost an accepted way of life, the 5ft 6in (1,676mm) gauge was initially the standard. Later, when the British authorities wished to add secondary routes, they found that the expense of broad-gauge track was an obstacle. So it was decided that the new lines, which had been carefully planned to connect with the broad-gauge trunk routes, would be of meter gauge. This meter-gauge network still co-exists with the broad gauge, and there are also several short narrow-gauge lines. The latter were limited to very local services, but a lack of co-operation between British government departments allowed the adoption of two different narrow gauges: 2ft (610mm) and 2ft 6in (762mm).

12
UNSCRUPULOUS OPERATORS

In 1857 the registrar of Britain's Great Northern Railway was found guilty of embezzling £0.25million sterling of the company's funds, and was sentenced to be transported to Australia. The railways, big businesses in which large numbers of employees handled money in offices remote from close supervision, presented great opportunities for the dishonest. As time passed, the companies found ways of regulating crime, and the huge burden of paperwork imposed on station workers is one consequence of this drive against dishonesty. Keeping elaborate records was the first step toward rooting out misappropriations.

However, while petty theft was energetically prosecuted, large-scale misuse of public money was sometimes permissible, provided no criminal intent could be proved. The big railway "kings" or "barons" were unscrupulous operators, who were intent on enriching themselves at the expense, ultimately, of people poorer than themselves. The USA was a far more sympathetic environment for these people than Britain, where sharp practice, once it became evident, was soon dealt with. In the US there was an element of public opinion that could be relied on to support the successful buccaneer, and, indeed, the names of the most successful "robber barons" have entered into American folklore in the guise almost of heroic figures, which they were not.

In Britain, George Hudson was the best-known and biggest of these men. His heyday was in the 1840s, after he had received a legacy enabling him to change from shopkeeper to railway-share speculator. Soon his bullying, wheedling and unscrupulous relationships with his fellow men brought him high responsibility and his sharp share dealings gained him control of 20% of the railway mileage. He also became a Tory member of Parliament. This gave him an additional advantage since it enabled him to speak his mind about rival railway companies; companies that threatened to build lines into the territory of his own railways or companies that had railways in territories which he himself intended to invade. Influencing Parliament to refuse railway proposals and dissuading investors from putting money into them were his main lines of attack.

By forcing down rival companies' shares, and then buying them up, Hudson acquired control of a succession of small companies, which he joined to form large railways, notably the North Eastern and the Midland. In doing this, he became part of a process of amalgamation that was demanded by the times, and his defenders claimed that, although he might be unscrupulous, his activities did at least bring beneficial reorganisations, which might not have otherwise occurred. At least it can be said that Hudson did the decent thing by dying in poverty. He may have ruined countless families, he may have wrecked numerous sensible railway schemes, but he did not last long. Once it was discovered that he had been paying dividends out of capital, and had enriched himself at the expense of his shareholders, his career was finished.

Right: **George Hudson, Britain's most notable railway manipulator.**

Above: **An 1845 cartoon from *Punch*, showing "King" Hudson receiving homage. The British press was quite rapid in its despatch of Hudson, whose "rule" was far shorter than that of his American counterparts.**

An early and fairly primitive form of corruption in the US railroad industry was supported by the practice of awarding state grants to railroad construction companies. So great was the public demand for railroads that legislatures, mainly state but occasionally federal, felt compelled to offer financial aid. The builders, having obtained such funds on the basis of inflated estimates, would then build as cheaply as possible and pocket the difference. When Americans celebrated the completion of the first transcontinental, the railroad they thought was finished was in fact only half-finished, and it would require years to complete the work that the builders had left undone.

Once an individual acquired enough shares to control a railroad, there were different ways in which he could milk it. Watering the stock was a preferred device; this was the secret printing of additional shares that could be sold on the unsuspecting market and which in effect increased the indebtedness of the railroad, while adding nothing to its assets.

Jay Gould, who was fairly typical of the American railroad barons of the late 19th century, milked the Erie Railroad in the 1860s before using his gains to finance the acquisition of a commanding number of Union Pacific Railroad (UP) shares. He then caused the UP to pay generous dividends, which were not backed by earnings, and sold his shareholding when, in consequence of those dividends, the share price rose high. This gain enabled him to buy the Kansas Pacific (KP), which was one of the UP's competitors. By threatening to reduce KP freight rates and to build a line paralleling one of the UP's, he forced the UP to buy up the KP. He then moved off with his gains to prey on some other railroads.

Gould and characters like him enriched themselves while impoverishing the railroads. Apart from the trail of personal ruin and suicide that they left behind as they devoured the savings or the tax contributions of their fellow-countrymen, their machinations left the USA with thousands of miles of railroad that were badly built, badly located and, in many cases, clearly unwanted. The Nickel Plate Railroad, which was built solely in order to parallel and hence damage the New York Central system, created by those other barons, the Vanderbilts, was only one example of a completely unjustified line. Its construction meant that dollars which might have been used to build more useful lines were dissipated to no purpose. The result was that the New York Central and other lines were in a weaker financial position when the time came to fight highway competition.

Building unwanted railways for short-term financial gain was not limited to the USA, for, in Britain, the Direct Portsmouth Line was built by a successful contractor, Thomas Brassey, in the expectation of selling it to the highest bidder among three other companies, which were already fighting for the Portsmouth traffic. On the whole, Britain and the USA were the most conspicuous victims of this parasitic aggression in which the interests of the railways' shareholders and clients were sacrificed to the greed of unscrupulous operators.

Such abuses became arguments for those who believed that state railways were preferable to private. Certainly the state railways of Belgium and Germany, despite the occasional scandal or misjudgement, represented successful attempts to construct sound railway networks for a minimum capital investment, while, in the British Parliament, the young Lloyd George argued that the Prussian State Railways operated far more efficiently than the British companies. Such arguments would be heard over and over again as, one by one, private railway companies were nationalized until the only major private systems left would be in North America and Switzerland.

13
BATTLE OF THE BRAKES

The first passenger death on a public railway seems to have been that of William Huskisson, the President of the Board of Trade, run down by *Rocket* at the opening of the Liverpool & Manchester Railway in 1830. It was his own fault. In the USA, the first fatality was of the fireman of the locomotive *Best Friend of Charleston* on the South Carolina Railroad, who, in an early essay in rationalisation, tied down the safety valve. The shattered locomotive was later rebuilt and renamed *Phoenix*, but no such resurrection awaited the fireman.

It was not until 1853 that an American railroad accident cost more than 10 lives, and, until 1856, the record for the worst accident lay in France, where in 1842 there had been a derailment, followed by a fire, on the Versailles line. The French railways had until then taken the precaution, from then on abandoned, of locking passengers into their compartments to prevent them jumping out of trains in motion. This was a practice that caused the incineration of 42 passengers in this disaster.

In Britain, the worst of the 19th century accidents was the collapse of the Tay Bridge in 1879, with 74 fatalities. In the USA, a burning culvert claimed 82 lives at Chatsworth, Illinois, in 1887, but this was eclipsed by Canada's worst accident, when a Grand Trunk Railroad train plunged over an open drawbridge at St Hilaire, Quebec, taking 88 lives with it. Such high fatalities were rare in accidents, but, in 1915, a British record was made when two trains of the Caledonian Railway collided, were run down by a third train, and caught fire. The official number of deaths was 227, but even this was not a world record, for, in that same year, a Mexican train fell into a gorge; 600 were killed.

Improved track more or less kept pace with higher train speeds, so the most frequent accidents were collisions. To reduce these, better signaling and brakes were required, and, by the end of the 19th century, the basic inventions had been achieved and applied to improve these two essentials.

Although British, continental and North American signaling techniques subsequently diverged, in the beginning there were basic similarities. Moving trains were kept separate by signalmen, who initially used flags and, later, mechanical signals to admit trains into the sections of track they controlled. The time interval principle was observed, with no train allowed to proceed behind another except after the elapse of a predetermined period of time. In Britain, where lines were usually double-track, this was not hard to apply, although it could only reduce, without eliminating, the danger of tail-end collisions. In North America, where lines were almost entirely single-track, strict observance of schedules was required.

The electric telegraph enabled a radical improvement to be introduced. On double-track lines the principle of space-interval, much safer than time-interval, was established. Known as the block system, the new technique treated the line between successive signalmen as a block and no train was allowed to enter one block before its controlling signalman had been informed by the next signalman that the previous train had entered the following block. So long as the signalmen and the enginemen kept by the rules, a collision was henceforth impossible. In practice, external circumstances might so disturb railwaymen that they broke

Right: **A proportion of European freight cars had a manual brake operated from a brake platform. The traveling brakemen were provided with a sheltered seat, as on this French mineral car.**

Left: **A three-position sema-phore signal in New South Wales.**

Below: **A British disk-and-crossbar signal of the 1840s. "Proceed" was signified by rotating the disc so it faced the oncoming train.**

the rules and caused an accident, but nevertheless the block system was a great step forward.

In the USA, the train-order system was made possible by the telegraph. Enginemen picked up from operators at stations written train orders, which had the effect of modifying the regular timetable. So, if a northbound train was late, a southbound train could be instructed to take the passing loop at a station farther down the line. Tall semaphore signals outside the operators' offices at stations informed enginemen whether or not there was an order to be picked up.

For multi-track lines, the American railroads, as the British, adopted semaphore signals. In Britain, these were generally two-position — a horizontal arm signifying "Stop" and a lowered arm meaning "Proceed" (technically these are as "lower quadrant" signals). Later, some railways preferred to raise the arm at 45° to indicate "Proceed" (these are known as "upper quadrant" signals). Advance warning, or distant, signals were placed at a generous braking distance in front of the "Stop" signals, to repeat the signal of the latter so that trains would have time to come to a halt. In the USA, the three-position semaphore became popular. With this, the arm was vertical for "Proceed," inclined upward for "Proceed with Caution," and horizontal for "Stop." This type of signal was also used occasionally in Britain and Australia.

The first block system was applied between London and Dover in 1851, but then spread slowly in Britain. The Camden & Amboy Railroad, in New Jersey, installed the block system in 1865, after a disastrous collision. Both countries used interlocking systems to prevent a signalman inadvertently setting his signals in conflict with those of the adjacent signalman. The first track circuits, in which a train in a block section short-circuited a weak electric current passing through one rail and thereby operated a device that held at "Stop" the signal controlling entry to that block, were introduced in the 1870s.

The Railway Department of the British Board of Trade recognized quite early the need for a continuous and automatic brake; continuous meant braking power distributed down the train, and automatic really meant fail-safe. In particular, the brake was required to function even when the train was split by a broken coupling.

In the USA, George Westinghouse patented an air brake in 1869, but his really effective version, acting automatically should the train split, appeared in 1872. In the 1880s most American passenger trains were equipped with it, but it was difficult to use on long freight trains because it braked the leading cars long before the rear cars, and this could cause derailments. However, further improvements, as well as tests conducted on the Burlington Railroad, led to its gradual application to freight trains.

The Westinghouse brake was operated by compressed air, stored in a reservoir and produced by a pump on the locomotive. In Britain, railway engineers had perfected a rather similar brake that used atmospheric pressure instead, the brake pump being used to exhaust air from the system. Technically, because it could use higher pressures, the air brake was superior, but it was resisted by many British railways because the vacuum brake seemed quite good enough and was already in service. The Board of Trade conducted brake trials at Newark in 1875, and, in 1878, the Board put gentle pressure on companies to fit continuous automatic brakes. Compulsion followed in 1889. This harder attitude owed something to the Hexthorpe accident in 1887 where two trains had collided; the enginemen had been tried for manslaughter but were acquitted after the judge had condemned the unreliable braking system with which they were provided.

But the Board, neither in 1878 nor 1889, specified which system was to be used, so companies took sides in a long "battle of the brakes" and the end result was that some railways chose the vacuum and others the air brake. This situation was later repeated in South Africa, although for different reasons. As the two systems were incompatible, special dual-fitted stock was needed in Britain for continuously braked services over railways using different systems. This really meant that such through services were not operated, the most conspicuous exception being the dual-fitted East Coast passenger trains from London to Scotland in which the southern participant, the Great Northern, used the vacuum brake, but the northern participants, the North Eastern and North British railways, used the air brake. This coexistence of incompatible brakes persisted in Britain for another 100 years. It might have all been different if George Westinghouse had not tried to bribe the LNWR's influential chief mechanical engineer to adopt the air brake. The latter, formerly inclined to prefer the air brake, was a person of extreme or even excessive integrity, and the financial inducement had the opposite effect to that intended.

Main picture: **American-style railroading with rooftop brakemen survived until the 1970s on this mountainous Peruvian line.**

Left: **A British "split" signal: lower-quadrant semaphores controlling a divergent junction. The train is about to diverge to its right.**

Below: **Inside a Canadian Pacific caboose in the 1950s, by which time only the conductor and rear-end brakeman normally rode there.**

14
LUXURY ON THE LINE

Although the last four decades before World War 1 saw first-class rail passengers treated to unprecedented privileges and luxuries, this period can also be regarded as one in which many of the older comforts enjoyed by the superior-class passenger were increasingly offered to the mass of passengers. In Britain, this process had started dramatically when the Midland Railway upgraded third class, allowing its passengers to travel in upholstered comfort on even the fastest of the trains. The soft furnishing of British third-class accommodation was distinctive almost until the present day; indeed, in parts of continental Europe, wooden seats may still be encountered in the lowest class of accommodation, on some secondary lines.

Above: **An American coach seat, with geared arms to allow re-positioning of the wooden back.**

Right: **A British magazine views the novel experience of traveling by Pullman sleeper on the Midland Railway.**

Below: **A royal vehicle maintained on French railways by the Russian Tsar.**

Bottom: **The all-Pullman "Overland Limited" in Nevada. This Chicago-San Francisco train was the first of the transcontinental luxury services and was operated jointly by the Chicago & North Western, Union Pacific, and Southern Pacific railroads.**

THE GRAPHIC

AN ILLUSTRATED WEEKLY NEWSPAPER

VOL. X.—No. 260
Regd at General Post Office as a Newspaper]

SATURDAY, NOVEMBER 21, 1874

[PRICE SIXPENCE
Or by Post Sixpence Halfpenny

Sleeping Car— going to Bed

Good night Ma

Dawn—Is it time to get up?

A Smoke

Private Room

Very refreshing

Confound it! How the Fellow Snores

Quiet Luncheon

American and British practice continued to diverge in passenger carriage design. The British still preferred compartments, while the Americans stayed with the open car and central aisle. British sleeping cars were for night use only, unlike those of the Pullman type, as distances traveled were relatively short.

The practice of attaching dining cars to the better trains led, in America, to a fundamental improvement. Access to the diner over the open platform ends of each car was inconvenient and even dangerous, with the result that a better means of crossing from one car to another was sought. The solution, patented in 1887, was invented by a superintendent at the Pullman Works. This was an open metal frame suspended at the end of each car and bearing against a similar frame on the adjoining car. Concertina bellows were attached to it to form a walkway. The previously open end platform was narrowed and enclosed to form a vestibule, making a completely enclosed passage between

Above left: **A US parlor car seat. The seat and back are of veneer, perforated for comfort, and the chair rotates.**

Above right: **Another parlor-car fitting, the cool water dispenser.**

Left: **Queen Victoria's royal vehicles, normally stored at Calais and available for royal visits to Europe.**

two carriages. For more than a decade the "vestibule train" was the most heavily advertised offering of US railroads.

Vestibules spread slowly to other countries. In Britain the better longer-distance trains were corridor trains with dining cars, and these were the first to be so equipped. Another American feature, which became popular in Britain for some decades, was the raised longitudinal central roof section, or clerestory, which provided extra window area and also a space to suspend the lamps.

Train lighting had developed from nothing, at the start of the Railway Age, to candles, oil lamps, and then gas lamps. Oil and gas were liable to ignite disastrously in accidents, so electric lighting had advantages of safety as well as of smell and convenience. Another fire peril on American railroads had been the car heating stove, typically wood-fired. The provision of steam radiators, using steam piped down the train from the locomotive, was, again, not only a convenience but also a step toward greater safety. In Britain, steam heating meant the gradual disappearance of the footwarmer. The latter was a metal canister, recharged at main stations, inside which a chemical process maintained moderate heat. It survived on Australian secondary lines until the 1980s, enabling diesel locomotives to haul trains designed for steam heat.

In the aftermath of train fires there were often short-lived public demands for all-metal passenger cars, and, by 1914, this solution was in sight. The reason, however, was not safety but the increasing cost of the kind of timber needed for making carriage frames, as well as the space-saving virtue of steel construction. By 1909, 50% of US passenger carriage orders were for all-steel types.

Additional comfort for daytime passengers on long-distance trains in North America was provided by the chair (or parlor) carriage, which offered more comfortable seating and often a beverage service. These carriages were often

Above: **Dining on the Burlington RR. Thanks to its connections with the Northern Pacific and Great Northern railroads, the Burlington connected Chicago with the Pacific coast.**

Below: **The newly invented electric suction cleaner at the service of parlor car passengers.**

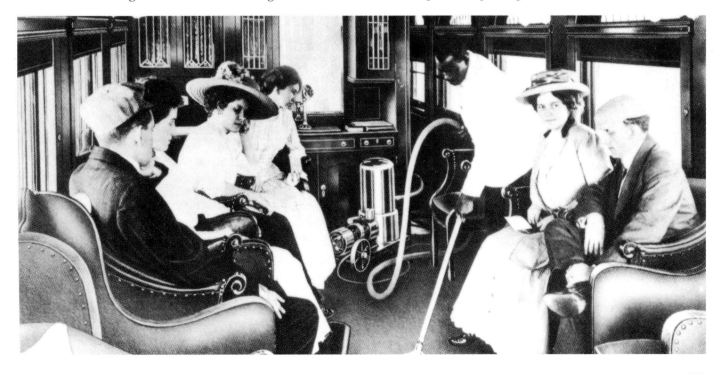

placed at the tail-end and were generally provided with an observation platform. They became a typical feature of the long-distance American train and could also be found in Australia, which also adopted several other American features. In Britain and other countries, where train journeys were relatively short, they were very rare, although the British did possess some observation carriages on scenic routes, such as the West Highland line in Scotland. Another North American feature was the business car. This was a vehicle, usually privately owned, that provided home comforts for those rich enough to own one. Most of them, including those used by railroad managers to tour their lines, were fairly simple, but there were others that were expensively and ostentatiously fitted out. One financier even had solid gold water pipes, which were said to be more economical than copper as they did not require polishing.

The carriages provided for royalty were also quite luxurious and several have found their way into railway museums. Queen Victoria, apart from having her own royal trains in Britain (many of the pre-Grouping companies produced royal carriages in the 19th century), kept two royal vehicles in France, at Calais, which she could use for her continental travels. Her son King Edward VII did the same, and while using one in Belgium, narrowly escaped death from an assassin's bullet. The tradition for royal trains continues in Britain to the present day with a dedicated rake of carriages in a distinctive purple livery, although time considerations and security now result in most royal journeys being undertaken by air or car.

Left: **The imperial flags and emblem were carried by locomotives hauling the Japanese royal train.**

Above: **Queen Victoria's personal saloon, part of the royal train provided by the London & North Western Railway.**

Right: **(1) Paris-Orleans Railway first class car of 1907. (2) Wagons-Lits restaurant car for international services. (3) PO Railway 1907 combination of first class, second class and baggage sections.**

15
TRAIN SERVICES

While almost all railways earned more revenue from freight than from passengers, progress in freight services was less noticeable, usually consisting of a steady increase in scale, with progressively longer trains, bigger freight wagons and, after the introduction of continuous brakes, an increase of average speeds. Passenger services at the end of the 19th century benefited from a general acceleration not only on the competition-oriented American and British railways, but also in continental Europe and Australia. The average speed of trains was highest, overall, in Britain, but the USA claimed to have the fastest trains in the world.

In North America, the most dramatic competition was between the Reading and the Pennsylvania railroads for the Philadelphia-Atlantic City traffic. The rail distance was 55 miles for one company and 58 for the other, and, in 1899, after two years of competitive scheduling, both lines were allowing 55min for the trip. In effect, this meant that for 50 miles or so the trains averaged around 65mph, which was a speed no British railway could match over that distance, although the London & South Western Railway did have a 60mph timing over 15 miles.

Elsewhere, in the USA, speeds were rising from their low averages of the 1880s. In that decade, only a handful of trains averaged more than 40mph, and these were mainly confined to the Jersey City-Philadelphia or Baltimore-Washington services. Chicago was 25hr from New York and 14hr from St Paul. But, at the end of the century, the Chicago & North Western Railroad was running to St Paul in 10hr, while two competing New York-Chicago overnight trains — the New York Central's "Twentieth Century Limited" and the Pennsylvania Railroad's "Pennsylvania Special" (predecessor of the "Broadway Limited") — brought the New York-Chicago timing down in 1902 to 20hr, which, in 1905, was reduced to 18hr. After this peak performance, however, there was a relapse to slightly longer schedules.

The New York Central was also the operator of the "Empire State Express," introduced in 1892 between New York and Buffalo (a distance of almost 440 miles). Excluding two stops for locomotive change, the schedule allowed 426min. As with most fast trains, the load was

small, typically only four cars, and it was this train, hauled by the celebrated No 999, which was said to have covered a mile in 32sec. No 999 was designed by William Buchanan and was initially built in 1893 with large driving wheels intended to facilitate high-speed running with light loads; on 10 May 1893 the locomotive hauled the "Empire State Express" over a measured mile at Batavia, New York, thus becoming the first officially recorded instance of a locomotive exceeding 100mph; it created a land speed record that was to survive for many years.

The practice of naming trains that were regarded as deserving special public attention became widespread in the USA, common in Britain, but less noticeable elsewhere. One of the earliest names was that of the "Irish Mail," which began running from London to Holyhead in 1848. Providing the mail service to the then British city of Dublin, it was required by the Post Office to maintain quite rigorous timings; as early as 1860 it was averaging 42mph. To help this train along, the technique of picking up and setting down mailbags at speed was developed, a practice that later came to the USA. By 1900, this train was averaging more than 50mph over the 265 miles, with only one intermediate stop for engine changing.

In Britain, the passenger services of the GWR were perhaps the most progressive at the end of the century. The GWR had introduced the first side-corridor train in 1891, and proceeded to accelerate its fast trains and introduce others. The final abolition of its broad gauge in 1892 had evidently infused a dynamic spirit into its management. Its best London-Bristol service covered the 118 miles in 2¼hr, and, in 1904, it introduced its "Cornish Riviera Limited," with a grueling schedule over the heavily-graded main line through Devon.

Most of the larger British towns were served by two or more companies, while between any two towns there was usually more than one route. Competitive pressures drove companies to provide faster services, so the increase of average speeds, unlike in the USA, was a process that lasted up to World War 1. The Caledonian Railway, for example, faced with competition from the North British, was running many 50mph trains as early as 1906, and also a 60mph train over the 32 miles from Perth to Forfar. In 1888 and 1895 there had been the "Races" from London to Scotland, in which for a few days the West Coast and East Coast companies sought to undercut each other's timings. Very

Main picture: **Late 19th century American rolling stock, still serving a Mexican branch line in the 1960s.**

Top left: **Carrying mail from northern France to southern Italy, this French postal car speeded communication between London and Britain's eastern empire.**

Top Right: **A French 20-ton mineral car.**

high, often unprecedent-
ed speeds were achieved in
these spontaneous bursts of intense com-
petition, although it is doubtful if they were enjoyed by the
passengers; the latter probably stayed away if they could,
and there is no doubt that the trains were reduced in size
day by day, being little more than 100 tons on the last days.
No disasters ensued, but risks were taken.

Another hotly competitive route was between
Plymouth and London on the days that transatlantic liners
berthed at Plymouth. Both the GWR and its rival, the
LSWR, ran fast "Ocean Mails" connecting with the ships. It
was during one such race to London in 1906 that the
LSWR's "Ocean Mail" hurtled off the rails on the Salisbury
curve, killing 24 passengers.

In continental Europe, too, trains were becoming faster.
In 1900 it was possible to cover the 540 miles from Paris to
Marseilles at an average speed of 45mph, although this was

in a luxury train at a fare
four times the third-class rate;
for the ordinary passenger there was a
train averaging 40mph. In other countries, whose railways
were not built for speed, the accent was put on comfort.
Russia had its "Trans-Siberian Express," which included a
piano among its attractions, while, in South Africa, the
"Union Limited," connecting with the British mailboat, and
the predecessor of the "Blue Train," had its beginnings in
1903.

Australia, in this period, was enjoying a foretaste of
interstate travel. After 1873 it was possible to journey by
train between Sydney and Melbourne, with a break of
gauge at Albury, and the two railways concerned, Victorian
Railways and the New South Wales Government Railways,
made a special effort with their Melbourne Cup race trains.
In 1891 they were able to provide Pullman 26-berth sleeping carriages, which included a two-berth ladies' cabin at

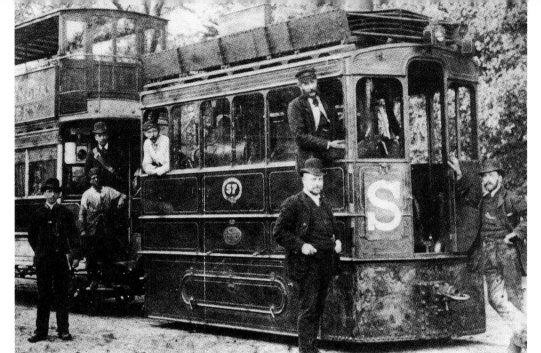

Opposite page, top: **The quality is not perfect but this is an early hand-colored postcard of the London & South Western Railway in about 1900.**

Opposite page, bottom: **Winter on the Philadelphia, Reading and New England RR.**

Left: **A city steam tram in Birmingham, England, in the late 19th century.**

Below: **An early type of British tank car.**

one end. They also provided the so-called "lavatory carriages," in which washrooms were made available for the first time to second-class passengers. By 1908 two regular daily trains were running from Sydney to Albury, the "Limited" and the "Express," with the timings requiring average speeds of 45mph on some sections. This route seemed to have a glowing future, and this expectation was not dimmed when the first airmail flight was organized from Sydney to Melbourne in the summer of 1914; the intrepid aviator required no less than 2¼ days to cover the route.

While railway companies were introducing long-distance trains that were faster and usually heavier than their predecessors, they were also encouraging the growth of short-distance traffic. Commuter services had been developing for several decades, aided by special reduced fares for workers. The trains were frequent and stopped at most or all of the stations on their comparatively short runs. They did much to change society, enabling people to live outside the cities in which they worked and instead to commute in, on a daily basis, to their places of employment. But they were often unprofitable, because they had sharp traffic peaks, between which the rolling stock was unproductive. Moreover, the intensity of these services meant that extra tracks had to be laid for them. So four-track lines on many of the routes out of London were created, and quadrupling was also required in the approaches to a few other cities. Indeed, such was the pressure that on certain sections six or eight tracks became essential. In the USA, much single-track line was doubled for the same reason, and often resignaled too. The process was not confined to Britain and the USA. Melbourne, Sydney, Calcutta and Johannesburg soon needed multi-track approaches, while cities such as Paris and Berlin also acquired intricate railway networks.

16
THE TRANS-CONTINENTAL LINES

The first American transcontinental route, despite the financial scandals that accompanied it, was an unquestioned success. It was evidently destined to be profitable; it was opening up for development vast tracts in the West as far as the Pacific, and, for a time, it did help to give Americans a sense of nationhood. The USA was a wide country, and there was room for more transcontinentals. Among these were the Atchison, Topeka & Santa Fe Railroad, which, by 1889, linked Chicago to the Pacific through Colorado and Kansas, having almost fought its way over the Raton Pass into New Mexico against the militant opposition of the Denver & Rio Grande Western Railroad (D&RGWR). The D&RGWR later joined with the Western Pacific at Salt Lake City to form another route to the Pacific. Then there was what became the Southern Pacific's line from New Orleans through Texas to Los Angeles. In the far north, the Canadian-born James Hill, not the worst of the railroad barons, managed to build two transcontinental lines — the Great Northern (GN) and the Northern Pacific (NP) — both running west to Seattle but taking different routes. Hill also controlled the Chicago, Burlington & Quincy Railroad, and naturally routed traffic originating on his GN and NP over that line. The Burlington's rival — the Milwaukee Railroad — in order to overcome this disadvantage, built its own extension to the Pacific, thereby finishing the last American transcontinental line. Its completion in 1909 was only seven years in advance of the Panama Canal, the opening of which took traffic from all the transcontinental routes.

Nation-building was a conspicuous objective of the Canadian Pacific Railway (CPR), for it was built to encourage British Columbia to join a proposed confederation of Britain's North American colonies rather than one day become part of the USA. The CPR was a difficult line to build, facing not only the Rockies but also expanses of swamp and muskeg around Lake Superior. But with strong financial and political support in London, setbacks were never allowed to kill it; the first through train from Montreal to the Pacific at Vancouver ran in 1886, taking 139hr for the trip. Two decades later a competing line, the Canadian Northern, was under way and, in 1915, was able to launch a Quebec-Vancouver service. Moreover, a third route of very high construction standards was also initiated. This consisted of a government project, the National Transcontinental Railway, which was laid from New Brunswick, over the new Quebec Bridge, and from there through virgin country to Winnipeg, where it linked with the Grand Trunk Pacific, which was building a line through the Rockies to Prince Rupert on the Pacific. This 3,543-mile route was completed in 1919, just in time to form part of the new Canadian National Railways, the government corporation formed to rescue Canada from the consequences of excessive railway construction.

The CPR was one of the inspirations behind the construction of the Trans-Siberian Railway by the Russian government, whose purpose was to consolidate the

Below: **In the early years of the Canadian Pacific, a train crosses Stoney Creek in British Columbia.**

Left: **On the newly-built Trans Siberian Railway.**

Below: **A bridge on the North Pacific Coast RR, a 3ft gauge line in California timber country.**

Russian hold on Siberia and its Pacific provinces by developing the eastern economy and supporting a fleet on the Pacific, as well as extending Russian political and economic influence in China. To save mileage, part of it was laid across Manchuria, over Chinese territory, and was known as the Chinese Eastern Railway (CER). Political sharp practice soon resulted in a Russian-owned branch line, the South Manchuria Railway (SMR), dropping south from the CER to Port Arthur, a Chinese seaport which became a Russian naval base. With such obvious expansionist purposes, it was hardly surprising that the Trans-Siberian would be immediately engulfed in the Russo-Japanese War, after which Russia was obliged to give up Port Arthur and the SMR.

Another political transcontinental, the Cape to Cairo Railway, was overtaken by events and never completed. It was the concept of Cecil Rhodes (the noted British explorer and imperialist, after whom the British colony of Rhodesia — now Zimbabwe — was named), who envisaged joining the railways in South African to the Egyptian Cairo-Luxor line by a route crossing Africa from south to north and consolidating British influence throughout its length. It was routed through Bechuanaland (now Botswana) so as to

avoid the Transvaal, which was then the anti-British South African Republic. It passed through Bulawayo, crossed the Zambezi by the celebrated Victoria Falls Bridge, but did not progress beyond Northern Rhodesia.

It was probably World War 1 and its aftermath that ended the Cape to Cairo dream. The Trans-Australian Railway was actually opened at the height of that conflict, in 1917. It was undertaken by a federal organization — Commonwealth Railways — following the federation of the Australian colonies in 1901. Its main purpose, as that of the Canadian Pacific, was to tie the most distant state in with the rest of the new nation. It linked existing railheads in Western Australia and South Australia and was 1,051 miles long. The choice of the 4ft 8½in (1,435mm) gauge, even though the two terminal states had systems of 3ft 6in (1,065mm) and 5ft 3 in (1,600mm) respectively, was intended to be a first step in standardizing the Australian railway gauge. It was a difficult line to build and to operate, because of water shortage, but natural obstacles were so rare that 297 successive miles of it could be laid perfectly straight across the Nullarbor Plain (the world's longest straight stretch), while the absence of stiff gradients enabled a single locomotive to haul heavy trains.

17
THE NARROW-GAUGE RAILWAY

As railway networks expanded, a point was reached when the main towns were served, but smaller and less prosperous communities remained isolated. Evidently, a cheaper type of railway was needed and the narrow gauge seemed the best solution, being considerably cheaper to build.

A big advantage of the narrow gauge, with its acceptance of sharp curves, was its ability to clasp the contours of a landscape. This meant that expensive earthworks and tunneling could be largely eliminated. Since rolling stock was smaller, it cost less, and the small size was no deterrent if heavy traffic was not anticipated. The narrow gauge did, however, present a problem: it could not exchange cars with adjacent, full-size railways. This was not serious for passengers, who were able to change trains at junctions in the usual way, but it did mean that freight had to be transhipped.

A definition of a narrow-gauge railway is not always easy, for one man's narrow gauge is another man's standard gauge. In the British colon, of Sierra Leone, for example, the railway network was of the 2ft 6in (762mm) gauge — a scale that would be regarded as tiny in most parts of the world. In South Africa, the main-line railways are of 3ft 6in (1,065mm), which would be regarded as a narrow gauge in many countries. In Japan, the standard gauge was also 3ft 6in (1,065mm).

Two British-built narrow-gauge lines had a great influence in popularizing the idea. The Ffestiniog Railway in Wales, laid for the transportation of quarried slate from the mountains down to the sea, was able to carry very heavy traffic even though it was only of 1ft 11⅛in (600mm) gauge. It was particularly noteworthy after 1870, when it began to use Fairlie's patent double-ended locomotives, designed especially for high-power outputs over sharply curved track.

The Barsi Light Railway in India, perhaps equally influential, was no short line, being 115 miles long. Of 2ft 6in (762mm) gauge, it was constructed by E. Calthrop, a theoretician of the narrow gauge. He used light rail, accepted a 15mph speed limit, designed locomotives with short wheelbases, low axle weights, but considerable power, and used high-capacity all-metal freight wagons of 15-ton

Main picture: **On the Russian narrow gauge. Eight-wheeler locomotives such as this were favored in modern times, hundreds being imported from Germany and Finland as post-World War II reparations.**

Left: **This 2ft 6in gauge machine was once a mainline locomotive in Sierra Leone, but now works on the Welshpool & Llanfair Railway in Wales.**

Below: **On the American-style 3ft gauge network in Yucatan. The 4-6-0 locomotive was built by Baldwin in 1916.**

Main picture: **A sugar cane railway in Queensland.**

Left: **Built in the Colorado silver boom, the 3ft gauge Rio Grande Southern was impoverished by the repeal of the Silver Purchase Act in 1893.**

Below left: **On the US-built Cuzco & Santa Ana Railroad in Peru.**

Bottom: **A British-built Pacific on the 2ft 6in gauge at Bangalore in India.**

capacity. In fact, his freight wagons were technically in advance of those used by most of the British main-line railways. After the Barsi line was built, Calthrop's reputation grew, and it was on his advice that the government of Victoria in Australia began to lay a series of 2ft 6in (762mm) gauge lines to supplement the main-line 5ft 3 in (1,600mm) gauge system.

The narrow gauge also became popular in India and South Africa for localities too poor to justify big investment. In South Africa, the narrow-gauge lines in Natal did much to encourage development, while the 177-mile Port Elizabeth-Avontuur line opened up a rich fruit-growing area.

In the USA, there was a "narrow-gauge fever" in the 1870s and 1880s. In Colorado, both the Colorado Central and the Denver & Rio Grande Western chose the 3ft (910mm) gauge as the largest practicable for that mountainous region. By 1883 the D&RGWR was running trains over a 770-mile heavily graded main line between Denver and Ogden. Although, in later years, it was steadily changed to standard gauge, the D&RGWR set a fashion, and, by 1900, only six states were without narrow-gauge lines. Most were of 3ft (910mm) gauge, but there were others. In Maine, the Sandy River & Rangeley Lakes Railroad had a 2ft (610mm) gauge network of over 100 miles.

France and Belgium also built narrow-gauge lines, the meter gauge being preferred. Austria, Germany and Switzerland used a variety of gauges and many of their narrow-gauge lines are still in use. The narrow gauge was also suitable for non-public railways, especially agricultural railways, which, in the period before the highway vehicle, began to appear on plantation-style, specialized, landholdings. The Decauville portable light railway, developed in France, was a 2ft (610mm) gauge system used by many

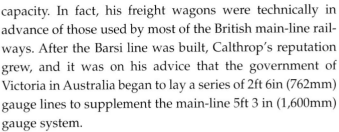

large farms in France, especially in the beet-growing areas. In many other parts of the world, including Queensland in Australia as well as the East and West Indies, 2ft (610mm) gauge sugar-cane lines, working only during the harvest season, were used.

The British were great proponents of the narrow gauge overseas, but were rather reluctant to employ it at home, preferring the light railway concept. The light railway is one where cheapness is obtained by employing lower constructional and operating standards while retaining, usually, the standard gauge. In return for allowing such railways to operate, the government imposed certain safety regulations that would have been intolerable for normal lines operating heavy trains at high speeds. The most important was a very low speed limit, which was necessary in view of the absence of signaling systems and of gates at highway crossings. There were, however, areas where the narrow gauge was important. These included several lines in Wales, such as the Welshpool & Llanfair and the Vale of Rheidol, and many in Ireland, then an integral part of the United Kingdom, with lines such as such as the Londonderry & Lough Swilly and the Country Donegal. In England, there were a small number of narrow-gauge lines that carried both passenger and freight services, these included the Lynton & Barnstaple and the Southwold railways, but these lines had largely closed by the outbreak of World War 2.

Above: **On a Deceauville-style portable railroad in France. This line, at Pithiviers, is a preserved section of a former agricultural network.**

Right: **Bosnia and Herzogovina had a substantial narrow-gauge mileage, which has since been regauged. The 0-8-2 locomotive is hauling a freight between Sarajevo and Dubrovnik.**

Far right: **Another scene on the Russian narrow gauge.**

18 IMPROVING THE LOCOMOTIVE

After 1875 steam locomotive development took two directions: consolidation and innovation. Consolidation meant the building of locomotives incorporating the advances of the previous decades, progress being measured by a steady increase in size, with its corollary of new wheel arrangements to bear the increased weight. Innovation meant radical technical advance in order to improve efficiency or to increase power without a proportionate increase of length or axle weight, both of which were restricted by limitations imposed by the track.

The 4-4-0 wheel arrangement, so long dominant in North America, was eventually succeeded there by the 2-6-0 and the 4-6-0, both of which could provide higher total weight on driving wheels and so more adhesion to allow the application of greater power without wheelslip. In Britain, the 4-4-0 would linger, some modern examples actually being built in the 1930s, but there, too, the type was superseded for passenger work by the 4-4-2 ("Atlantic") and the 4-6-0, with the 4-6-2 ("Pacific") making a cautious appearance before World War I. In the USA, the 4-6-2 arrived earlier and was soon adopted by many railroads. Its greatest manifestation was probably the "K4" type of the Pennsylvania Railroad, which produced a very high power output on test and was used for the Railroad's faster passenger trains over several decades.

The 4-6-2 had the advantage that the low rear axle allowed a wide firebox to be fitted. This, in turn, increased the all-important grate area, which determined the sustainable power output. The 4-6-0 had a narrow firebox, which is perhaps why it did not have a long life as a top passenger locomotive in the USA. In Britain, however, and in those countries like Australia and India, which closely followed British practice, the 4-6-0 had a long reign. In some cases the limiting rear axle was moved well back behind the firebox, producing an irregular spacing of the driving wheels that was also to be seen in other wheel arrangements. The 4-6-0 did have one advantage over the 4-6-2, in that a greater proportion of its weight was on the driving wheels, so it was less prone to slip. The GWR retained the 4-6-0 design until the end of its independent existence and the nationalized British Railways perpetuated its designs

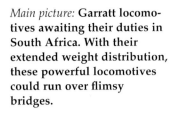

Main picture: **Garratt locomotives awaiting their duties in South Africa. With their extended weight distribution, these powerful locomotives could run over flimsy bridges.**

Left: **A Camelback passenger locomotive of the Lackawanna RR. Mounting the cab on the boiler was necessary because of the wide firebox, designed to burn local anthracite.**

Below: **The first of a class of large Pacific locomotives built by the Canadian Pacific Railway in its own workshops at Montreal.**

Main picture: **A Shay flexible-wheelbase locomotive at work in Bolivia.**

Right: **The standard Prussian passenger 4-6-0, of which over 3,000 units were built.**

Far right: **The small high-pressure cylinder of a French Nord Railway compound locomotive. This class was called "Les Grands Chocolats," because of their brown paintwork.**

for a brief period after 1948, while the South African railways, faced with the 1 in 40 (2.5%) gradient over the Hex River Pass and the long 1 in 66 climbs of the Durban line, used the 4-6-0, as well as the 4-8-0, design for many years.

For freight work, the British railways would continue to build simple inside-cylinder 0-6-0s for many years, although larger 0-8-0s and 2-8-0s were also built for mineral traffic. The latter had the advantage that they could use the same components as the 4-6-0 just as, in America, the popular 2-8-2 freight locomotive could use standard parts shared with the 4-6-2. In America the 2-10-0 and 2-10-2 soon made their appearances on lines with stiff gradients or heavy trains, but 10-coupled locomotives were regarded as excessive in Britain, and did not make their appearance until World War II.

British railways, because of their shorter distances and numerous branches, were large users of tank locomotives which, because they did not have tenders, could run in either direction and therefore did not need to be turned at the end of their usually short runs. One variety of tank locomotive, the Forney tank, did become popular in the USA. This carried its water not in side tanks but behind the cab, and was used for suburban workings.

The low thermal efficiency of the steam locomotive, with most of the energy potential of the coal going unused up the chimney, began to concern engineers as the railways' coal bills grew. One method of improving efficiency was "compounding," in which steam used by a cylinder was led, not to the chimney, but to a second low-pressure cylinder, where it could give up more of its power. Various permutations were used. In Britain, on the Midland Railway, which produced a successful 4-4-0 compound early in the 20th century, there was a high-pressure cylinder between the frames, exhausting into two outside low-pressure cylinders. On the London & North Western Railway, whose compounds were generally unsuccessful, there were two small high-pressure outside cylinders, exhausting into a wide low-pressure cylinder in the middle. In Germany and Russia, in particular, the outside cylinder "cross-compound" became popular. This had a small high-pressure cylinder on one side and a big low-pressure cylinder on the other. The system was not very

suitable for the faster engines, because it was impossible to equalise the power output of the two cylinders. Despite this disadvantage, the cross-compound locomotive was built in large numbers, the Russians having an 0-8-0 version, which finally totalled about 8,000 engines, a world record at the time.

In America, the Vauclain compound was briefly popular, and included the record-breaking 4-4-2s of the Reading Railroad. In the Vauclain scheme there were four outside cylinders, with the high-pressure ones placed directly above the low-pressure. But with ruggedness, reliability and simplicity being regarded on American railroads as more important than coal and water economy, compounding was not especially popular in the USA. It was developed to the highest degree in France, aided possibly by the better technical training of French enginemen, who could be trusted to get the best out of these more complicated machines. The du Bousquet layout became the most popular in France; this had four cylinders, the high-pressure ones being outside.

Meanwhile, Wilhelm Schmidt of the Prussian State Railways was developing another line of attack — the locomotive superheater. This was a bank of steam elements, which led the steam, on its way from the boiler to the cylinders, through a reheating process that raised its temperature far enough to prevent condensation when it entered the cylinders. By eliminating condensation, greater power was

obtained from a given quantity of steam. It was soon found that superheating produced economies as good as compounding, and by a much cheaper method. This is one reason why railways in Britain did not use the compounding process for long, even though trials held on the Midland Railway suggested that, although a superheated engine was more efficient than a compound in most conditions, a superheated compound was the most efficient of all.

One of the earlier advocates of compounding was Anatole Mallet, a professor of engineering in Paris, who designed a type of articulated locomotive to exploit it. This later became known as the "Mallet" locomotive and it had a boiler that was attached to a power unit (that is, cylinders and driving wheels) at the rear but merely rested on the second, forward, power unit, which was therefore free to swivel independently from the rest of the locomotive. This enabled a larger number of driving wheels to be used, thereby keeping the critical axle weight low in relation to the weight available for adhesion. The weakness of the "Mallet" locomotive was the flexible steam pipes and steam joints needed to connect the swivelling forward unit with the boiler. By making the forward unit the low-pressure part of a compound locomotive, this problem of steam escape was largely overcome.

In France and Germany, the "Mallet" took the form of tank locomotives for sharply curved lines, typically narrow gauge. In the USA, the Mallet idea was adopted on a large

Left: **The Canadian Pacific was an early user of the 2-10-0 type, especially over its western, mountainous, lines.**

Top left: **The Great Western two-cylinder 4-6-0 type, incorporating American features and shaping the later development of British locomotives.**

Center left: **A Mallet compound locomotive, built by Baldwin in 1911. The different diameters of low- and high-pressure cylinders are clearly visible.**

Above: **A late 19th century New South Wales 2-8-0 at the coaling stage.**

scale for heavy freight locomotives, enabling the railroads to go beyond the conventional 2-10-0 and 2-10-2 (although the Union Pacific did use some 4-12-2 engines, 12 driving wheels in a rigid frame were really too many for curved track). The first American "Mallet" was an 0-6-6-0 built for the B&O, which was so successful that other railroads began to order larger versions. In 1920 the Virginian Railway would reach the limit of the compound "Mallet," with a series of 2-10-10-2 locomotives in which the low-pressure cylinders were 4ft (1,220mm) in diameter; cylinders bigger than this were impossible to accommodate, so subsequent more powerful "Mallets" were simples (that is, non-compound, so all cylinders were high pressure). Interesting, but not very successful, variants of the "Mallet" included a series built by Baldwin, in which greater flexibility was obtained by actually using a jointed boiler, and the "Triplex" of the Erie Railroad, which had three power units, the extra one carrying the tender.

The British engineer Herbert Garratt devised a successful alternative to the "Mallet." The "Garratt" locomotive was also articulated, but the boiler was slung between, rather than above, the two power units, and both of the latter could swivel. This produced a type that was more flexible than the "Mallet" and also had ample space below the boiler in which a firebox and ashpan, with really good air circulation, could be fitted. The "Garratt" design was first supplied to a narrow-gauge line in Tasmania, but was later built in large numbers, especially for railways in the British Empire. A Russian commentator later wrote that the British "had invented the Garratt to save the wages of

locomotive crew in their colonies"; the grain of truth in this was that the "Garratt" could be regarded as two locomotives driven by a single crew.

South African Railways were enthusiastic users of "Garratt" locomotives, and, in the early 1920s, held comparative trials between "Garratt," "Mallet" and conventional units. In these, as could have been expected, the "Garratt" performed best, thanks largely to its efficient boiler. Despite its advantages, however, the "Garratt" was never bought for North American railroads. The latter preferred to stick with the "Mallet," thereby exhibiting the kind of managerial inertia that was later to prove so costly.

Just as the "Garratt" design patents were taken up by one particular builder, Beyer Peacock of Manchester, so was another innovatory concept, the "Shay" locomotive, adopted by the Lima Locomotive Works in Ohio. Ephraim Shay designed this locomotive to work on rough forestry lines, where the rails were light, badly laid and sharply curved. This very successful type had its cylinders placed vertically on one side of the boiler. They drove a crankshaft which was coupled to rotating shafts. These in turn, by means of bevel gears, transmitted their rotary motion to the wheels on that, right-hand, side of the engine. The wheels were in two four-wheel bogies, which were free to rotate, so sharp curves were no problem, while the long space between the two bogies spread the locomotive's weight. It was only the decline of the US logging industry that brought an end to "Shay" production in 1945. The last surviving "Shays" were in Bolivia, Taiwan and the Philippines, and were active in the latter were until the 1990s.

Left: **The first Garratt locomotive, built for Tasmania but shown here in England, on display in the National Railway Museum at York.**

Right: **The final flowering of the du Bousquet four-cylinder compound locomotive was a pair of 4-6-4 units. These remarkable machines were never developed, because du Bousquet died prematurely. No 3.1102 is displayed at the French national railway museum.**

19 RAILWAY ELECTRIFICATION

Although it would not be until the 1920s that the really big railway electrification schemes would be started, by 1900 the major technical problems had been solved and the main obstacle to electrification was the high cost of the initial equipment. Although burning coal in a generating station and using the electricity for traction provided more horsepower per ton of coal than the conventional steam locomotive, the cost of the generating plant, sub-stations and the conductor rails or overhead conductors to feed the locomotives was prohibitive except where there was a high volume of traffic over which these capital costs could be spread. Also, at a time of rapid technical progress, there was an understandable reluctance to embark on electrification schemes, which, within a few years, would be obsolete. However, exceptions were made where there were short lengths of line, which, perhaps because of the heavy gradients or long tunnels, were especially difficult for steam traction.

The German Dr Ernst Werner von Siemens had operated a small electric locomotive at the Berlin Trade Exhibition of

1879, but Volk's Railway in Brighton, England, became the first public electric railway when it opened in 1883. This short sea-front line, which still exists, used cars similar to tramcars, drawing current at low voltage from a third rail (although when originally opened power was derived from one of the two running lines). In the USA, during the 1880s, two electric locomotives were built by Leo Daft, while van der Poele showed how current could be conducted to the train by an overhead wire. Frank Sprague developed the idea of what he called the multiple-unit train, in which several electric motors along the train could be controlled from one cab.

In 1890, one of the London underground railways replaced steam locomotives with electric, and, five years later, the B&O built an electrified line at Baltimore connecting its western and northern main lines. The city authorities had rejected a proposal for an elevated line, so a tunnel was dug instead. This was electrified, because of the smoke problem, and electric locomotives hauled the trains, complete with their temporarily inactive steam locomotives, through the underground section. This electrification was imitated by several other North American lines. In New York, the city authorities, tired of the smoke nuisance from the New York Central trains using the Park Avenue tunnel to reach Grand Central Terminal, prohibited the use of steam traction south of the Harlem River. The New York Central decided to electrify and, unlike the B&O, which used overhead conductors, it opted for a third rail, carrying 600V dc; the 35 locomotives did have a tiny pantograph, but this was only to pick up overhead current at places where points interrupted the third rail.

The New Haven Railroad, which shared the tracks into Grand Central, was not content with merely electrifying for a few miles, and decided to convert its main line out of New York as far as New Haven; this 72-mile stretch was ready by 1914, using the 11,000V ac system offered by the Westinghouse Corporation. This voltage was also chosen by the Norfolk & Western Railroad when it electrified its steeply graded line through the Elkhorn Tunnel in West Virginia. Meanwhile, the Milwaukee Railroad had begun to electrify difficult sections of its new main line, while the Canadian Northern Railway, which had envisaged electrification from the start, was burrowing through Mount Royal to provide an outlet to the north of Montreal. The tunnel was completed in 1918 and the 2,400V dc overhead system, designed by General Electric, was later extended to permit the introduction of electric commuter services.

In Britain, by World War I, several railways had begun to experiment with short electrification schemes and several different, incompatible, systems were in use. In 1904, two third-rail 600V schemes were started — the Lancashire & Yorkshire (L&YR) Railway's 37-mile Liverpool-Southport commuter line and the North Eastern Railway's Newcastle scheme, whose 32 miles were expected to carry heavy

freight as well as passenger traffic. It was already realized that high-voltage systems were potentially more economical, but they presented technical problems. The Midland Railway's 10-mile Lancaster-Heysham electrification was at 6,600V ac, as was the London, Brighton & South Coast's eight-mile South London scheme. During the war, the LNWR's 630V dc scheme, using third and fourth rails, came into use in the north London suburbs, as did the L&YR's 1,200V third-rail Manchester-Bury project and the London Suburban 650V dc third-rail scheme of the London & South Western Railway (LSWR). It was the latter, even then not the technically best system, which was destined to expand after the war as the Southern Railway (which replaced the LSWR at the Grouping of 1923) expanded third-rail electrification through many of the south London suburbs and ultimately onto the main lines toward Portsmouth and Brighton..

In France, a variety of systems was tried in the south and, in 1900, the Paris-Orleans Railway began a 1,500V overhead conductor scheme from the capital to the southwest. This did not progress far before the war, but it was to be the nucleus for France's first major main-line electrification. In Germany, where the steam locomotive was well-entrenched as a very reliable performer burning cheap local fuel, electrification was not much favored. Overhead conductors were frowned upon by the military authorities, who argued that a break in the wire could bring trains to a standstill for many miles, which would be a weak link in mobilisation plans. However, the Prussian State Railways did begin a 15,000V ac project through the Silesian mountains which was completed in 1928, only to be dismantled and taken east, lock, stock and barrel, by the victorious Russians in 1945.

Left: **A British-built electric locomotive of the 1920s, initially used in Montreal docks.**

Top: **German electric locomotive of 1909, built for the 5,500V line to Oberammergau.**

Above: **A British electric locomotive of 1915, built for the second stage (1,500V) of the North Eastern Railway electrification.**

Right: **The successful Pennsylvania RR "DD1" electric locomotive design of 1910.**

PART THREE

FEELING THE STRAIN 1914-1945

Left: General Motors demonstration "F3" freight locomotive. Over 1,500 units were built between 1946 and 1949.

20
WORLD WAR I

Between the Franco-Prussian War of 1870-71 and the outbreak of World War I in 1914, railways had been a key factor in several other conflicts. In Africa, the British Royal Engineers had laid lines to Khartoum to support the victorious campaign against the Dervishes of the Sudan and then, in 1899, came the Boer War in South Africa.

The campaigns of this war extended over a vast area, with hundreds of miles separating the ports of the Cape, through which the British forces passed, from the territories where most of the war was fought. To prevent the railways and the military working at cross-purposes, the British established a Department of Military Railways, which matched military requirements with actual railway capacity. The lines were almost entirely single-track, with capacity limited, and so it became usual to despatch troops on foot while reserving the trains for their supplies.

In their initial retreat the Boers destroyed much of their railway track, but, when they turned to the offensive, they rarely restored it. Being traditionalists, they preferred horse transport, and, even when a railway was available, they often made no use of it. They became adept at disablement,

however, and on railways close to the war zones the British had to send out parties each dawn to check that Boer commandos had not damaged the track during the night.

Rudimentary armored trains were fitted out, typically consisting of a locomotive in the middle, open wagons with armored sides for the infantry, and a flatcar at the head-end with a gun. These were less successful than had been hoped, because they were unwisely regarded as a form of cavalry and sent on incursions into enemy territory. However, unlike cavalry, they had to go back the same way as they had come, which gave opportunities to a wily enemy. It was while riding in an armored train that the young Winston Churchill was captured by the Boers, who had blocked its line of retreat.

Soon after the Boer War came the Russo-Japanese War of 1904, which demonstrated the strategic importance of railways. Although the barely finished Trans-Siberian line was equipped with extra crossing loops and the train service speeded up, the Russians were able to assemble and supply a strong army only in the final months of the campaign, after they had lost the key battles. This was the first major war in which 2ft (610mm) gauge transportable railways of the Decauville type were employed. Laid behind the front lines, they were used for bringing up troops and supplies, as well as for evacuating the wounded.

The big continental military powers depended on railways for their security, which rested on fast mobilization and deployment. For Germany, liable to face a two-front war against France and Russia, fast mobilization was the basis of the Schlieffen Plan, which envisaged a concentration of troops against France before Russia could mobilize, and then, after France's rapid defeat, a quick railborne redeployment to the east to face the Russians.

Right: **A depot for narrow-gauge field railways behind the British lines on the Western Front in World War I. Shells are being loaded.**

In peacetime Germany, platforms and paved station areas were built as military loading points and exercises were regularly held to test the readiness of the railways. Railways had a military member on their management councils, and facilities were inspected each year. A mobilization schedule, revised annually, detailed down to the last carrier pigeon the movement of the army and its supplies. There were two phases: the mobilization phase, in which special trains would take reservists from their home stations to their military depots, and the deployment, in which units would be taken from their depots to allotted places on the frontier.

France, Austria and Russia had similar, though less detailed, mobilization plans. In the years preceding 1914, the Russians, helped by French advice and money, had been improving their western railways, and also placing their regular army formations nearer the frontier. By that year, the Russian plan could mobilize 66% of its immense army in just three days longer than the Germans needed to mobilize their whole army. Thus the several weeks difference in deployment times that the Schlieffen Plan relied on could no longer be expected. This was alarming for the German General Staff, which now saw that a victorious war against the Franco-Russian alliance was fast becoming impossible. It was this realization that engendered the "now or never" spirit among the German staff in 1914.

Once the war started, the belligerents' mobilization and deployment plans worked faultlessly. Even the bureaucratic, creaking, Austrian administration managed to field its troops in the expected time, while Russia achieved mobilization and deployment several days earlier than planned.

At Cologne, for two weeks, six westbound military trains per hour rumbled across the key railway bridge over the Rhine. To utilize all their railway lines, the German troops had to be spread over a long expanse of frontier. This, in turn, meant that one arm of their offensive passed through neutral Belgium, with dire diplomatic consequences, while in the south, the Duchy of Luxembourg had to be captured for the sake of its key railway junction. A sin-

gle armored train, sent in as war was declared, did this. The violation of the neutrality of Belgium, which had been guaranteed by the British amongst others, resulted in the British declaration of war and brought the British Empire into the conflict.

Later, when the German army moved into France, the plans went astray. The offensive outpaced the speed with which the railway battalions could restore and operate the captured French and Belgian railways, with the result that many German formations were reduced to living off the land, which had some effect on their fighting capacity.

The transportation of the British Expeditionary Force (BEF) to Southampton was faultless, and, as the war progressed, the supply of the BEF in France was taken over by the Railway Operating Division (ROD) of the Royal Engineers, which was composed, for the most part, of soldiers recruited from the home railways. British locomotives and rolling stock were sent to work over the French lines

Above: **British troops sent against German South West Africa depart from a South African station.**

Left: **British soldiers go home to England on leave during World War I.**

Right: **British wounded are brought to the rear by field railway.**

Below right: **Heavy shells make their precarious way by field railway to the gun sites.**

between the Channel ports and the British sector of the front. At Richborough, in Kent, a new port was built to handle train ferries carrying loaded freight wagons to France.

Meanwhile, as the war progressed, the British railways were burdened with unprecedented demands. Wisely, the government had set up the Railway Executive Committee (REC) to control the activities of the scores of railway companies. Being made up of railway managers, the REC had a good idea of what could and could not be done, and therefore worked very successfully. One consequence was that, because the different railways were co-ordinated and wasteful competition eliminated, they seemed to work far more efficiently than they had in peacetime.

Traffic took new directions. In particular, the poverty-stricken low-traffic Highland Railway was flooded with traffic, for it was the closest line serving the Royal Navy's base at Scapa Flow (albeit still requiring transhipment by boat across the Pentland Firth to the Orkney Islands). The

"Naval Special" ran daily over the more than 700 miles separating London from the northern tip of Scotland. Meanwhile, to enable trains to carry more passengers, restaurant cars were removed from almost all services in Britain. Exhortations to Britons to refrain from traveling for pleasure and holidays, however, were largely unheeded even after a sharp deterrent rise in fares. Railway workshops turned over much of their production to munitions work, with the result that much maintenance was deferred.

For the American railroads, the war really began in 1915, with increased traffic resulting from the flow of supplies ordered by the belligerent powers. Among these supplies were 2ft (610mm) gauge locomotives ordered for the field railways of Britain, France and Russia. The railroads also did well in 1916, with their expeditious southward movement of National Guard units during the Mexican crisis. However, when traffic became heavy, bottlenecks developed, and the companies were in a poor position to deal with these. Co-ordination was the obvious technical solution, with railroads agreeing to route freight over unusual routes so as to reduce congestion. But the anti-monopoly legislation of the previous decades prohibited this kind of co-operation and, moreover, the companies were unwilling to divert part of their freight over competitors' lines. It was the spring of 1917 before the railroads felt able and willing to set up their Railroads War Board. This effected some useful changes but, with the USA entering the war, with labor unrest on the railroads and with the blizzards of late 1917, a traffic crisis developed, and the federal government took over the railroads, setting up the US Railroad Administration (USRA). Then events in the USA closely paralleled what had happened in Britain: the rail network began to work incomparably better. Services were pooled, standard USRA locomotives were ordered for use on all railroads, competing city ticket offices were closed and so on. However, on the whole, this success (and in particular the reasons for it) was not publicized.

When the US Army landed in France in 1918 it was accompanied by its own railroad service. Soon the US Transportation Corps was operating trains not only behind the American sector of the front, but also between the Atlantic ports and the Western Front. Most of the American railroad operating troops were professional railroaders and made a good impression, but later reinforcements appear to have been of lower quality. When the war ended, the railroad troops were required to stay on for another year and, dispirited, they soon made themselves a nuisance by ignoring French railway instructions and regulations, stopping their trains to make unscheduled calls at station buffets and, it was alleged, molesting travelers.

Above: **Soldiers of the White Army in the Russian civil war, traveling in a Finnish boxcar.**

Left: **One of many field railway locomotives supplied by American builders to the Russian army.**

21
POSTWAR
UPHEAVAL

World War I marked the end of an age for the railways as well as for society in general, but, whereas in western society a brave new world seemed to be dawning, for the railways a brave old world had just disappeared. Gone were the prewar certainties, the knowledge that railways were indispensable, progressive and profit-making. The war had hastened certain processes and had revealed others, for example the slow decline of profitability, that had been partly hidden before.

To varying degrees, the railways of the belligerents had been worn out. Hardest hit, perhaps, was Belgium, which had been occupied throughout the war. Most of the Belgian locomotives had been evacuated to France but some had even been sent as far as Russia; by no means all came back. The German railways were run down, and, after the war, they were administered by the Allies for some years. In Britain, the railways had carried extra traffic during the war and had deferred much maintenance and investment. The government had prevented them raising their rates in line with inflation and, moreover, had forced them to grant wage increases. When the war ended they expected promised compensation payments, but the government refused, and only after lengthy argument was a compromise reached.

The American railroads were not released from federal control until 1920, by which time many USRA locomotives had been placed into service. There had been a call for railroad nationalization, since federal control had greatly improved their performance, but the Transportation Act of

1920 simply strengthened the Interstate Commerce Commission (ICC) which from then on was allowed to set minimum as well as maximum railroad rates. The ICC's stated intention of persuading small companies to merge into larger ones had no result.

In Britain, there were also calls for nationalization, for the same reasons. In the end, there was a compromise. The 123 companies were obliged by the 1921 Railways Act to amalgamate into four large enterprises (there were a number of minor companies that were not to be "Grouped" at this time; the majority of these retained their independence until nationalization in 1948). Of the old companies, only the Great Western Railway survived, considerably enlarged by the acquisition of a number of Welsh companies. Largest of the new companies was the London Midland & Scottish Railway (LMSR), which absorbed, among others, the London & North Western, Midland and Caledonian railways. Second biggest was the London & North Eastern Railway (LNER), which embraced the Great Northern, Great Eastern, North Eastern, North British and other railways. Smallest of the "Big Four" was the Southern Railway (SR), which served southern England and which was distinguished from the others in that most of its revenue came from passengers, rather than freight.

In Germany, where the old state railways had continued even after the proclamation of the German Empire in 1871, there was at last the long-awaited amalgamation into a national network, the Deutsche Reichsbahn (DR), which tended to imitate the practices of its largest constituent, the Prussian State Railways.

In France there was already one state railway, the État, which had been formed to take over the burden of several loss-making lines in the west, and, in 1938, the remaining main-line railways would be nationalized to form the French National Railways (Société Nationale des Chemins de Fer Français — SNCF). Numerous other local companies, however, continued to exist. The French were not alone in having both state and private railways coexisting. In Sweden and Switzerland, the process of converting private to state railways was incomplete, while Denmark retained a network of state-owned lines alongside numer-

Right: **A Paris-bound commuter train of France's Est Railway**

ous small companies. In Holland, the two companies — one private and one state — were not joined into the Nederlandse Spoorwegen (NS) until 1938. In the new Irish Free State, the railways were amalgamated into the Great Southern Railways, which, in 1945, became the nucleus of the state-owned Coras Iompair Éireann (CIE). Private ownership continued in Northern Ireland, until the British railways were themselves nationalized in 1948.

In Canada, when the war ended, there was the profitable and self-confident Canadian Pacific alongside other lines with uncertain prospects. These included the Canadian Government Railways, which had been formed to take over the ailing Intercolonial Railway, the private Grand Trunk, whose line ran from Montreal to Toronto, the Canadian Northern, which was expanding into a coast-to-coast railway, and the Grand Trunk Pacific, which operated its own main line to the Pacific in the west and also the connecting, government-built National Transcontinental. Duplication of routes was quite blatant; for example, the Yellowhead Pass in the Rockies had two competing lines side-by-side. Government action, or inaction, was largely responsible for this overbuilding, but, when the Grand Trunk ran into financial difficulties in 1919, the Canadian government at Ottawa refused to help. Its British board of management thereupon voted itself five years' salary and sold the company to the Canadian government. In 1923 the main railways, with the exception of the Canadian Pacific, were amalgamated into a crown corporation — Canadian National Railways — which, under the vigorous leadership of its American president, Henry Thornton, became a smart and coherent enterprise.

In South Africa nationalization was achieved by a different route. At the end of the Boer War, the British Army's Department of Military Railways became the Imperial Military Railways, which took over the captured railways of the Transvaal and Orange Free State. These lines then became the Central South African Railways, which, in 1910, on the formation of the Union of South Africa, joined with the Cape and the Natal government railways to form a new company — the South African Railways & Harbours.

Australia was different because, in the Commonwealth Railways (owner and operator of the Trans Australian line), it already had a national federal railway coexisting with the state government railways. Full-scale nationalisation was not practicable because the state governments were unwilling to hand over their railways to Canberra. Not until political mismanagement had turned the state railways into serious financial burdens did the Australian states consider seriously the idea of handing them to the Commonwealth Railways (later the Australian National Railways). By the mid-1980s the Tasmanian and the South Australian government railways had joined the ANR.

The reorganizations in Europe and Canada probably helped the railways in their struggle against the new competition from road vehicles. World War 1 had advanced the onset of highway competition by some years for, when it ended, there were thousands of ex-soldiers who had learned to drive and thousands of army motor trucks for disposal at knockdown prices. The consequence was a multiplication of small-scale highway operators, some of which developed into large companies that began to skim away the railways' traffic. Specializing at first in the most highly rated traffic, highway operators could deliver door-to-door, offer cheaper rates and, because trucks did not need to wait in yards for a train to be assembled, a faster service. The railways retaliated, in particular agitating at the political level for fair treatment, by which they meant that highway operators did not pay for, or repair, the roads they used and were not obliged to carry any traffic that was offered, as the railways were. In continental Europe, this political effort had some success; governments realized that if railways lost their high-rated traffic they might be unable to operate low-traffic lines or carry their bulk traffic so cheaply. In Britain, where the highway lobby was, and remained, strong, the railways' pleas were less successful.

Short of political help, the only recourse was to compete on price and service. Fast freight trains — such as the LNER's "Green Arrow" service — and more specialized freight wagons were among their policies, as were efforts to cut down costs so as to give scope for rate reductions. In some ways, the competition, therefore, benefited the railways, for it obliged them to do things that they had previously neglected. Cost accounting, for example, had hitherto languished in a prehistoric condition both in the USA and Britain, with railway companies quite ignorant of how much it cost to carry various categories of freight.

The coming of the internal combustion engine was only one advance that helped to rob the railways of their reputation as technological pacemakers. Now the railways seemed old-fashioned and not so essential. In conscious and unconscious reaction to this feeling, managements began to seek ways of altering their public image. The streamlined passenger train was the most blatant effort to recapture a spirit of modernity, but there were others too. Progressive artists were hired to design posters and advertising. A few railways used such artists to design a whole house-style for liveries, signs, maps and all other railway features susceptible of redesign. The Southern Railway in Britain introduced a malachite green livery and began to reconstruct its stations in the modern idiom, with extended use of concrete and other up-to-date materials. In the USA, although many companies still preferred to build ponderous, monolithic railroad stations, there were others which were more ambitious, hiring architects to build stations with a hint of the futuristic about them. Cincinnati Union Terminal was perhaps the best-known, but not the only one, of these extremely up-to-date stations.

22
THE
STREAMLINERS

The first streamlined train, the "Windsplitter," appeared in the USA as early as 1900. On trial over the B&O, it averaged 87mph for several miles, although greater speeds had been hoped for, and the project was abandoned. Paradoxically it failed because, as with the later streamliners, its sole purpose was to reduce wind resistance. This was a very unrealistic aim, and streamlining, when it finally blossomed in the 1930s, justified itself in terms not of wind resistance, but of publicity.

Wind pressure can require vastly increased horsepower to overcome it, but this arises, not from head winds but from strong side winds, which push the train against the leeward rail, causing the wheel flanges to grind. There is little a designer can do to reduce this, except strive to pre-

Below: **The end of the streamlined steam train era was marked by this Chesapeake & Ohio RR train, built after World War 2 but, because of dieselization, never put into its intended service.**

sent a train with clean, smooth, sides. Head-on resistance is negligible up to about 70mph, and, even above that figure, it builds up slowly. No doubt the 126mph speed record won by the streamlined British locomotive *Mallard* would not have been achieved in the absence of streamlining, but, at that speed, streamlining probably only accounted for about 5mph. The "Windsplitter" seemed to recognize this, for it was the train, rather than the locomotive, that was streamlined. But the rolling stock was heavy and speeds did not exceed 90mph.

The first of the later generation of streamliners were self-propelled, rather than locomotive-hauled, trains. In 1933 the Budd Co built a two-car, vaguely streamlined, train for the Texas & Pacific Railroad, but the main public interest in this was focused on the French-designed Michelin pneumatic tyres. In France, modernistic railcars incorporating racing-car technology and designed by Bugatti were attracting attention, and it would not be long before the GWR in Britain would introduce single-unit streamlined diesel railcars.

The first two examples of the long-distance, main-line, streamlined train appeared in the USA almost simultaneously in 1934. Both were three-car and articulated (that is, adjoining carriage ends shared the support of a single truck). The streamlining was only one of their advanced features. Others included the power units, which were 600hp internal combustion engines. The first to appear was the Union Pacific's M-10000, built of aluminum alloy by Pullman Standard and powered by a distillate engine. It was followed some months later by the somewhat larger M-10001, which was diesel powered. Meanwhile, the Burlington Railroad had introduced its *Zephyr*, similar in

concept but powered by electric motors supplied from a generator driven by a General Motors diesel engine. This was the first of the streamliners to enter regular service, plying between Lincoln, Nebraska and Kansas City. The two Union Pacific streamliners toured much of the USA, breaking speed records now and again to retain public attention, before entering regular service, with M-10000 running between Kansas City and Salina, a short run, and M-10001 becoming *City of Portland*, running between Chicago and Portland in less than 40hr.

As a publicity enterprise, the streamliners were wildly successful. They were associated in the public mind with speed (for 60mph schedules were typical) and with modernity. Civil airliners at this time were only just becoming metal monoplanes and their radial engines were far from streamlined, so in terms of sleekness the train was outmatching the airliner, and, in some ways, resembled the racing car. Soon, most big railroads were introducing streamlined trains. The first non-articulated streamliners, the "Rebels" of the Gulf, Mobile & Northern, were built by the American Car & Foundry in 1935. Placed on the St Louis-New Orleans service, they were the first streamliners in the south and also the first to carry train hostesses.

Many of the new streamliners were steam-hauled, the typical low-cost expedient being the clothing of existing locomotives in an outer skin, which, all too often, resembled nothing more speedy than an upturned bathtub. Even cheaper was the bullet nose, preferred by several economy-minded managements (including, after World War II, the Indian Railways, which operated no really fast trains but ordered hundreds of the fast-looking "WP" class Pacific locomotives).

Above: **Some 120 of these "coupe-vent" locomotives were built before World War I, streamlined to cope with the "Mistral" wind of southern France.**

Left: **A diesel railcar of Britain's Great Western Railway; the streamlining was more for style than effect.**

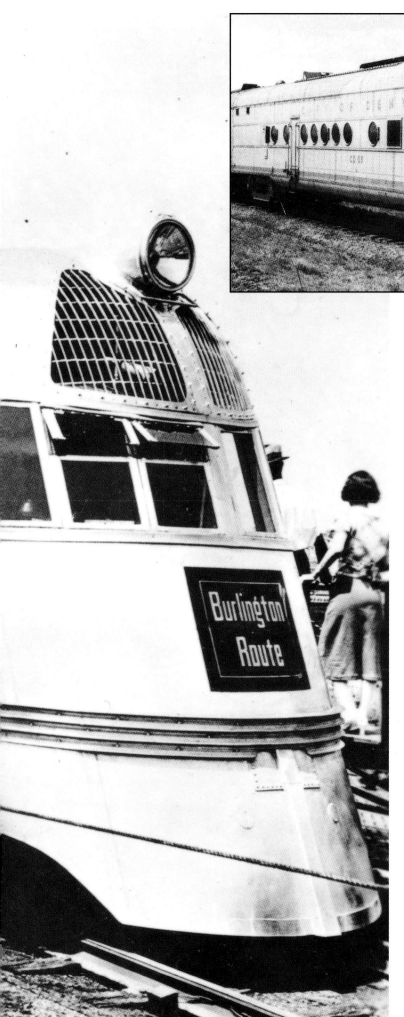

Main picture: **The original Burlington RR *Zephyr*, built in 1934 and consisting of three cars powered by a 600hp diesel engine.**

Above left: **One of 10 Canadian National streamlined locomotives built for the Montreal-Chicago service overtakes an older CNR locomotive at Toronto.**

Above: **The Union Pacific/Chicago & North Western *City of Denver* of 1936.**

To provide reserves, there were many more streamlined locomotives than streamlined trains, and the surplus engines were used to haul non-streamlined trains, giving passengers the useful impression that they were traveling in a streamliner. Some railways built streamlined locomotives but not streamlined trains. Among them were the Canadian National and its American subsidiary, the Grand Trunk Western, which employed 10 streamlined 4-8-4 locomotives between Montreal and Chicago. In Australia, the Victorian Railways had some streamlined Pacifics for use on the "Spirit of Progress" Sydney-Melbourne interstate express, while the New South Wales Government Railways streamlined the first five of its war-built "38" class Pacifics. But it was the post-World War II SNCF which took the image-building idea to ridiculous excess, when they rebuilt some superannuated 4-6-0 locomotives, embellishing them with bullet noses and smoke deflectors that were not far removed from angels' wings. These locomotives were then placed at the head of crack trains, the "Trains Drapeaux," between Paris and eastern France.

It was in Britain that the streamlined steam train attained its greatest sophistication. The London & North Eastern Railway, aware of the successful German high-

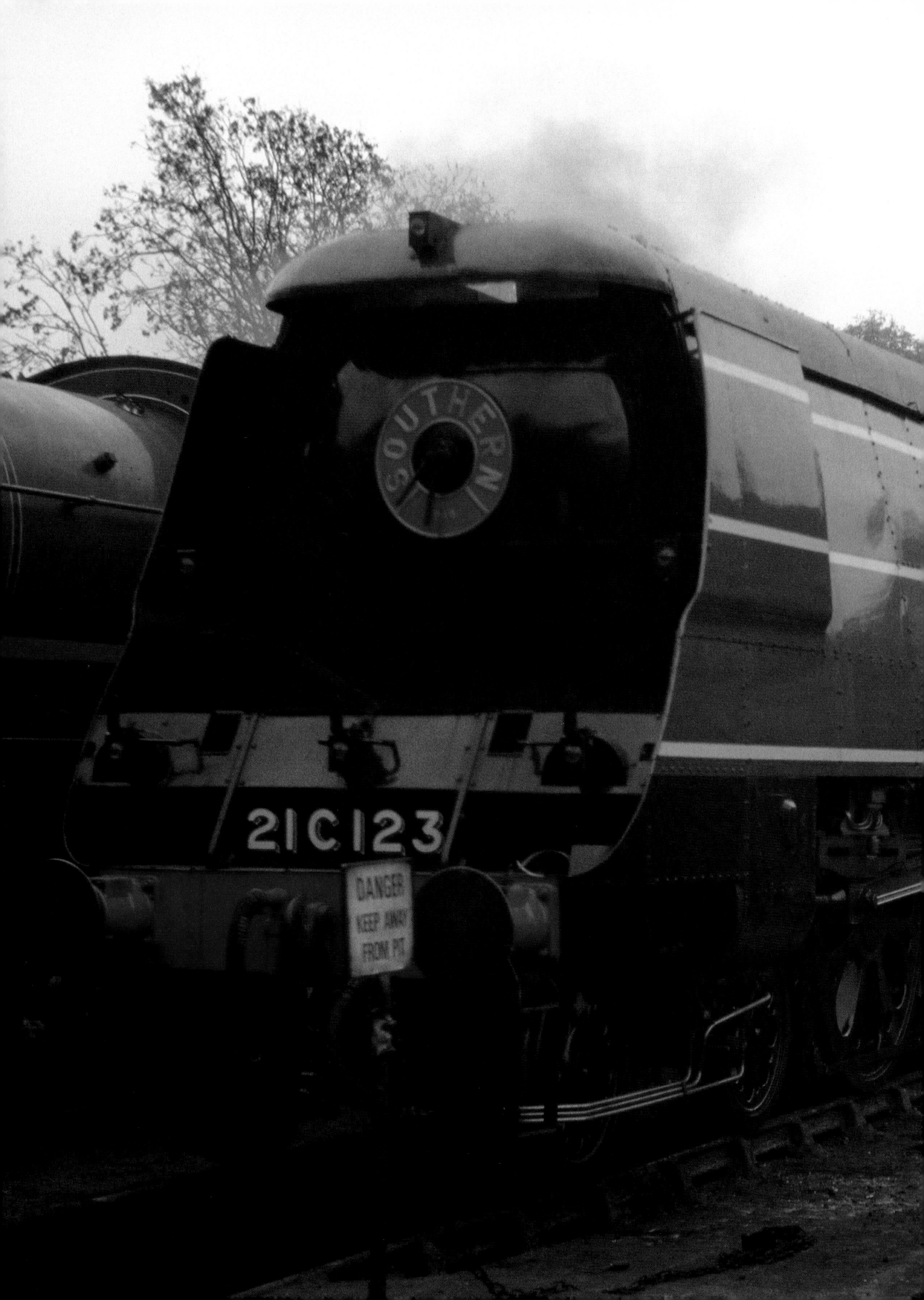
SOUTHERN
21C123
DANGER
KEEP AWAY
FROM PIT

Main picture: **One of the many "air-smoothed" 4-6-2 passenger locomotives built by Britain's Southern Railway in the 1940s.**

Above: **Sheep in lamb's clothing; the old but streamlined locomotive type used for the French "Trains Drapeaux."**

Below: **Germany's *Flying Hamburger* about to make a record-breaking run.**

speed two-car diesel railcar *Flying Hamburger*, envisaged a similar train. However, on the advice of its chief mechanical engineer, Nigel Gresley, it decided to introduce a steam streamliner instead. The result was the "Silver Jubilee" London-Newcastle service introduced in 1935, hauled by a new class of streamlined Pacific locomotives. On a trial run, this train ran 43 miles at an average of 100mph. In 1937 came the "Coronation," hauled by the same locomotives and providing a high-speed London-Edinburgh service over the East Coast main line. Meanwhile, the LMSR responded on the West Coast route with the "Coronation Scot," also hauled by streamlined Pacifics, which reached 114mph on trial.

Main picture: **The Union Pacific's first streamliner, M-10000.**

Above: **A London & North Eastern Railway streamlined Pacific leaves Kings Cross Station in London.**

Below: **The LMSR "Coronation Scot" on its way from London to Glasgow.**

23
TRAIN SERVICES

Although the streamliners attracted public attention, they were only a small minority of trains. For the average railway client what was important was the general level of service. The interwar period was a time when the customer was beginning to see that the railway was rarely the only option. Highway operators were offering a good cheap service for many commodities and, while passengers might rarely fly, many could elect to buy a car, or if too poor to do either of these, could still travel on the intercity bus, less comfortable but cheaper than the train.

Partly because of this competition, partly because the radical improvement brought by the streamliners filtered down to other, lesser services, and partly because there were technical advances, railway passenger and freight train services did improve quite significantly in the interwar years.

Average train speeds increased. The speed records that were periodically broken were not in themselves helpful to passengers, but they showed that the locomotives, trains and tracks were capable of higher speeds than before World War 1. By the early 1930s, the world's fastest regularly scheduled train was reckoned to be the "Cheltenham Flyer" of the GWR in Britain, which in 1932 was accelerated to an average of 71.4mph over the 77 miles from Swindon to London. Later, the LNER's "Coronation," by covering the 188 miles from London to York in 157min, slightly surpassed this average. By then, the US streamliners were in service with, for example, the Milwaukee Railroad's steam "Hiawatha," which regularly exceeded 100mph, and the Burlington's diesel "Denver Zephyr," which, on one occasion, covered the 1,017 miles from Denver to Chicago at an average speed of 83mph.

Elsewhere in North America there had been occasional regressions, usually taking the form of slowing down trains that had been over-accelerated in the heat of competition. The competition between the New York Central and Pennsylvania railroads for the New York-Chicago overnight Pullman traffic had resulted in both the "Twentieth Century Limited" and the "Broadway Limited" offering 18hr schedules between the two cities. In the 1920s, the schedules were of 20hr, the two companies having chosen to compete in terms of service and advertising, rather than speed. In Canada, the Canadian Pacific and Canadian National did something which the anti-trust laws prevented US railroads from doing; they actually colluded with each

Below: **A GWR fruit car. Because of low temperatures and short distances, British railways did not need to refrigerate fruit; good ventilation was enough.**

Above: **Parlor car of the Burlington RR's "Nebraska Zephyr." Fluted alloy sheathing became a feature of passenger stock supplied by the Budd company.**

other to dampen competition. In the early 1920s, the two companies had competed strongly on the trunk Montreal-Toronto route, where the single-track CPR paralleled the double-track CNR. The CPR, in an unsuccessful effort to match the CNR's six-hour timing for the 335 miles, did manage to schedule a train over 124 miles of the course at an average speed of 68mph, which was a world record at the time for a regularly scheduled train, but soon afterwards the two companies agreed to run "pool trains." These were jointly operated, each company providing a share of the locomotives and cars. The Ottawa-Toronto service was included and later the Montreal-Quebec route.

Many railway managements, aware that the automobile and the aircraft could not compete in terms of space per passenger, introduced or renovated luxury trains of moderate speed in which the journey could be regarded as a holiday, rather than a necessity. Many of the Pullman trains, running over US railroads alongside the more glamorous streamliners, came into this category, especially the long transcontinental trains with their observation cars and sophisticated dining-car menus. This tradition was also alive in Europe, where the pre-1914 international sleeping-car trains, like the "Orient Express" and "Nord Express," had set high standards for supplementary-fare passengers. New trains were introduced in Europe, often providing accommodation for the less wealthy. Among them was the "Golden Arrow," introduced in the 1920s between London and Paris. It was a day service and was unusual in that it provided Pullman rather than Wagons-Lits vehicles. It really consisted of two trains, one on the British and one on the French side, with a steamer connection across the English Channel. Another introduction was the "Train Bleu," which provided an opulently luxurious service from Calais and Paris down to the French Riviera. In the mid-1930s the "Night Ferry" was introduced. This was a Wagons-Lits sleeper train, which joined London with Paris and Brussels,

with the train making an overnight Channel crossing aboard a train ferry.

What was perhaps the most luxurious of the interwar trains was the "Blue Train" of the South African Railways. This magnificently-equipped train was introduced in 1939 and provided a dust-proofed, air-conditioned environment for its lucky passengers; lucky, because not only was a high price payable for using this train, but also because places were strictly limited — to provide space for the various on-board services, barely 100 passengers were carried and reservations had to be made long in advance. This train covered the 999 miles from Cape Town to Pretoria in 27hr; it was not an especially fast train, but that schedule compared favorably with the 44hr needed by the fastest train on this route in 1910.

In Australia, the late 1930s witnessed the introduction of two notable luxury trains. The "Spirit of Progress" was brought in by the Victorian Railways in 1937 and ran from Melbourne to Albury, where it connected with the New South Wales Government Railways' "Sydney Express." It was very much in the style of the American streamliner, with its cars air-smoothed and made of lightweight alloy. It was usually a train of 12 vehicles, and was scheduled at an average of 53mph. Meanwhile, Commonwealth Railways was operating a transcontinental service between Port Pirie and Kalgoorlie at an average speed of 28mph. The train provided first-class sleepers with 20 passengers per car and second-class with 36. Its parlor car had a piano and the first-class passengers could take a shower. As on an ocean liner, which it somewhat resembled, the fare included the price of meals.

Main picture: **A "pool train" jointly operated by the Canadian National and Canadian Pacific railways. This Montreal-bound train is leaving Toronto behind a CNR locomotive.**

Above: **The "Laurentian" (Montreal-New York) is hauled over the New York Central's "Water-Level Route" along the River Hudson by an NYC 4-6-4 locomotive.**

Above right: **The locomotive of a Spanish lightweight "Talgo" train.**

In most countries, there were creditable efforts to improve the speed and comfort of trains on secondary routes. Two interesting solutions to the problem of high speed running over curving track appeared during this period. The Canadian Pacific designed and built some locomotives of the unusual 4-4-4 wheel arrangement, providing high power output with a minimum rigid wheelbase, and, in Spain, the "Talgo" train appeared. The latter was a light-weight train with a low center of gravity, with one axle per vehicle; the non-axled end of each car resting on the axled end of the next. This solution was very successful in Spain, but less so elsewhere until the 1990s.

Although it was their passenger services that were most in the public eye, the majority of railway owners were more concerned about their competitive position against truck operators. To meet the competition, the fast-freight train was the favorite weapon. The first American fast overnight freight was the 1931 "Blue Streak" of the Cotton Belt Railroad, which was soon imitated by other railroads. Many of these ran at passenger train speeds and some had specially painted cars. Technically, the US railroads were better equipped than the British to operate fast, or "hot-shot," freights. The automatic "buck-eye" coupler had been imposed on all American railroads by federal law as early as 1893. Apart from speeding up train formation and saving the life and limb of yard-men, it also enabled higher outputs to be transmitted down the train without fear of broken couplings. Moreover, in North America, the automatic brake was added to freight wagons. The situation was different in Britain, where the crude, loose, hook-and-link coupling was still fitted to most freight wagons, which, on the whole, were lacking automatic brakes. The British railways' solution was to classify freight trains in accordance to the proportion of cars fitted with continuous brakes and screw couplings, ranging from Class 1 (all vehicles with automatic brakes) to Class 9 (slow freights with hand-brakes only). Class 1 freights were introduced between the important traffic centers in Britain and were fast enough to offer delivery of consignments the next morning. Fortunately, British railways relied for most of their freight revenue on the bulk consignments for which rail transport was so suitable: coal, ores, timber and building materials. These were carried at low rates and did not face highway competition. At the same time, however, the practice of maintaining goods yards every few miles along the tracks meant that there was much small-scale shunting of individual, often half-loaded, freight wagons by regular pick-up freight trains, which was a high-cost, low-revenue operation. Most — even the smallest — country stations had small goods yards until the 1960s; it was only when the nationalized British Railways embarked on freight concentration schemes, with a reduced number of freight stations and reliance on road transport for pick-up and delivery, that most of these wayside yards were to close.

24
STEAM LOCOMOTIVE DEVELOPMENT

In the USA, locomotive design was dominated by William Woodard's "Superpower" designs, built by the Lima Locomotive Works. Facing competition, the US railroads required higher horsepower so as to offer faster schedules without reducing train size. Woodard solved this problem by incorporating a four-wheel trailing truck, which allowed very big fireboxes to be used. His first venture was effectively a 2-8-2 built as a 2-8-4 and many 2-8-4s, or "Berkshires," were subsequently built for the railroads. His 2-10-4 for heavy freight, 4-6-4 for fast passenger traffic and finally the 4-8-4, or "Northern," for heavy mixed traffic,

followed. Apart from the large firebox, served by mechanical stokers, which became commonplace in North America between the wars, Woodard introduced other improvements, including a jointed connecting rod.

Alongside the "Superpower" locomotives, the "Mallet" type of articulated locomotive continued to thrive. The Union Pacific improved its front suspension in the "Challenger" class, enabling it to handle quite fast trains, including passenger trains on occasion. It was a development of the "Challengers," the Union Pacific's "Big Boy" 4-8-8-4s, that claimed the title of the world's biggest steam locomotives, weighing almost 600 tons in working order with tender, and able to handle 3,600-ton trains. These machines were a compelling illustration of the wide divergence between American and British and European practice. Rugged, huge and tolerant of poor maintenance, they were designed for hauling very heavy loads with best possible reliability. In Europe, on the other hand, the accent at this time was on fuel economy, high performance in terms of power/weight ratios and an acceptance of features demanding careful and frequent maintenance.

In Britain, the blend of American, British and continental practice that had resulted in a superb range of locomotives for the GWR had its culmination after World

Left: **A "cab-in-front" Mallet locomotive of the Souithern Pacific RR. The location of the cab preserved the loco-motive crew from excessive smoke inhalation when the locomotive was working hard in tunnels.**

Below: **William Stanier's "Princess Elizabeth" design for the London Midland & Scottish Railway.**

Main picture: **Grand Trunk Western RR locomotives. The unit on the right is one of the USRA standard World War 1 designs.**

Far left: **A Central RR of New Jersey short-distance passenger locomotive.**

Left: **A compound "Mallet" locomotive in pusher service on the Norfolk & Western RR.**

War 1. The GWR continued with 4-6-0 designs, enlarging them to produce the outstanding "Castle" and "King" passenger locomotives, and introducing a good mixed-traffic locomotive with the "Halls." The interwar years were, perhaps, most noteworthy for the proliferation of mixed-traffic designs, the idea being that a locomotive with driving wheel diameters halfway between the 4ft 7in (1,400mm) of typical freight locomotives and the 6ft 8in (1,980mm) of fast passenger locomotives would be capable of hauling all trains except the very heaviest freights and the very fastest passenger trains. Such locomotives would consequently spend more hours in traffic, and so produce economies. The idea had arisen earlier; indeed, the American 4-4-0 in the 19th century was long regarded as a dual-purpose engine, but it

was only in the cost-conscious 1920s and 1930s that the fast mixed-traffic: locomotive became widespread in Britain.

Unlike the GWR, the LNER and LMS preferred Pacific locomotives for their faster passenger trains. The LNER adopted the type designed by Nigel Gresley, of which *Flying Scotsman* became the most famous example. Improved, and with streamlining, this three-cylinder design developed into the "A4" class, one of which, *Mallard,* holds the authenticated world speed record for steam traction at slightly over 126mph. Gresley was an innovative designer and introduced wheel arrangements that were quite novel in Britain. For mixed traffic, his "Green Arrows" had the 2-6-2 arrangement, and he also designed several 2-8-2s, such as *Cock o' the North*, for heavy

Above left: **4-6-4 and 4-8-2 compound locomotives at the Gare du Nord in Paris.**

Above: **William Stanier, chief mechanical engineer of the London Midland & Scottsh Railway.**

Above right: **Sir Nigel Gresley, designer of the record-breaking *Mallard*.**

Below: **The last compound Mallet design of the Norfolk & Western RR, built in the company's own workshop.**

passenger service. Gresley's 2-8-2 designs were not very successful and were rebuilt by Gresley's successor, Edward Thompson, as Pacifics. Thompson himself reverted to the 4-6-0 arrangement for his own mixed-traffic class, the handsome, but unremarkable, "B1."

The LMS was plagued by animosity and acrimony between the managers and engineers who had come to it from the constituent companies. When former Midland Railway men took charge of locomotive policy, they seemed more interested in scrapping LNWR designs than in producing plans for new locomotives. However, new locomotive designs did emerge such as the "Royal Scot" class 4-6-0, produced to a design of the ex-Midland Chief Mechanical Engineer Sir Henry Fowler, who was CME of

the LMS between 1925 and 1931. Finally, in the early 1930s, William Stanier, a GWR man trained at Swindon, was appointed Chief Mechanical Engineer and produced a range of successful types that first incorporated, and then improved upon, GWR design features. For heavy passenger work he introduced two types of Pacific: the "Princess Elizabeths" and then the "Duchesses." Some of the latter were originally streamlined and one of them, *Duchess of Abercorn*, produced 3,300 indicated horsepower on test — a quite remarkable output for a locomotive of that size. Among Stanier's other successes were his Class 5 mixed-traffic 4-6-0 — nicknamed "Black Fives" — and Class 8 freight 2-8-0; examples of both types remained to the end of steam in Great Britain in 1968 and a number can still be seen operating on Britain's numerous preserved railways.

The fourth and smallest of the British post-Grouping companies, the SR, was developing its electrified suburban network and, from the mid-1930s, extended the process of electrification to the Brighton and Portsmouth main lines. As a consequence, innovation in steam locomotive design was less dramatic than elsewhere. In the first two decades of the SRs existence, many 2-6-0 mixed-traffic locomotives were built, as were several classes of 4-6-0s such as the "King Arthur" and "Lord Nelson" types. But in the 1940s, despite the war, a new Chief Mechanical Engineer, Oliver Bulleid, produced two startling designs. His "Q1" class of 0-6-0 was a remarkably ugly machine, designed with a view to saving metal, while his Pacifics — the "Merchant Navy" and the more numerous, but smaller, "West Country" and "Battle of Britain" types — were extremely

Far left: **Oliver Bulleid, one of the more innovative British locomotive designers.**

Left: **Sir Henry Fowler, better at workshop organization than locomotive design.**

Right: **Chapelon's "141P" 2-8-2 locomotive for French railways; weight-for-weight, this was one of the world's most effective designs.**

Right centre: **A pair of GWR two-cylinder "Hall" type 4-6-0s, which in the 1920s established the pattern of British mixed-traffic locomotives.**

Bottom: **The Boston & Maine RR's final class of 4-6-2. Built by Lima in 1937, these had a high power/weight ratio and were used for fast merchandise as well as passenger trains.**

WORLD RAILWAYS

Main picture: **One of the LMSR's "Duchess" class of four-cylinder Pacifics.**

Right: **A "V2" class three-cylinder mixed traffic 2-6-2 of the London & North Eastern Railway.**

Right and Below right: **Two views of the GWR "Castle" design of four-cylinder passenger 4-6-0 locomotive, an outstanding British design.**

WORLD RAILWAYS

Main picture: **The first of the LMSR "Princess" type locomotives arrives in London for inspection by the company's directors.**

Right: **Two British companies revived the old 4-4-0 wheel arrangement in the 1930s. This is one of the successful "Schools" class of the Southern Railway.**

Below: **A three-cylinder "Jubilee" class 4-6-0 of the LMSR.**

innovative. They were enveloped in a smooth shroud to reduce air resistance, their three cylinders were controlled by a valve gear operated by chains and working in an oil bath, and they had American-style disc driving wheels. Many of them were rebuilt as less complex locomotives after the war.

In Germany, the new unified railway, DR, followed the Prussian locomotive tradition; priority was given to simplicity and reliability, producing locomotives that had a lower power/weight ratio than those of other countries, but which were well liked by the men who had to operate them. The outstanding design was the Class 50 2-10-0 that became the basis for the "Kriegslok," built by the thousand and used in most parts of German-occupied Europe during World War 2.

But it was in France that the most exciting developments took place. Here André Chapelon introduced, or reintroduced, so many improvements that his rebuilding of certain existing locomotives could almost double their power outputs while hardly changing their weight. He was a protagonist of compounding, but that was not the secret

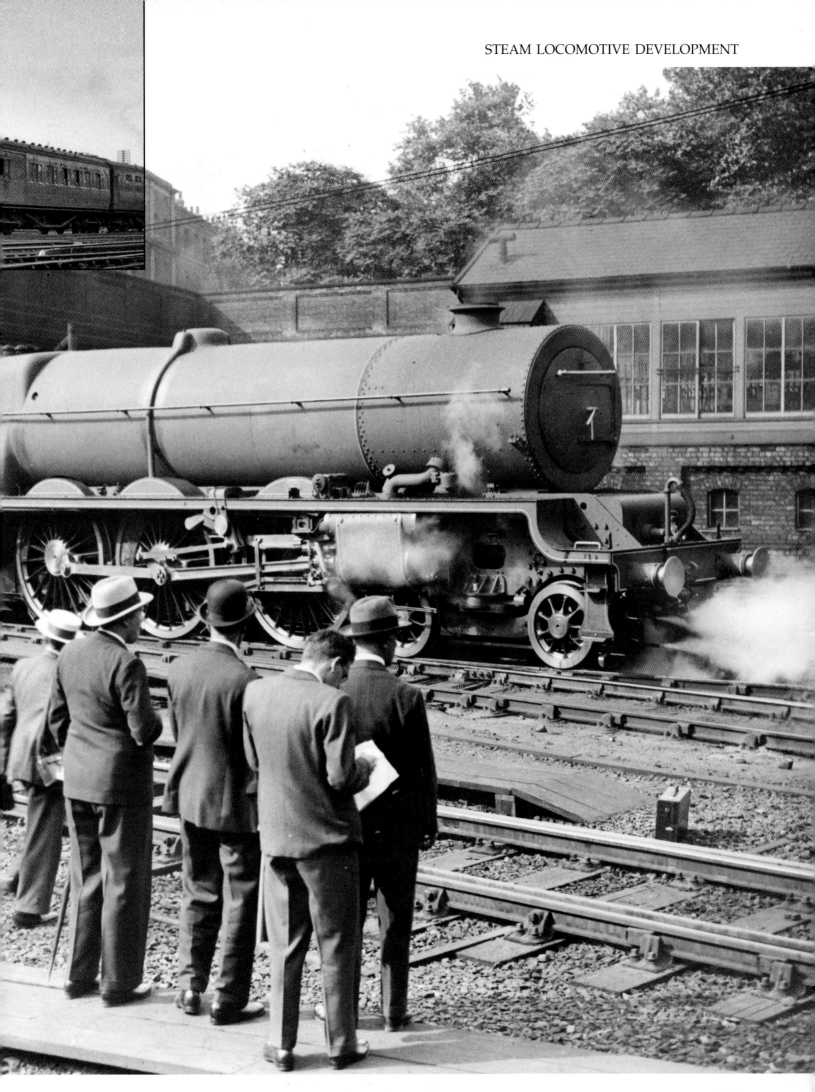

Main picture: **The Southern Pacific's main passenger locomotives were 4-8-4s, of which this is one of the later versions.**

Above left: **A "Big Boy" of the Union Pacific, reputed to be the world's biggest steam locomotive.**

Above: **A "Royal Hudson" 4-6-4 of the Canadian Pacific.**

Below: **A B&O 2-10-2 of a class built in the 1920s.**

of his success. He widened and smoothed internal steam passages to conserve energy, he incorporated feedwater heating and higher temperature superheating. His work also dramatically improved draughting; his "Kylchap" exhaust, usually including a double chimney (that is, with two orifices), provided a draught that was strong and smooth, powerful enough to draw ample air through the fire, but not powerful enough to drag coal particles with it. This "Kylchap" exhaust was fitted to some British locomotives, including the very successful rebuilt version of the "Royal Scots." Chapelon's mixed-traffic "141P" class 2-8-2 was probably the world's most successful design in terms of the power/weight ratio.

Main picture: **In the final steam decades, the Canadian National relied on this class of 4-8-4 for heavy passenger and freight work.**

Above: **A typical British 4-4-0 of the Southern Railway, crossing Brighton Viaduct.**

Below: **A Class 50 2-10-0 of the German State Railway.**

25
UNORTHODOX STEAM POWER

The requirement for ever more horsepower within the existing limits of axle weight, wheelbase and width, meant that many engineers began to seek radical alternatives to the conventional steam locomotive. The "Mallet" and "Garratt" types had themselves been radical solutions in their time, but they were both approaching the limits of their development and, moreover, perpetuated the inherent economic weakness of the steam locomotive — its inability to convert more than about 6-10% of coal's potential energy into tractive effort.

Steam turbine locomotives received a good deal of attention for, in theory, they promised better thermal efficiency and, because of their smooth operation, less

Below: **Fireless locomotives were periodically charged with high-pressure steam. This is a German unit, exported to a Soviet Union oil refinery.**

"hammerblow" on the track. But, for maximum efficiency, they needed a condenser to convert used steam into warm feedwater and, for reverse working, they needed either complex gearing or a second turbine. In Britain, the Ramsay-Macleod turbine locomotive of 1924, of the 4-4-0+0-4-4 wheel arrangement, was fairly successful but its power/weight ratio was too low to make it worthwhile. On the LMS, while the "Turbomotive" 4-6-2 had parts in common with the "Princess Elizabeth" class of conventional locomotives, it also had a small reverse turbine and a main turbine producing 2,600hp. It worked quite well from 1935 to 1951, but, being a single and special unit, when it needed repairs these tended to take a long time, so its utilization rate was low. It was ultimately to be rebuilt as a conventional locomotive before being written off in the disastrous Harrow & Wealdstone accident in October 1952. In the USA, the Pennsylvania Railroad's Class S2 6-8-6 turbomotive suffered from the same problem. It was technically successful, but, because of time spent out of service, could not compete with diesels. The Swedish Ljungstrom turbine locomotives were the most successful. These had a single turbine driving through gearing and had a remarkably low water consumption. One sent to Britain worked reasonably well but was soon withdrawn, while several others worked for a long time and successfully in Sweden.

Steam-electric locomotives used steam to generate electricity, which was then fed to electric traction motors. This idea emerged as early as 1890, with the Heilmann locomotive of the French Western Railway. The later British Reid-Ramsay locomotives were similar, but had

condensers. They worked satisfactorily, but the power/weight ratio was low. On the eve of World War 2 the Union Pacific in the USA was trying two steam-electrics with very high boiler pressure and watertube boilers; they seemed promising but the war put an end to their trials. After World War 2, the Chesapeake & Ohio (C&O) and the Norfolk & Western (N&W) railroads, both of which were in close contact with the coal industry, tried steam-turbine-electrics as alternatives to diesel traction. The three built for the C&O in 1947-48 were unsuccessful, but No 2300 of the N&W lasted longer. This, at 586 tons, was the world's biggest single-unit locomotive, possessing a watertube boiler and 12 powered axles.

Attempts to combine the flexibility of the steam loco-motive with the thermal efficiency of the diesel were uniformly unsuccessful. The British Kitson-Still of 1927 had eight opposed cylinders, which worked on a four-stroke diesel cycle, aided by steam acting on the passive side of their pistons when extra power was needed. In the 1930s and 1940s, the Soviet Railways expended much effort on their "Teploparovozy." These had conventional boilers, which supplied steam to cylinders that had opposed pis-tons. When a sufficiently high speed was reached, the central parts of the cylinders were switched from steam to diesel combustion, so that steam propelled the pistons on their inward stroke and diesel combustion on their out-ward stroke. Unlike many other more hopeful innovations, these follies received ample financial support, but, after 10 years of glowing reports, they were acknowledged to be failures; the basic problem of equalizing the thrust of the diesel and steam impulses was never solved satisfactorily.

High-pressure steam locomotives, which used steam not at the conventionally low 150-300psi railway pressure but at 400-1,000psi, thereby increasing both power and fuel economy, were tried by several railways, especially in Germany. Worldwide examples include *Fury*, an LMS 4-6-0 which suffered a fatal steam burst, No 10000 of the LNER, which was a compound with watertube boiler, *L. F. Loree* of the Delaware & Hudson Railroad and No 5905 of the Canadian Pacific.

Condenser locomotives for use in arid regions had some success. Henschel of Germany specialized in these and the company's designs were adopted by Soviet Railways for mass production of a 2-10-0 type for use in the Central Asian deserts. The same design was used for the massive "25" class of 4-8-4 for the South African Railways. In World War 2 the Russian design was "copied back" to provide the German forces in Russia with their own condenser locomotives.

The Franco-Crosti and Crosti locomotives were also quite successful. In these the exhaust steam passed through one or two drums to pre-heat the boiler feedwater. This did bring a fuel economy, but also higher maintenance costs, so it was only in Italy, where coal was expensive, that these locomotives were used extensively, although the nationalized British Railways experimented with them on a small batch of Class 9F 2-10-0s in the 1950s. The Italians claimed savings of over 17% in fuel terms with locomotives fitted with these boilers; experience in Britain, however, was that the savings were much smaller — of the order of 3 or 4% — and the locomotives fitted with the Crosti boilers were eventually converted to conventional form.

The Pennsylvania Railroad adopted the duplex drive locomotive (first used on the B&O in 1937) and its 52 4-4-4-4 locomotives became the basic steam passenger type in the years before the introduction of diesel power. These distinctive locomotives, which resembled non-articulated "Mallets," were virtually 4-8-4s in which the four driving axles were split into two two-axle units, each powered by its own outside cylinders. This layout lessened the track stresses experienced by heavy locomotives traveling at high speed.

Among other innovations, one which proved exceptionally useless was the 4-14-4 designed by Soviet engineering students in the 1930s and foisted onto an unenthusiastic Soviet Railways management. There were 14 driving axles in a rigid frame. This was a world record, for good reasons, as with that length of wheelbase the locomotive was only safe on straight track. An even stranger prototype was the three-unit, four-boiler 0-6-2+2-4-2+0-4-2+2-6-0. This was designed by an Italian but built and tried in Belgium.

Far left: **LNER No 10000, with its watertube boiler.**

Left: **The Norfolk & Western RR's steam-turbine-electric No 2300.**

Below left: **One of the Pennsylvania RR's duplex drive locomotives.**

Main picture: **A pair of condensing locomotives on South African Railways. The big tenders had an array of cooling vents.**

26
THE LOCOMOTIVE EXPORTED

In the early days of railways, companies would buy the locomotives that happened to be on offer by the outside builders either at home or abroad. Thus the Stephensons' "Patentee" type could be seen at work in several countries. As new locomotive works were opened, different schools of locomotive design became evident. The divergence of American practice came quite early, the bar-framed, haystack-firebox imports from Edward Bury being the starting point and, when locomotive works were opened in France, Germany and Belgium, railway engines began to assume national characteristics.

Sometimes the divergences were fundamental, but sometimes only superficial, being marked by preferred designs of components, such as chimneys and cabs. Within a given country, too, individual railways might develop their own sub-style of locomotive. This was particularly the case when a company had its own locomotive works. In Britain, most railways built their own locomotives, which

could usually be distinguished from those of other companies by their details and style. In North America a few railroads built their own. Amongst these were the Pennsylvania and Canadian Pacific railroads, both of which developed a very distinctive corporate style for their locomotives.

In the 20th century, the French locomotive was very distinctive, not only because of the wide use of compounding but because of the somewhat refined design of components. French enginemen were the best trained in the world, and they were entrusted with locomotives that American railroads would have found impossibly delicate. In Austria, the tradition established by Karl Gölsdorf was unique. Faced with the need to provide high power and low axle weights, this designer built engines with very light frames and boilers, which were sharply tapered to save weight at the front end and were designed for low pressures so that thin plates could be used. He also omitted running plates and splashers to save weight. Such gaunt, but effective, engines were not seen outside central Europe.

When locomotive builders exported their products they were, in effect, exporting their style and their technology. Thus it was not surprising that French-style locomotives should appear in Spain, North Africa, and Indo-China. Throughout the British Empire, locomotives of identical types could be encountered, many of which were produced in the great locomotive-building cities of Manchester and Glasgow. The German style of locomotive spread to the Russian Empire, while American locomotive practice could be seen in South America, and even in parts of the British Empire; for railways in Canada, New Zealand, Australia and South Africa occasionally bought American.

There was also considerable cross-fertilization. In the early 20th century George Jackson Churchward, the locomotive superintendent of the GWR in Britain, designed a

Above: **The US "Andes" design was used by several South American railways but, unusually, this 1948 example was built for Bolivia by a British company.**

Left: **This postwar Soviet "LV" class 2-10-2 incorporated many American features.**

Below: **In turn, "LV" class drawings were used to create the Chinese "QJ" class, in whose design Russian engineers participated.**

range of very distinctive locomotives that combined British, American and French features. From America he took the tapered boiler resting on a smokebox saddle that consisted of two castings, each containing one cylinder and half the smokebox saddle, and also the 2-6-0 wheel arrangement, which he used for the first British mixed-traffic locomotive. His leading four-wheel bogie was of French origin, his firebox was of an improved Belgian Belpaire type and he paid great attention to providing wide, smooth, internal steam passages, a fundamental improvement which he probably arrived at himself, although the proportions of chimney and blast-pipe, so important for good steaming, were derived from the theoretical work of the American Professor Goss. This new range of locomotives soon proved itself superior to those of other British railways, which eventually copied some of its features. Another facet of Churchward's designs — again

derived from practice in the USA — was standardization of parts so that interchangeability became practical.

A sudden and wholesale adoption of American practice occurred in interwar Russia, up to then influenced mainly by Germany and Austria. There had been hints in the 1920s of the emergence of a new, Soviet, school of design, but this was cut short by the upheavals of the 1930s. After a Soviet delegation had visited the USA, an order was placed with Baldwin and Alco for five locomotives each, but the visiting Soviet engineers were arrested on their return, confined with their drawing boards, and quickly produced designs for a 2-10-2 freight locomotive and its "Josef Stalin" 2-8-4 passenger version. These, mass-produced in Soviet factories, were American both in design and detail. After World War 2, Soviet engineers helped the Chinese to introduce new locomotives of their own and the Chinese "QJ" class 2-10-2 had evident similarities with the postwar Soviet

"P36" class 4-8-4 and "LV" class 2-10-2, which were themselves influenced by their American-style predecessors.

In Australia, the New South Wales Government Railways, after almost a century of British practice, built their own design during World War 2, the Class 38 Pacific, intended for long runs without engine-change. In South Australia, the interwar years witnessed the phenomenon of new locomotives twice as big as their predecessors — designed in Australia, built in Britain, but American in style. A final class, mixed-traffic 4-8-4s, clearly imitated the Pennsylvania Railroad's 4-4-4-4s.

Another case of British-built locomotives taking an American form was a number of 2-8-0s built for railways in the Andes. These lines had been engineered by Americans, who specified an American-built 2-8-0 design. These were built by US locomotive companies, but, after World War 2, further orders were placed in Britain, with the manufacturers there copying the American design. There was an earlier parallel to this — during World War 1, British locomotive builders built French-designed engines for France.

South African locomotives in the 20th century were recognisably South African, although mainly built in Britain. The design work was by South African engineers, who evolved their own style; the large-diameter boilers, with chimney and other boiler fittings of low profile, had a distinctive air on 3ft 6in (1,065mm) gauge tracks.

Had it not been for the advent of the diesel, world steam locomotive development would have probably produced a trend toward the American style, especially with the good impression made by the American-built 2-8-2 locomotives exported during (and soon after) the war. These included the "141R" class for France, the "59" class for New South Wales and many "MacArthur" engines. The American emphasis on ease of maintenance was appreciated in postwar conditions. Even British postwar designs included American labor-saving devices such as rocking grates, as well as a preference for outside cylinders and valve gears with their easier access.

Main picture: **British-built locomotives on Argentine's Buenos Aires Great Southern Railway.**

Far left: **A 4-6-2 of the Bolivian State Railway, imported from Germany before World War 1.**

Left: **Purely American in inspiration, the Soviet Railways "FD" 2-10-2 was mass-produced in the 1930s.**

27
THE INTER-WAR ELECTRIFICATIONS

It is, perhaps, surprising that the railways of America and Europe did not electrify more than they did in the interwar years. In many cases there were sound economic reasons for continuing with steam traction and the Depression of the 1930s deferred many schemes, but inertia on the part of railway managements and their political or financial overseers was a large factor.

In terms of proportion of total mileage electrified, Italy led the way. Coal was expensive in that country, there was a highly developed tradition of electrical engineering and electrified railways created precisely the kind of image Mussolini sought for his regime. The result was not only a high mileage of electrified line, but the development of hydro-electric generating schemes. Passenger services could be accelerated and luxurious, extra-fare, electric train-sets were introduced, one of which averaged 102mph on trial over the Florence-Milan route in 1939.

The Italians selected the 3kV dc system, which was marginally superior to the French 1,500V dc used for the interwar electrifications from Paris to Toulouse and Bordeaux as well as the shorter length from Paris to Le Mans. The USSR began with 1,500V dc but later changed to 3kV dc, the higher voltage enabling sub-stations to be placed farther apart and, in practice, allowing more power to be supplied. This was an important factor when several trains were drawing current from the same stretch of overhead conductor. In Germany, where locomotive coal was plentiful and the steam locomotive well-liked, there were short electrification schemes in the mountainous areas, especially Bavaria, and the north-south trunk line from Magdeburg to Leipzig was also electrified.

But, as might be expected, it was countries with ample hydro-electric sources and steeply graded lines that gained most. In Sweden the 280-mile Lapland Railway, carrying heavy iron-ore traffic over difficult terrain, was electrified in 1923 and, two years later, the Stockholm-Göteborg main line was converted. Other conversions followed. In Switzerland and Austria progress was also fast. Indeed, the Swiss electrical engineering industry with its advanced companies like Oerlikon and Brown Boveri made many advances in electric locomotive technology, including a

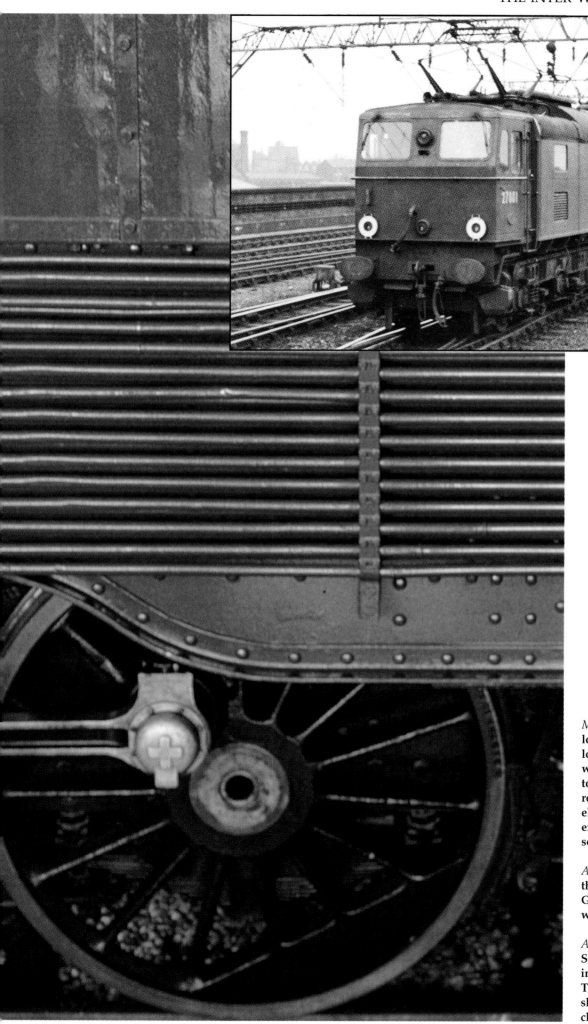

Main picture: **Early electric locomotives used steam locomotive type driving wheels, which were coupled to transverse jackshafts rotated, through gears, by the electric motor. In this Swiss example the jackshaft can be seen at the left.**

Above left: **Over 200 units of this "E94" class were built for German and Austrian railways between 1940 and 1956.**

Above: **Britain's Manchester-Sheffield electrifcation was interrupted by World War 2. This view is from the 1960s, shortly before the line was closed.**

WORLD RAILWAYS

Main picture: **A distinctive "GG1" locomotive of the Pennsylvania RR leaves Washington for New York.**

Right: **One of the first French electrifications, the Paris-Orleans main line.**

Far right: **A British-built locomotive for the Great Indian Peninsula Railway's electrification out of Bombay.**

system for transmitting power from motor to axle that, for the first time, made it possible for electric locomotives to run at very high speeds — an important innovation.

Sweden, Germany, Austria and Switzerland all chose 15kV ac, which had the advantage of widely spaced sub-stations, less loss in transmission and lighter conductor wires, but required each locomotive to carry a rectifier to provide the direct current required by the traction motors. At the other end of the voltage scale was the Southern Railway in England which, alone of the four British post-Grouping main line companies, pursued electrification schemes with great enthusiasm.

The SR was primarily a passenger-carrying railway and most of its passengers were short-distance, particularly on the commuter lines into London. Heavy traffic flows, the need for high power outputs to guarantee rapid accelera-tion from frequent stops and the new company's quest for a modern image were clear recommendations for electrifi-cation. Consequently, the SR went ahead, using the existing LSWR suburban scheme as a basis. This was a third-rail system, with a fairly low voltage. Such a system is very suited to commuter railways, for the traction motors can take their current directly from the conductor rail, with no need for heavy auxiliary equipment. Moreover, the third rail, with its wide cross-section, is well adapted to carrying the powerful current needed when closely spaced trains are accelerating from stations.

The SR electrification provided a network of electrified lines to the south of London, and then began to embrace longer-distance routes, from London to Brighton and, later, from London to Portsmouth. The third-rail low-voltage system was less suited to these distances, but was accepted for the sake of uniformity. The SR found that electrification, enabling a faster and more frequent service, attracted new passengers to the railway (a phenomenon that would later be known as the "sparks effect"), and land prices rose in the

area served by Southern Electric (as the network became known). Although a handful of electric locomotives were built primarily for freight, Southern Electric passenger services were provided by electric trains, with one or more multiple units (groups of cars, some powered, with a cab at each end) coupled together to form a train of the required length. Elsewhere in Britain, schemes were drawn up, but capital was not forthcoming to make them a reality. The LNER finally started work on two schemes (near Sheffield and on the main line from London Liverpool Street), but these were interrupted by the war. The LMS had inherited electrified lines from a number of its constituent companies; other than modernize stock when necessary, it did little to extend its electrified network.

Throughout the world, conversion of heavy-traffic suburban lines was typically the first move in the electrification process. In the USSR, the Moscow and Leningrad networks were electrified in the 1930s. In India, two routes out of Bombay were converted. In South Africa, schemes at Cape Town and Durban were started in the 1920s, the former at 1,500V dc and the latter at 3kV. When the Witwatersrand area was later converted at 3kV, that voltage was established as the future standard. In Australia, electrification began of the Sydney and Melbourne networks, both at 1,500V dc.

These suburban schemes later became parts of longer-distance electrifications. Indeed, in the smaller countries like Belgium and Holland, two suburban networks could meet and provide an intercity electrification, as happened between Brussels and Antwerp and between Amsterdam and Rotterdam via The Hague. In the USA, the Pennsylvania Railroad's suburban electrification out of

Above: **One of the German "E94" design locomotives, as operated by Austrian Railways.**

Right: **The Swiss "Ae4/7" design of the 1920s, which made the transition from outside coupling rods to individual axle drive.**

Top right: **One of the first electric trains built for the Brussels suburban electrification.**

Far right: **An early Japanese electric railcar.**

128

New York was a stimulus for the conversion of the main line down to Washington and Harrisburg, a scheme whose last section was ready in 1939. Before then, in 1934, the first of the classic "GG1" semi-streamlined electric locomotives had been assembled. These were the forerunners of a 139-strong class that would handle all the heavy passenger traffic of this line until the 1970s.

As a result of the high capital cost of electrification, it was suitable only where traffic was dense or where it was the best solution to technical problems. In North America, traffic density was low except on a few lines in the east, but there were heavily graded lines in alpine terrain in the northwest. Here the Milwaukee Railroad electrified 656 miles and the Great Northern 74 miles of their transcontinental lines, although these sections were "de-electrified" after World War 2.

American electrification was characterized not only by its sparsity, but also by the variety of different systems employed. The Pennsylvania Railroad scheme used 11kV ac, with Westinghouse supplying the electrical equipment. Westinghouse's competitor, General Electric, equipped the Milwaukee and Great Northern electrifications, the latter at 11kV but the former at 3kV dc. The Virginian Railway also used 11kV for the conversion of 134 miles of its coal-hauling main line.

US electric locomotives also took a variety of forms. The pre-World War 1 Norfolk & Western electric locomotives used three-phase motors; technically convenient, they allowed the locomotive to operate at only two speeds (14mph and 28mph). On the Milwaukee Railroad huge bipolar locomotives could be seen, contrasting starkly with the rough-hewn poles that carried the conductor wires.

28
THE COMING OF
THE DIESEL

In a fast-moving age, it is strange that the internal-combustion (primarily diesel) locomotive took longer than the steam locomotive to gain acceptance. It is less strange that the first attempts were built before the German Dr Rudolph Diesel had invented his engine, for the diesel was only an improved version of the existing internal-combustion engine. A British 12hp four-wheel dockyard locomotive built in 1894 is regarded as the pioneer. This was followed by six other locomotives built for British government arsenals. Petrol motors were also tried and, but for World War 1, the Trans-Australian Railway would have acquired a petrol-electric locomotive, in which the engine drove a generator that in turn supplied the traction motors, as in the later diesel-electrics.

Above left: One of General Electric's gas-electric locomotives for the Dan Patch line.

Centrer left: A pioneer American diesel-electric yard locomotive built for the Central RR of New Jersey in 1925.

Right: The Great Western Railway pioneered diesel railcars in Britain. This unit is hauling a trailer.

Below: A "Doodlebug" gas-electric railcar of 1924, one of a series built by Electro Motive and used by several US railroads.

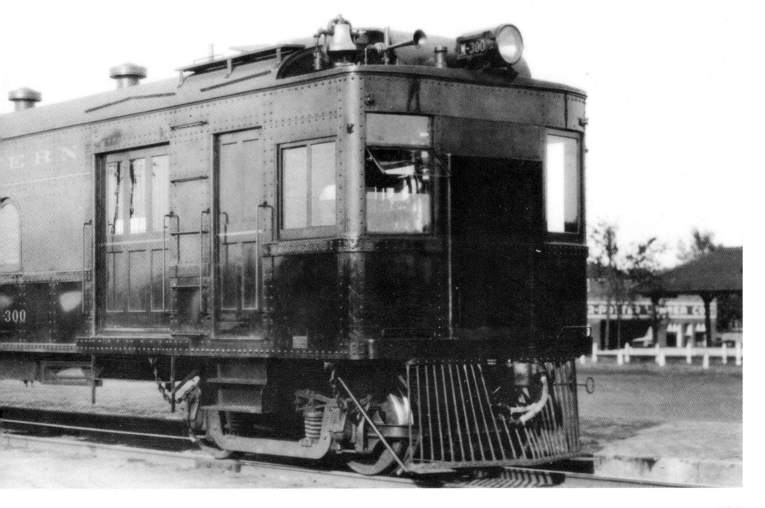

Elsewhere in the world, a Swedish short line acquired some diesel-electric railcars and, in 1912, the Prussian State Railways tried to operate the world's first main-line diesel locomotive. This failed for a number of reasons, one of which included a chronic inability to start the engine.

Meanwhile, in the USA, the internal-combustion engine was being used to power railcars, offering reduced operating costs for light-traffic branch lines. The McKeen railcar, bought by several lines, used a petrol engine and chain drive. Then the General Electric Co, inspired by a successful British railcar, which used an 85hp petrol engine to drive a generator, produced its own petrol-electric railcar, of which about 90 were sold before World War 1. From this railcar design, General Electric created three 400hp petrol-electric locomotives for the Dan Patch short line, which used them successfully for its passenger trains.

Soon after the Russian Revolution, Lenin approved the building of experimental diesel locomotives as a way to revolutionize Soviet Railways. One of these, sponsored by the leading Russian railway engineer, Georgii Lomonosov, was built in Germany and was a 1,200hp diesel-electric, while another was built in Leningrad, using a Vickers engine intended for a submarine. Both were finished in November 1924, but Lomonosov's worked satisfactorily while the other did not. The Lomonosov locomotive, a 2-10-2 rigid-frame machine, may therefore be regarded as the world's first successful main-line diesel. The USSR subsequently built several similar units, examples of which worked in Central Asia until the 1950s.

One of the Russian designers, Alphonse Lipets, emigrated and joined the American Locomotive Co (Alco). This firm had co-operated with General Electric in the construction of some diesel-electric yard locomotives. One of these, No 1000, which was built in 1925 for the Central of New Jersey Railroad, is regarded as the first commercially successful diesel-electric locomotive in the USA and was destined for a long life. By 1928, Alco was interested in manufacturing higher-power diesels and its first order came from the New York Central, which took three 750hp units for light-traffic lines. Even after 1937, when new working rules made it difficult to use one-man crews on yard diesel locomotives, they were an attractive proposition because they could work almost 24hr daily; that is, a single diesel could replace two steam locomotives. For most of the 1930s, therefore, Alco found a healthy market for its diesel yard locomotives. These usually had engines of 300hp or 600hp, although Alco's introduction of the turbocharger subsequently enabled the latter to be rerated to 900hp.

In 1940 Alco built the first dual-service diesel locomotive. This rode on two six-wheel bogies and had two engines, producing 2,000hp. An immediate success on the New Haven Railroad, where it hauled passenger trains in the day and freights at night, it led to the first road-switcher, which combined the functions of a main-line and yard locomotive.

Above right: **A pioneer French main-line railcar.**

Right: **French metre-gauge local railways were enthusiastic users of railcars. Here one such railcar is being coupled to a trailer.**

Below: **One of the successful English Electric yard locomotives. Most were used in Britain, but this is a Netherlands Railways' example.**

Meanwhile General Motors (GM), the automobile company, bought up the Electro-Motive Corporation, which marketed and designed petrol-electric railcars. It also bought a maker of diesel engines and, with this combination of experience, entered the diesel locomotive market. GM provided power for the "Burlington Zephyr" and other streamliners and also began to make diesel shunters. It insisted on producing a standard design, allowing no variations, in order to contain the diesel locomotive's rather high capital cost. In 1939 GM built a diesel-electric freight locomotive consisting of four units and having an output of 5,400hp. It demonstrated this over many American railroads, which were impressed by the convenience of its use. Orders began to arrive for the production version, known as the "FT," and General Motors was further helped by the war, because federal regulations named it as the only builder of main-line diesel locomotives.

Meanwhile, other countries were experimenting with diesel traction. In Britain, the GWR built a fleet of diesel railcars, while manufacturers tried to interest railway companies in diesel locomotives. Armstrong-Whitworth built some satisfactory diesel trains for Brazil and the Argentine, and Beardmore powered a diesel-electric locomotive for Canadian National Railways. The English Electric Co developed a 300hp diesel engine for railway use and this powered a very successful design of shunting (yard) locomotive that was used in Britain, exported to the Netherlands and forms the basis of today's "08" class type shunting (yard) locomotive on Britain's privatized railway network.

A theoretical drawback of the diesel locomotive was the difficulty of converting the high-speed rotary action of the engine to the slow revolutions of the driving wheels. Using electricity as a medium solved this problem, but necessitated the provision of a generator; in effect, this meant that one locomotive carried two power units, which added to cost and weight. Methods of mechanical or hydro-mechanical transmission were worked out for low-power locomotives

Main picture: **A fast railcar design introduced by the French Nord Railway in 1936.**

Left: **The General Motors "FT" demonstrator locomotive of 1939.**

Far left: **A German main-line diesel train.**

Below: **Elevated driving cupolas were a feature of several French railcar designs.**

— such as yard switchers — and, in Germany, hydraulic transmissions for powerful locomotives were devised. They were used in the record-breaking "Flying Hamburger" twin-unit train and in a 1,500hp main-line locomotive built in 1935. Germany also built diesel railcars and diesel switchers in large numbers, but they became problematic in World War 2 as a result of limited oil supplies.

Diesel railcars were also developed in France. The most spectacular were the Bugatti high-speed railcars, covering the Paris to Deauville run of 137 miles in two hours. A variety of railcars were built, some for fast service and some for lightly used branches. A few experimental diesel locomotives were also tried, but were not outstanding.

Frichs, a Danish company, scored a modest success with its main-line diesel-electric locomotives supplied to the Thai railways. They worked in Thailand for more than two decades, and were popular because they burned oil rather than the high quality teak consumed by Thai steam locomotives.

29
THE LINES BEHIND THE LINES

The British railways had a dress rehearsal for war in 1938, when the Munich Crisis saw them running evacuation specials out of the cities as well as troop trains, all without disrupting normal services. In Britain, and to a greater extent in the USA, the war showed how much spare capacity the railways possessed. Even the evacuation from Dunkirk, which meant the spontaneous generation of hundreds of troop trains, was accomplished by the British railways without any reduction of normal services, apart from those around two of the southern ports:

A Railway Executive Committee of senior British railway managers, similar to that which had been so successful in the previous war, was established before war started and worked well. Once again, the railways seemed to perform more efficiently in wartime than in peacetime, although the difference was not now so marked. What was new was that in World War 2 the railways were expected to continue their work under air bombardment and with a nightly blackout.

An early sign of war was the fitting of locomotives with gas detection panels that would change color should the train pass through a cloud of poisonous gas. Station lights were kept switched off and white lines painted along

THE LINES BEHIND THE LINES

Main picture: **A surviving example of the German "Kriegslok" war service locomotive.**

Left: **The locomotive of a Russian armored train.**

Below left: **The GWR encourages its workers to hand in waste material for recycling.**

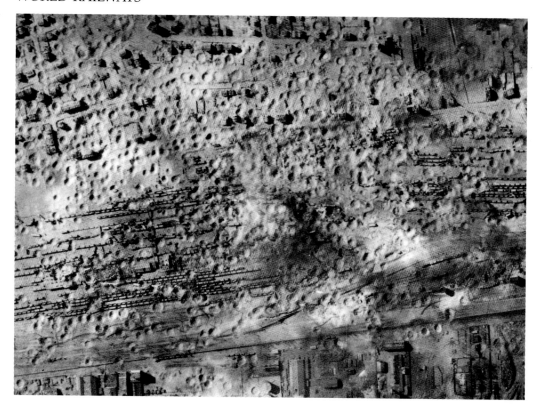

platform edges in partial compensation. Dim blue bulbs replaced the white lights in passenger vehicles and opaque black borders were painted on windows. Heavy bombing of Britain started in 1940 and, in total, about 400 railwaymen were killed on duty. In early May 1941, seven of the London terminals were out of action for some time. As the war progressed and as the threat of aerial attack receded so the level of damage declined, but the war was never far away, as the arrival of the German flying bombs and rockets in 1944 demonstrated. Though these were nerve-wracking, they caused little damage to the railways.

The British railways handed some of their locomotives to the War Department for service overseas and, in return, they later received standard war-built locomotives. The Stanier LMS Class 8F 2-8-0 was chosen as the wartime production type and was built in several workshops. Meanwhile, the Ministry of Supply was designing its own locomotives for military service. Based upon the "8F" design, these "Austerity" locomotives took into account the need to save metal and working hours in their construction and the need to cope with difficult operating conditions on the continent of Europe, where most were expected to work. A small 0-6-0ST (saddle tank) was also built along with a heavy freight locomotive of the unusual (for Britain) 2-10-0 wheel arrangement. Later, the railways had the use of the US Transportation Corps 2-8-0 until it was needed to serve the American Army in Europe. This was a simple locomotive, with a tendency to suffer boiler explosions when in the hands of unwary crews.

The British government ordered from American builders several hundred 2-8-2 locomotives of traditional US design, but with some British features. Most went to India and others to the Trans-Iran Railway. The latter,

which ran from the Persian Gulf to the Caspian, was taken over by the British and Russians after Hitler's invasion of the USSR. The Russians operated its northern part and the British (after 1944, the Americans) its southern part. It was an important route for supplying the Russians, especially after its very difficult operating conditions had been

alleviated by the introduction of diesel locomotives built in the United States.

Hitler's invasion of Russia in 1941 was hampered by his reliance on road transport. Having expected the Red Army to collapse because of the allegedly defective railway system, he discovered that his own advance was held back because his highway transport could not cope with the inadequate Russian roads and too little provision had been made for the Wehrmacht's rail transport. Russian locomotives had been withdrawn or demolished and, having few locomotives of the right gauge, the Germans were unable to adequately supply their drives against Moscow and Leningrad.

French, Dutch and German railways suffered badly during the war. In the case of France, bomb damage was supplemented by the far more precise destruction wreaked by the Resistance.

The US railroads, having learned a hard lesson in World War 1, co-ordinated their activities so well that there was no need for another government take-over. They easily handled the upsurge of traffic in the east, when German submarines brought coastal shipping to a virtual standstill, and they coped with the huge burden of troop and supply movement as the nation mobilized. Line capacity was ample, but passenger vehicles were sometimes scarce, so troops had to be often moved in converted boxcars. Military supply railways were the concern of the Corps of Engineers until 1942, when the US Transportation Corps was formed. Like the British, the Americans took their own railway operating units with them in the European campaign. This, again, was a repetition of World War 1 practice. There was a major change, however: fronts were not static in World War 2, so there was no need for narrow-gauge front railways.

PART FOUR

NEW DIRECTIONS: 1945 TO THE END OF THE CENTURY

Left: **A Conrail freight train passes through Champaign in Illinois.**

30
REORGANIZATION AND MODERNIZATION

No railway system emerged from World War 2 in total ruin — but the western lines of the USSR had suffered badly and in the Netherlands the railways were in such a poor state that the government decided not merely to restore them, but to rebuild based on electric traction. In Germany destruction was widespread because the bombs had been directed against a system already feeling the effect of wartime scarcities.

In Britain, actual damage had been relatively limited, but the arrears of accumulated maintenance and replacement were enormous. To a much lesser extent, the American railroads were also suffering from the effects of heavy wartime traffic imposed on lines, which had not been properly maintained or renewed because of the wartime scarcities.

It was in these run-down conditions that the railways of North America and Europe had to face the onslaught of renewed competition. The war, far from holding back the development of highway and air transport, had done much to stimulate them. Moreover, postwar governments for one reason or another decided to invest huge sums in highways and airports. In Europe, however, where the importance of a healthy railway system was usually recognized, some governments did legislate to prevent truck transport driving the railways to the wall. Such legislation typically imposed limits on the number of licensed highway operators and restricted their share of the traffic.

In North America and Britain, the railways were less protected. In the USA, federal highway construction gave considerable advantage to the road haulage industry, while an enormous program of works by the Army's engineers created virtually new waterway systems along the eastern seaboard, while several river systems were also refurbished. At the same time, continental distances, the availability of cheap surplus transport aircraft and the eagerness of civic authorities to finance new airports soon had their effect on railroad passenger traffic. In Britain, road operators (both passenger and freight) benefited from road improvements (and, from the late 1950s, the construction of the motorway network), while paying very little toward their construction and upkeep through taxes and license fees. In both countries the railways were hampered by regulations directed against competitive rate cutting and so began to suffer.

By the late 1940s, it was clear that the railways of Britain and North America were in decline and the failure of governments to remedy this by ensuring a fairer competitive framework implies that this decline was quite acceptable to those governments. Neither in Britain nor the USA were the railways held high in public esteem. Apart from the cardinal sin of appearing old-fashioned, they suffered from citizens' unpleasant memories of recent wartime travel.

While legislation tied one hand firmly behind the railways' backs, the powerful railway trade unions gripped tightly the other hand. Thus, the American railroads' natural reaction to competition — re-equipment to provide better service at lower cost — met unnatural obstacles. Introducing diesel power should have brought some reduced labor costs by eliminating locomotive firemen, but the struggle on this issue was long drawn-out. As was so often the case, the various railroad companies failed to present a united front; this had been crucial in 1935, when they had not supported the Burlington Railroad in its contention that the diesel "Zephyrs" did not need firemen. The Canadian Pacific strike of 1957 and the US rail strike of 1963 emphasized that the locomotive fireman would be drawing his pay for many more years. The 1963 strike did have an interesting outcome when the Florida East Coast Railroad (FEC) broke ranks and refused to accept union-imposed working practices any longer; the FEC abolished firemen and other surplus train staff and went on to become one of the most efficient railroads and also one of the safest, despite occasional sabotage by its enemies.

Under union pressure, many states had legislated full-crew laws, by which railroads were compelled to attach a minimum number of workers to all trains operating in a given state. This meant that trains, which, technically, could be handled by a single man, had to have a complement of five or seven. Meanwhile, steam-age pay systems were not allowed to wither. A full day's work for a locomotive crew was still 100 miles. This had been fair enough in the days when trains only averaged 10-20mph, but, in the 1950s, it meant that fast trains needed to change crews approximately every two hours. Whereas a single truck driver might take his cargo 600 miles in a day, a train moving 600 miles might need to pay a day's wage to about 40 crewmen.

In the face of such waste, the technical advantage of steel wheels running on steel rails was of little avail. High-cost operation, the decline of heavy industries (which traditionally supplied the railways with their bulk traffic), managerial inertia (partly due to the labor and legislative obstacles that crushed any initiative) all combined to produce declining traffic, line closures and general depression in the railway industry. In 1916, the peak year for US railroads, railwaymen represented 4% of the American labor force, the railroads carried 75% of all freight and 98% of passengers. But in 1966, although freight traffic was double that of 1916, it was only 43% of the total. Passenger traffic was only 50% that of 1916, even though the American population had doubled and railroad workers represented only 1% of the total workforce.

Railroad bankruptcies and amalgamations were one result. Among amalgamations, that of the rival New York Central and Pennsylvania railroads, joined later by the New Haven Railroad, only made things worse, and the new company, Penn Central, soon collapsed. This bankruptcy, and the perilous state of other eastern railroads, did at last persuade the federal government that something needed to be done. The Consolidated Rail Corporation (Conrail) was formed in 1976 under federal auspices to combine the lines of the Penn Central, Erie-Lackawanna, Reading, Central of New Jersey, Lehigh Valley, and Lehigh & Hudson River railroads. With a small measure of co-operation from the unions and some sensible management, as well as government sympathy and finance, Conrail began to reduce costs and produce revenue, enabling it to be offered to private purchasers as a going concern. Earlier, federal intervention had created Amtrak, to operate a national system of passenger services.

Compared to other countries, the US railroad system was organizationally fluid. Mergers were always under discussion; those that became reality in the postwar decades included the combination of the Burlington, Great Northern, Northern Pacific and Spokane, Portland & Seattle into the Burlington Northern Railroad. The once rival Seaboard Railroad and Atlantic Coast Line merged to form the Seaboard Coast Line, which later, as part of the CSX System, joined with the Baltimore & Ohio, Chesapeake & Ohio, Louisville & Nashville and other railroads. The Norfolk Southern combined under a single management the two giants: the Norfolk & Western and the Southern. In the same period, several companies disappeared through bankruptcy, including the New York, Ontario & Western, the Milwaukee and the Rock Island railroads. At the same time a number of new short lines appeared, often taking over sections of bankrupt companies.

By the 1980s, some easing of the US railroads' situation was evident. Deregulation and, in particular, the Staggers Act freed the railroads of much federal supervision. It became easier to close lines and withdraw services. Above all, the railroads regained much of their old freedom in rate-setting, which enabled them to respond more flexibly to price competition. The unions began to make concessions with selected acceptance of two-man crews for certain trains and an agreement to dispense with cabooses.

In Britain, the "Big Four" companies in 1948 became the state-owned British Railways (later British Rail [BR]). Nationalization occurred, however, not because the government favored railways, but because it opposed private ownership; similarly, the coal and electricity industries, along with much of the road haulage industry and other sectors of the economy, also passed into the hands of the then Labour government. Railways were mishandled in the postwar decades, largely because of a reluctance to grasp nettles.

Unwilling to accept, as in continental Europe, that railways were a public service worthy of subsidy, yet at the same time unwilling to accept that they should abandon loss-making services, successive British governments had no clear-cut railway policy but seemed to expect BR to make a profit and provide uneconomic services. As the railways staggered from crisis to crisis, the governments, anxious to be seen doing something, made successive organizational changes that did little except unsettle management and clients. Once, in the early 1960s, at a time when road transport was exceptionally strong politically, the government decided that profit should come first. This resulted in a report, *The Reshaping of British Railways* (known colloquially as the "Beeching Report" after the then chairman of British Railways, Dr Richard Beeching, who compiled it), in 1963, after which thousands of miles of route and thousands of stations were closed, although an effort was made to provide modern freight services by eliminating many of the wayside goods yards. As usual, when essential decisions are taken too late, the policy was taken too far and, with an obsessional zeal, the BR administration proceeded to close not only loss-making facilities but also lines and stations which, given time and effort, could have contributed to revenue.

After this period of sacrifice, BR settled down to digest its ill prepared modernization plans (in 1955, BR had launched a massive scheme to replace steam locomotives). It still faced a number of hindrances. The press, mainly hostile to nationalized industries, was so keen to condemn BR that useful criticism was swamped by a sea of petty and often fabricated aspersions. The railways had no real representative in the government. Ostensibly they were the responsibility of the Minister of Transport, but the latter, apart from averaging barely two years in office before being transferred elsewhere, headed a department that was more interested in road transport than in rail. On top of all this BR, unlike the previous companies, was not allowed to raise capital. It had to rely on government money for investment and for subsidy (a concept of support for unremunerative passenger services was accepted only after 1968). Funding for investment was rarely forthcoming without protracted negotiation and interference, so projects that could have produced a good rate of return in terms of improved efficiency were simply not attempted. In the 1980s British railway investment per mile of route was about 25% of that of Belgium,

From time to time, under Conservative governments, there was talk of privatization, but first the problem had to be solved of persuading private investors to purchase BR's loss-making, as well as the potentially profitable, businesses. Meanwhile, Japan adopted a viable scheme for restructuring the loss-making Japanese National Railways into companies in 1987 and, in Europe, Sweden became a pioneer; in 1988 Swedish State Railways (SJ) was divided into separate track (BV) and operating (SJ) managements, the latter no longer having a monopoly of train operation.

31
TRIUMPH OF THE DIESEL

After the war ended, more and more US railroads decided to stop placing orders for steam locomotives. They had been impressed by the performance of the GM diesel locomotives produced in limited quantities during the war and, free of government control over purchases, aimed to eliminate the steam locomotive. GM, benefiting from its privileged position as monopoly supplier during the war, expanded its output but soon began to face competition. Alco, the steam locomotive company, partnered General Electric to become the second-biggest builder, while the two other big locomotive companies in the country, Baldwin and Lima, tried but failed to make a success of diesel traction. Meanwhile, Fairbanks Morse used a US Navy opposed-piston diesel-engine design to power its "Trainmaster," a high-horsepower (2,400hp) unit which failed to make much impact thanks to GM's dominant market position.

General Electric, which was also an independent producer of its own designs, specialized in a 44-ton yard and branch-line diesel locomotive, which was an exceptionally low-cost unit because American working regulations allowed a one-man crew for diesel locomotives of less than 45 tons. After leaving its partnership with Alco, GE introduced its own main-line diesel locomotive in 1960, the

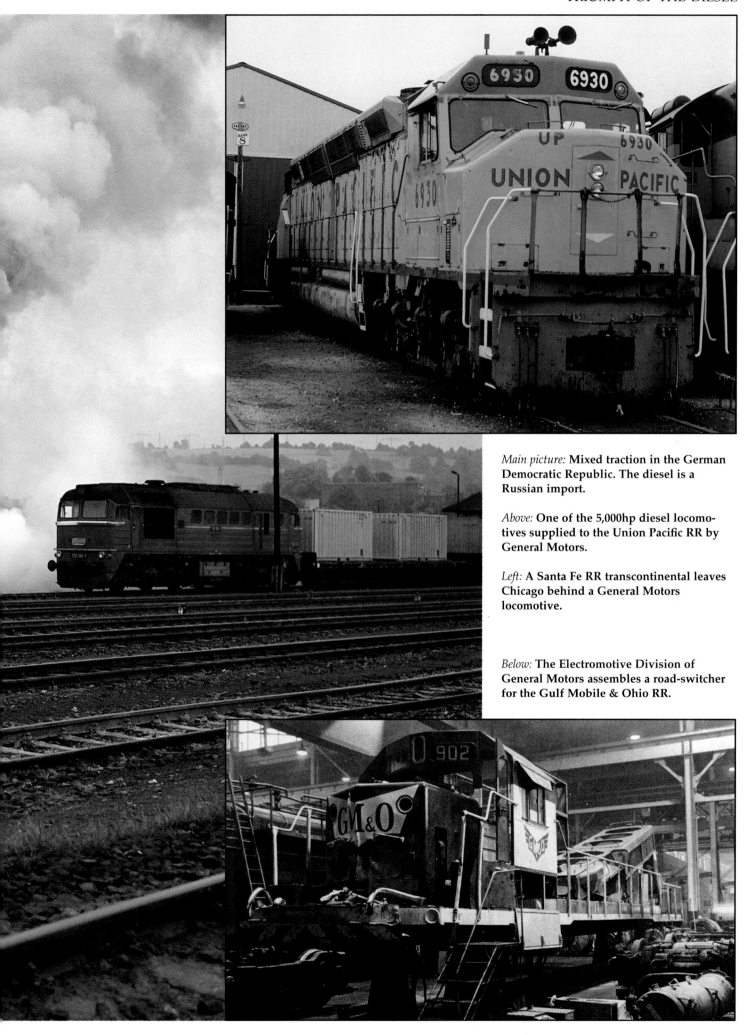

Main picture: **Mixed traction in the German Democratic Republic. The diesel is a Russian import.**

Above: **One of the 5,000hp diesel locomotives supplied to the Union Pacific RR by General Motors.**

Left: **A Santa Fe RR transcontinental leaves Chicago behind a General Motors locomotive.**

Below: **The Electromotive Division of General Motors assembles a road-switcher for the Gulf Mobile & Ohio RR.**

WORLD RAILWAYS

Main picture: **On the eve of its 1948 nationalization, the LMSR ordered two main-line diesel units for trial.**

Right: **The British "Deltic" locomotives provided more than 3,000hp in a single unit.**

Far right: **Built in Sweden for Norwegian Railways, this locomotive was essentially a General Motors design.**

Below: **A US export to southern Africa, the Benguela Railway's class of General Electric locomotives.**

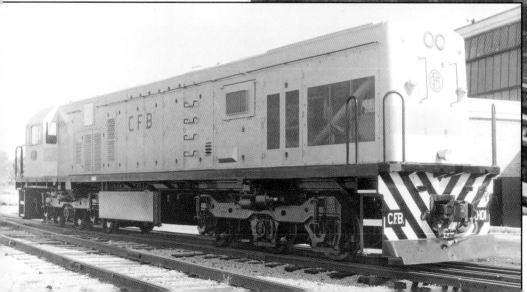

"U25B" 2,500hp road-switcher. The result of years of research, the "U25B" had electronic controls, a body that was largely maintenance-free and pressurized (therefore dust-free) equipment compartments. Its excellence enabled GE to win a foothold in the market despite GM's dominance. For a time Alco's Canadian subsidiary, Montreal Locomotive, continued to build Alco designs, as did the Indian Railways' diesel locomotive plant set up earlier by Alco, but the American market and export trade was held by GM and GE from now on.

Initially, the main-line locomotive market was dominated by the "cab" type of locomotive, in which the body was the full width of the locomotive and was streamlined; "A" units were provided with a streamlined cab while "B" units were cabless and intended to be attached to "A" units. It was this facility of adding units to form a multiple-unit locomotive controlled by a single crew, plus the high availability of the diesel, that made it so popular among railroad operators. Later, the more functional road-switcher (in which the machinery was enclosed in a narrow hood, with external inspection walkways) superseded the cab units. Horsepowers varied from 1,200 to 3,600 per unit, although the Union Pacific bought some locomotives of 5,000hp.

In many cases, the diesel locomotive was a cost-saving innovation, which enabled managements to put off, for a few more years, long-needed changes, and this was part of the reason for the rapidity of its adoption. Steam locomotives were written off needlessly early and, by the mid-1950s, the coal-hauling Norfolk & Western Railroad was the only major American railroad still faithful to steam, a stronghold that was soon breached. The locomotive builders then switched to more powerful units, in order to create a second-generation market. They also benefited from a trade in exports, typically with countries supplied with the necessary dollars by American or international finance institutions.

Above: **An Alco locomotive, built under license in Spain.**

Main picture: **Russia's Class TEP60 single-unit passenger locomotive, of which over 1,300 units were built from 1961 to 1985.**

Below: **Another Alco locomotive, this one supplied to Pakistan in the 1950s.**

Main picture: **General Motors units head New York Central RR passenger trains at Buffalo in 1957.**

Far left: **Another design of 5,000hp units for the Union Pacific. General Electric built just 40 of these.**

Left: **In the 1970s US railroads began to buy high-horsepower diesels of 3,000hp or more. This is one such, supplied to the SP by General Electric.**

In many cases the diesel locomotive was oversold. Whereas in US conditions it usually had substantial operating and economic advantages over the steam locomotive, this was not necessarily true everywhere. Many Third World railways, whose governments had been attracted by the sales talk of US corporations, found themselves saddled with fleets of diesels that were largely unserviceable, as soon as they had run off their initial mileages. Shortage of spare parts, of skilled engineers and of proper maintenance facilities contributed to this situation.

In the more developed countries, the US builders often set up their own works or licensed overseas builders to produce their designs. General Motors of Canada built GM designs for the Canadian railways, while Montreal Locomotive built Alco types. In Sweden, Nohab stopped building steam locomotives in favor of diesels incorporating GM technology and so did two Belgian companies. In Australia, Clyde Engineering built its own versions of GM designs while Goodwin produced what were essentially Alco locomotives. GM designs were also constructed in South Africa.

In much of Europe, however, US locomotives were excluded. The German diesel locomotive industry, building on past experience, evolved its own range of designs, many of which used hydraulic instead of electric transmission. Such transmission dispensed with the need to carry heavy electric generators on each locomotive, but eventually it was found that the advantage of this was, for main-line units, more than outweighed by heavier maintenance expenses. In France and Italy, too, home industry produced its own designs, whereas the Spanish National Railways preferred to buy Alco or German designs. Russia went its own way, having absorbed American technology from a few US units imported during the war.

Some railways adopted policies of massive and rapid dieselization while others planned to replace the steam locomotive gradually. Some US lines, British Railways and many Third World railways came into the first category while the French, German, South African and Australian railways were among those which took the more considered approach, introducing the diesel gradually.

British adoption of diesel power, introduced in the Modernisation Plan of 1955, stands as an example of how not to do it. BR had initially decided to remain with the steam locomotive and dieselization proposals, being studied by the companies on the eve of nationalization were not pursued energetically. Then, seeing the success of dieselization in the USA, BR decided to make up for lost time. Domestic locomotive builders were gratified by massive orders for diesel locomotives of an excessively wide range of designs. The result was the multiplication of a few good but many inferior types. At the same time, the government ensured that no American builders would participate in this activity. This had the effect of excluding the most experienced diesel locomotive designers and builders from this transformation of BR and contrasted with the former companies' long-standing willingness to seek examples from overseas. The British approach to adopting diesel power was, therefore, an enormous misallocation of investment. Recently built steam locomotives were sent for scrap long before the end of their natural lives and were soon joined by new, but defective, diesel locomotives. Not only was BR faced by a multitude of designs, it also investigated both electric and hydraulic traction, with the Western Region (effectively the old GWR) being supplied with large numbers of diesel-hydraulic locomotives, most of which had very short lives. However, the French and German railways were more rational, conserving their steam locomotives while the main lines were being electrified and, thereby, avoiding over-investment in diesels.

Among British successes was the development of the ac/dc locomotive, in which an alternator was fitted instead of a generator; modern electronics having eased the problem of converting ac (easier to produce) to dc (better for the traction motors). The prototype ac/dc unit was subsequently sold for study by Soviet engineers.

In the mid-1980s GM locomotives did at last move on British rails, when the quarrying company, Foster Yeoman, bought four advanced-technology units to haul its roadstone trains over BR track. These acquisitions had an invigorating effect on BR's traction engineers.

Main picture: **The most numerous British Rail diesel, the Class 47, used for both passenger and freight work.**

Inset, top left: **One of a series of gas-turbine locomotives built by General Electric for the Union Pacific in the 1950s.**

Inset, top right: **Diesel and steam traction co-existing at Ottawa's main passenger terminal in 1957.**

32
POSTWAR ELECTRIFICATION

The postwar decades were years of widespread electrification. However, this trend was hardly felt in the Americas. Indeed, in the USA there was a perceptible de-electrification as railroads discovered that after dieselization, it made sense to replace their electric locomotives with diesel. By 1975 the electrified US mileage, which had once reached 3,100 miles, was down to less than 2,000 miles, much of which was commuter line. The US situation, so out of order with the rest of the world, arose because electrification, which required an expensive infrastructure, was most economic on lines of high traffic density and such lines were rare in the USA with its long, relatively low-traffic, routes.

The major US electrification remained that of the former Pennsylvania Railroad line from New York to Washington and Harrisburg. Extension of this line to Pittsburgh was proposed but not attempted. Electric Amtrak passenger services were operated over this line, as they were over parts of the former New Haven Railroad's electrified route, but they were hauled by locomotives designed in Sweden, electric locomotive technology having languished in the US from lack of orders.

Advanced technology was, however, employed on two specialized electric railroads. The first was the Muskingum Electric Railroad, opened in 1968 over 15 miles to transport coal to a generating station. It used high-voltage (25kV ac) current which, at 60 cycles, corresponded to the public grid supply. The success of this line encouraged the building of another, longer, power station line. This was the 78-mile Black Mesa & Lake Powell Railroad in Arizona, which used the exceptionally high 50kV ac. Both these lines used rectifier locomotives supplied by GE.

Another, longer, 50kV electrification was undertaken in South Africa for the 535-mile Sishen-Saldanha ore-carrying railway. But, on the whole, it was the French who led the way in electric railway technology during the postwar decades. With over 2,000 miles of electrified route open before the war, SNCF had accumulated enough experience to plan the electrification of all its main routes, beginning with the Paris-Lyons Mediterranean trunk line. At the same time, SNCF was successfully introducing the then-novel 25kV ac system on the heavy-traffic Metz-Thionville line in eastern France.

It had always been realized that a high-voltage ac system would lower the cost of electrification, but the problem had been the need to rectify the current to make it suitable for the low voltage dc traction motors of the locomotives. The postwar development of lightweight rectifiers provided a simple and fairly cheap solution for this. Next, the French used the system for the Paris-Lille electrification and then for all of their subsequent electrification schemes except for some that were continuations of older 1,500V dc schemes.

In due course dual-current locomotives, capable of working over the old and new systems, were introduced to eliminate engine-changing where the two systems met.

Right: **On the 25,000V electrified western main line in Hungary. The "V43" class locomotive was designed by a European consortium but built in Hungary from the 1960s.**

Later, several European railways introduced quadri-current locomotives, capable of operating not only on the high-voltage ac system, but also on the older 1,500V dc system of Holland and France, the 3kV dc system of Belgium, as well as the 15kV ac system of the German railways — an important change.

Other railways that accepted the disadvantage of supporting two different electrification systems were Soviet Railways (which was to have more electrified mileage than any other railway) and India; the French experience with 25kV ac was so favorable that even though these countries had substantial dc mileages they willingly moved to the higher voltage. Others, including Italy at 3kV, the Scandinavian and central European block of countries using 15kV ac and, in Australia, New South Wales and Victoria at 1,500V dc stayed with their old systems. Queensland, however, starting fresh with electrification in the 1970s, opted for 25kV. In South Africa three systems coexisted, with the 25kV and 50kV systems for new electrifications and the 3kV system preserved on the older conversions.

British electrification was held back by shortage of investment funds, but this had the advantage that the first long main-line scheme, that from London to Birmingham, Liverpool, Manchester and Glasgow was begun after the virtues of 25kV ac had become apparent and this system was adopted. Existing electrifications, undertaken by the old companies, met varying fates. The Manchester-Sheffield scheme, over the Pennines, started by the LNER at 1,500V, remained largely unaltered, but eventually this route was closed (in 1981) and the western extremity, which served communities close to Manchester, was converted to 25kV. The LNER commuter scheme, initially from London to Shenfield, was undertaken at 1,500V and was later extended; the route was subsequently converted to 25kV. The dense third-rail network of the old Southern Railway was retained and adopted for extensions to the Kent Coast in the late 1950s and to Weymouth (progressively from the

Above: **The German current-invertor Type 120 electric locomotive. When introduced in 1979 this was the world's most powerful four-axle design, at 5,600kW.**

Left: **The French National Railways introduced the "CC-7100" class in 1952, and in 1955 one of them broke a record by reaching 205mph.**

155

1960s through to the mid-1980s), even though this system was not really suited to the longer-distance services.

The electrification at 25kV ac of the West Coast main line, from London to Birmingham, Manchester, and Liverpool, not only reduced operating costs but enabled a new service of more frequent, faster and brighter trains to be run, thereby attracting considerable new business to the railway. It was soon extended northward to Glasgow, where some commuter lines had already electrified. After this, despite the obvious success of electrification, new schemes were more modest, comprising outer-suburban lines from London to Royston, near Cambridge, and from London to Bedford. The latter was completed in the early 1980s and was followed by the electrification of a second route to Cambridge as well as an extension of existing electrification from London to Colchester through to Ipswich and Norwich. In this period too, the electrification of the East Coast main line from London to Edinburgh was begun, thus ultimately releasing diesel-powered high-speed trains for service elsewhere.

Progress during the 20th century in electrical engineering was so rapid that electrification schemes adopted in one decade could be obsolescent in the next. There was a price to be paid for early innovation; the third-rail lines of southern England, once so progressive, had become technically disadvantaged by the 1980s. Some of the innovations were applicable to locomotives rather than to whole systems. For example, new kinds of electronic control, thyristor control for ac units and chopper control for dc locomotives, enabled power to be increased in a continuous flow, rather than in a series of steps. Such a smooth transition helped to reduce wheelslip and, therefore, represented a real increase in a locomotive's tractive power. Electronics also gave birth to the current invertor, which enabled three-phase ac traction motors to be used in place of the traditional dc type. The ac motor wears better in service and a batch of current-invertor locomotives, Class 120, was tried on German Railways. New third-rail trains planned by British Rail for the 1990s were to incorporate this innovation.

Main picture: **An Amtrak Northeast Corridor train enters Washington terminal, hauled by an "AEM7" type locomotive. This class, supplied by General Motors from 1979, was based on a Swedish design.**

Left: **Introduced in 1964, the Swiss "420" class numbers more than 280 units, and is suited for both passenger and freight work.**

Below: **The German Type 103 was the standard traction for fast services, until the appearance of the high-speed trains.**

33
SURVIVAL OF STEAM

On the eve of dieselization the locomotive works at Swindon in Britain conducted trials of different chimney and exhaust arrangements, revealing that, with very careful design of draughting, the steam locomotive's efficiency could be noticeably enhanced. The problem had always been that the intermittent exhaust from the cylinders, used to provide a draught for the fire as it left the blastpipe to exit through the chimney, was difficult to harness in such a way that it would provide a draught that was strong, steady and unlikely to pull unburned coal particles from the grate. Various types of wide and double chimneys had appeared during the interwar years, but perfection was still a long way off. An important step in the right direction was the postwar "Giesl Ejector," in which the exhaust steam was channelled through seven nozzles, each aimed upwards at a distinct part of the chimney orifice. Locomotives fitted with this device, recognizable by their elongated chimneys, extracted considerably more energy from the coal they burned. But the invention came too late

to extend the life of steam traction in Britain and America, although it did find a role in central Europe and India.

One of the countries where steam traction survived for a long time was the Argentine and here the engineer L. Porta continued the tradition of the Frenchman Chapelon by designing better blast-pipe and chimney arrangements, known as the "Kylpor" and "Lempor" chimneys. He also experimented with the combustion end of the locomotive, replacing the conventional firebox with a gas-producer grate in which the coal was kept at a fairly low temperature, gas being extracted from it and then burned at a higher level. These ideas were taken up by the South African Railways' engineer P. Wardale, under whose auspices an orthodox 4-8-4, No 3450, was rebuilt on Porta's principles in 1980. This appeared to give substantial economy combined with higher maximum power output and, in the mid-1980s, Wardale was in China, helping to redesign the standard 2-10-2 that was still being built there. However, there were no substantial long-term results from this work.

As for the orthodox steam locomotive, this was still in regular service in many parts of the world in the late 1980s. Indeed, new steam locomotives were still being built in China, where steam traction would continue into the 21st century, despite extending electrification and dieselization. In the late 1980s, the "QJ" class 2-10-2, a derivative of a Soviet Railways' design, was still being produced by the Datong Works, while the Tangshan Works, restored after a

Below: **The massive Chesapeake & Ohio RR "Alleghenies" were introduced in 1941 and lasted until 1956. They were the heaviest class of steam locomotives ever built.**

Left: Two "WP" Pacifics meet in India. Designed mainly in the USA, but built in several countries, this type initially handled almost all major Indian long-distance passenger trains and some units survived into the 1990s.

Below left: The Norfolk & Western was the last American operator of streamlined steam trains. This is the "Powhattan Arrow," linking Norfolk with Cincinatti.

Below: On Indian Railways, an elderly British-built ten-wheeler enters Baroda in 1970, passing a more modern "WP" Pacific.

disastrous earthquake, were producing a type of 2-8-2 steam locomotive.

In India, dieselization and electrification took their toll, and production of steam locomotives finished in the 1970s, although spare components continued to be produced. By the mid-1980s, the older British-built types had largely disappeared and steam traction was confined to a handful of more modern designs. On the broad gauge, these were the "WG" 2-8-2, a freight locomotive of British inspiration that had been mass produced at the new Chittaranjan Locomotive Works in the 1950s and 1960s, and the bullet-nosed "WP" 4-6-2, designed in the USA and constructed in several countries. On the meter gauge, it was the postwar "YG" 2-8-2 and "YP" 4-6-2 classes that survived the longest, although on both gauges American-built 2-8-2s, acquired during and after the war, were still active in the late-1980s.

Steam traction also remained important in parts of Africa. In the Republic of South Africa diesel power was adopted at a pace which seemed irrational, given that country's dependence on oil imports and its abundance of coal. Steam traction was increasingly confined to certain areas and to certain classes of locomotive, of which the massive Class 25NC 4-8-4 was very prominent. The "Garratts" were early casualties, although, in common with other withdrawn designs, some of them were sold for use on colliery railways.

In Zimbabwe, there was something of a steam renaissance. Imported diesels, producing extremely low productivity indices, thanks to shortage of spare parts and lack of good maintenance facilities, proved inadequate and steam locomotives, side-tracked for scrap, were taken into

Above: **The last substantial inter-city steam service in Europe was that between Berlin and Dresden, in the German Democratic Republic. This train was photographed in 1975.**

Below: **Bolivia imported its final steam locomotives from Britain and Japan. This 4-8-2 is heading out of the capital, La Paz, in 1968.**

Left: **In the final years of German steam the predominant locomotives were of the 2-10-0 type. Here are three of them at a depot near Hanover.**

Below: **In sub-zero weather steam locomotives were sometimes drafted in to replace diesels, as in this scene where Canadian National steam power has taken over the passenger services out of Stratford, Ontario, in the 1958-59 winter.**

Above: **The "Britannia" type Pacific (nearest camera) was the passenger locomotive built for the nationalized British railways.**

Above right: **"QJ" locomotives of Chinese Railways, hundreds of which remain in service.**

Main picture: **Streamlined and non-streamlined versions of the New South Wales "C38" Pacific handle an excursion near Bathurst in 1971.**

works and restored to traffic. Thus the "Garratts" of the former Rhodesian Railways gained a fresh lease of life, as they also did in neighbouring Zambia. Farther north, in the Sudan, famine produced another implicit acknowledgement that the blandishments of the diesel salesmen should have been resisted more stoutly. When international aid produced the grain to relieve the famine of the southern Sudan it was found that the railways could not handle the traffic, for here too, the new diesel locomotives were failing, with 75% out of service. As this was an emergency, in which realities had priority over image-building, it was decided to renovate the steam locomotive fleet. A number of quite modern British-built 2-8-2 locomotives were sent to a works in South Wales for refurbishing, while other steam locomotives were also repaired and returned to traffic by the Atbara works in Sudan itself. The units repaired in South Wales were also modernized with "Lempor" exhausts, after which their fuel costs were comparable to those of diesel locomotives.

In 1977, the DB in West Germany withdrew its last steam locomotives, having wisely kept steam traction alive in the years of large-scale electrification so as to avoid over production of diesels. BR had ended steam traction a

WORLD RAILWAYS

Previous page: **The postwar mixed-traffic design for Polish Railways, a handful of which are still in service.**

Main picture: **Australia's last regular steam passenger train, the Newcastle-Singleton commuter service, photographed in 1970.**

Right: **The last French steam commuter service was from the Gare du Nord in Paris.**

Far right: **The last regular steam-hauled freight service in Victoria, Australia, shown leaving Geelong behind a British-built 2-8-0 in 1970.**

Bottom right: **Servicing a Garratt locomotive in New South Wales.**

Below: **A narrow-gauge locomotive sent after World War 2 to Yugoslavia by the UN's relief organization.**

decade before and steam had also disappeared from SNCF. In Austria, Portugal and Italy steam hung on a little longer, but, by the mid-1980s, European steam traction was largely confined to Eastern Europe. Poland, in particular, still operated many steam services. In Yugoslavia, East Germany and Romania there were still pockets of steam operation; Romania even preserved on its books a few remaining veterans of the Prussian "P38" 4-6-0 type. The USSR and Hungary also had a few steam locomotives in service, mainly for yard work and extra trains. The Turkish railways, meanwhile, repeatedly announced the forthcoming end of steam, but, somehow, steam traction survived there, having proved less dispensable than expected.

While regular steam traction had disappeared on North American railroads, in South America it still lingered on in the 1980s. Paraguay, which was too impoverished to modernize its railways, relied on British 2-6-0s, supplemented by second-hand locomotives bought from the Argentine. Bolivia and Peru had already adopted diesel power, and Chile was about to, but in the Argentine and Ecuador there were still regular steam-hauled services. Steam could also be found in Uruguay, while Brazil and the Argentine each had coal-hauling lines devoted entirely to steam traction.

Main picture: **A Bolivian 4-8-2 interrupts daily life in Oruro.**

Above right: **A Canadian National freight train approaches Winnipeg in 1957.**

Bottom right: **German Pacifics await their duties at Osnabrück in 1966.**

Below: **Paraguayan woodburners at their depot in Asuncion.**

Main picture: **Indonesian street scene, 1972. The locomotive is a German-built 4-4-0.**

Above left: **Heavy South African motive power at the Bloemfontein depot.**

Above: **South African short-wheelbase yard locomotives at Capetown docks. Unusually, these postwar locomotives were designed and built in South Africa.**

Far left: **Chinese locomotives at Changchun in 1988. The unit on the left is plainly of American inspiration, where-as the more modern locomotive blends Japanese and Russian features.**

Left: **Indian "WP" Pacifics at Baroda.**

Below left: **A British Rail Southern Region Pacific takes water at Southampton.**

Right: **The final German Pacific design, built in the German Democratic Republic.**

Below: **The last British passenger locomotive design. This remained a lone prototype.**

Bottom: **British and US practice in New South Wales. The nearer locomotive is a US 2-8-2 similar to those built for wartime service.**

34

THE PASSENGER TRAIN: CRISIS AND SURVIVAL

Despite growing car ownership, the railways in Western Europe, after some difficult years, succeeded in holding and even attracting passengers with vastly improved services and careful fare setting. But in the USA and Canada, despite the efforts of some passenger-conscious companies, the passenger train remained such a loss-making proposition that the railroads were finally allowed to abandon the business altogether, being required only to make their tracks available for passenger trains operated by government-inspired and subsidized passenger train corporations, notably Amtrak in the US and Via Rail in Canada.

Meanwhile, in both Europe and North America, the responsibility for popular but loss-making suburban services was increasingly handed over to local authorities, which, having learned that expensive highway construction brought more problems than it solved, were willing to make a financial contribution to enable peak-hour traffic to move by train rather than by automobile. Thus, many city terminals were enlivened by trains, operated by the mainline railways, but painted in the liveries of the various local passenger authorities that sponsored and subsidized them.

In most of Western Europe, including Britain but not Ireland, the railways responded to difficulty by providing better services over their main lines, while neglecting or abandoning their secondary services. This effort to a large extent succeeded in not only holding, but developing, the passenger market. In Britain, for example, the railways began to derive most of their income from passengers and not from freight, as previously.

Above right: **The former Buenos Aires Great Southern terminus in 1968, with mixed steam and diesel haulage of commuter services.**

Right: **Diesel and electric passenger trains at Barcelona.**

Below: **A Spanish "Talgo" lightweight train near Almeria.**

Main picture: **Amtrak's "South-West Chief" halts at Albuquerque in New Mexico.**

Above: **A Japanese electric commuter train at Kyoto.**

Below: **Dutch passenger trains at Amsterdam.**

In North America, the picture was quite different, with freight revenue forming an ever-increasing proportion of the railroads' total income as passenger services declined. In the immediate postwar years, most US railroads made a determined effort to rejuvenate their passenger services. New rolling stock was purchased, which, hauled by cab-type diesels, could be plausibly described as streamlined. By 1948, the railroads were operating 250 such streamlined trains and about 33% of the passengers benefited from them; a proportion that would grow in subsequent years. Some new eye-catching trains were introduced. The "California Zephyr," for example, operated jointly by the Burlington, Denver & Rio Grande and the Western Pacific railroads, was a stainless-steel train timed to allow

passengers to enjoy the Feather River Canyon and other spectacular scenery. The "Lark" of the Southern Pacific provided a 12hr overnight trip between San Francisco and Los Angeles. It was all-Pullman and had a magnificent dining unit consisting of three carriages with articulated suspension. However, it needed no fewer than 21 members of crew, while carrying fewer than two bus-loads of passengers.

Novel rolling stock was also introduced. The first dome car, followed by many others, was introduced on the Burlington Railroad in 1945; passengers could climb into an overhead glass-topped section to look at the scenery. The Santa Fe Railroad soon went one better by providing what in effect were double-deck carriages on its "El Capitan"; passengers sat on the glass-enclosed upper deck, leaving

Top left: **An experimental low-slung train tried by the Pennsylvania RR in the 1950s.**

Far left: **A Grand Trunk Western commuter train pulls out of Detroit in 1958.**

Above: **The "Scarborough Flyer," one of several British named trains connecting London with holiday resorts.**

Left: **For some communities, cheap railway travel remained essential. This scene is in a Mexican branch-line train.**

the lower deck for sleeping and other services. The Burlington Railroad was also the first to use the "Slumbercoach." This enabled coach-class passengers to use sleeping accommodation, formerly the preserve of those buying first-class tickets. For a small supplement, they could use one of the tiny sleeping compartments of this vehicle which, ingeniously arranged, accommodated 40 passengers. Another success was the Budd car, or Rail Diesel Car (RDC), introduced in 1950. These self-propelled railcars came in four configurations and could run as single units or be coupled together to form trains. They reduced operating costs considerably and thereby enabled services to be maintained on secondary and branch lines.

But the gap between costs and revenues widened. The final blow was the decision of the US Post Office to transfer mail traffic from rail to road whenever possible. The guaranteed mail contract had been a vital part of railroad passenger revenue and, with its loss, passenger deficits could only rise.

1967 was perhaps the beginning of the end. The Illinois Central and the Pennsylvania railroads added coach-class accommodation to their hitherto all-Pullman "Panama Limited" and "Broadway Limited" services, implicitly acknowledging that the airlines had scooped the market for the higher class of passenger. The Erie-Lackawanna Railroad's old-established "Phoebe Snow," connecting New York with Chicago, was cut, while the pride of the NYC, the "Twentieth Century Limited," disappeared from

Above: **A German diesel-hauled train exchanges passsengers at a ski resort. Some railroads provide scheduled "ski trains" in season.**

Above right: **An Amtrak transcontinental train takes up passengers.**

Right: **Amtrak, persuading passengers that train travel was not just transportation, but an experience, provided some of its trains with these "Sightseer Lounge Cars."**

the timetables as the NYC announced that it intended to discontinue all its longer-distance trains.

The Frisco Railroad, meanwhile, became a freight-only railroad and by 1967 the proportion of railroad mileage carrying a passenger service fell to 32%, compared with 71% in 1947. In the next decade, railroads presented a succession of "train-off" petitions to the authorities and, by the mid-1970s, it was evident, despite the continuing persistence of a few managements, that the long-distance passenger train was about to disappear from the American scene. To prevent this, in 1971 the federal government established Amtrak. This was to operate passenger trains over the tracks of the railroad companies, the latter receiving a fee and dropping their own surviving passenger trains.

Over the years, Amtrak developed its own image and bought new rolling stock, which included double-deck

Above: **The "South Yorkshireman," introduced after World War 2 by British Railways and connecting Sheffield with London. It is hauled by a mixed-traffic ten-wheeler.**

Right: **One of the celebrated "Castle" class locomotives built by the Great Western Railway rests at Swansea after bringing in a train from London.**

"Superliner" carriages for its western routes, where the loading gauge were more generous. Its operations were divided between the North East Corridor route (Washington-New York-Boston), whose tracks it owned and reconstructed, and where the train service was frequent and profitable, and its other routes, which were a selection from the long-distance passenger network once offered by the railroads. As its losses were made up by government subsidy, its choice of routes was changeable, being affected by the need to keep its deficit as low as possible and by the political pressures that could be placed on it to maintain services to one or another city. By the 1980s, some states had begun to pay Amtrak for the operation of intrastate trains. California, for example, subsidized a San Francisco-Los Angeles service.

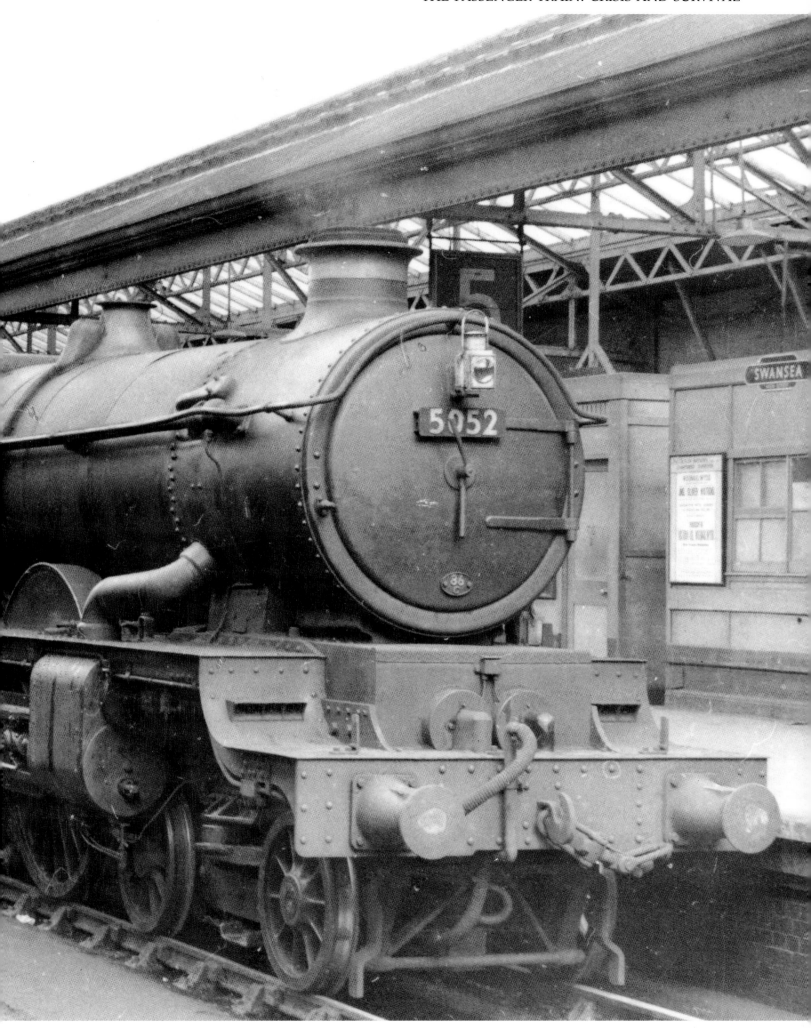

Above: **Passenger trains at Vienna's Ostbahnhof in 1982.**

Right: **Canadian Pacific commuter trains ready to leave Montreal in 1958.**

Opposite page, Top: **A passenger train operated by ViaRail, Canada's equivalent of Amtrak, leaves Montreal in 1983.**

Opposite page, center: **A Budd rail diesel car of the New York Central RR near Niagara in 1957.**

Opposite page, bottom: **An unusual boarding procedure for a New York-bound Amtrak train.**

In Canada, Via Rail was set up to relieve CNR and CPR of their long-distance passenger services. In the 1960s, CNR had made a great effort to save its passenger services, offering fare reductions on off-peak days, complimentary meals for first-class passengers and new trains, such as the "Rapidos," which, for example, reduced the Montreal-Toronto schedule to five hours for the 335 miles. These measures did attract passengers, but the increase was not enough to clear the deficit. Via Rail was less glamorous than Amtrak and was obliged to soldier on with outdated equipment in addition to paying the two companies a high price for the use of their tracks and maintenance facilities. Its only leap forward, the purchase of a fleet of Canadian-built fast diesel trains, the LRC ("Light, Rapid, Comfortable"), was clouded when these trains proved to be victims of multiple design defects. Nevertheless, Via Rail did preserve passenger services on most of the main lines, including the transcontinental route through the Rockies.

Meanwhile, great things were happening on British Railways, which was anxious to dispel the old public image of grimy, slow and overcrowded trains. A few diesel Pullman trains were operated in the 1960s, but these were overshadowed by the electrification from London to Birmingham, Liverpool, Manchester and Glasgow, which permitted the introduction of a fast and frequent service, attracting far more new passengers than had been expected. With this encouragement, other plans were made. The term "InterCity" was adopted as a brand name intended to signify a better-than-usual service; as such, it was highly successful, with DB copying it for their own new passenger service and with its echo in the later "Euro-City" marketing device.

35
INTERNATIONAL AND HIGH-SPEED TRAINS

Because of the out-of-town situation of airports, city center-city center rail transit times are usually less than air transit up to distances of about 250 miles. Most European passenger journeys are shorter than this, so it has been the private automobile rather than the airliner that has been the main rival. To keep businessmen on the trains, the Western European railways introduced the Trans-Europ Express (TEE) service; a network of extra-fare trains using ultramodern equipment and providing the best possible and most reliable service. These operated both nationally and internationally, acquiring a high reputation before, in 1987, being replaced by the "Euro-City" network. "Euro-City" trains, operated by most of the then members of the EEC plus Switzerland and Austria, were air-conditioned and had a minimum average speed of 56mph, except in mountainous regions.

Meanwhile, a handful of the traditional prewar international trains, including the long-lived "Nord Express," soldiered on and were supplemented by a new concept, which carried both passengers and their cars. This concept was enthusiastically pursued for a number of years by British Railways, whose Motorail service linked London with Scotland and with the southwest. Gradually, however, the improvements in the national road network, which made car travel much quicker, allied with increasing costs, led to the end of these services, although one of the privatized companies — First Great Western — attempted to reintroduce the concept in the late 1990s. This type of service also appeared in the USA, serving Florida.

The old "Orient Express" ceased to run, but its name was taken by a high-fare traditional luxury train for the tourist trade, operating between London and the Mediterranean. Another interesting international train was the "Catalan Talgo." Operating between Madrid and Geneva, this took one of the unique Spanish "Talgo" trains, with adjustable axles to suit the two gauges, into France and Switzerland.

The quest for higher speeds continued in Europe. At first it was the French "Mistral," running over electrified lines from Paris to Marseilles, that held the main records, being scheduled to average 84mph over the 195 miles from Paris to Dijon. In 1954, SNCF, in special trials with electric locomotives, reached a maximum speed of 151mph.

Unprecedented high speeds were reached in Japan on the new Tokaido line, opened in 1964. This, later extended,

was a standard-gauge route, unlike the other Japanese main lines, which are of 3ft 6in (1,065mm) gauge. Its trains could reach a maximum of 130mph, while averaging 112mph between Yokohama and Nagoya. The concept of building an entirely new railway for high-speed passenger trains was later adopted by the French for their Train à Grande Vitesse (TGV) service. The first such route, from Paris to Lyons, began operations in 1981 with 13 daily trains capable of reaching 162mph and consequently providing the world's fastest average intercity speeds.

In Britain, there was a preference for running high-speed trains over existing track, despite the interference from other traffic and the presence of relatively sharp curves. The diesel-powered HST, having a permanently attached locomotive at each end, went into service on the Western Region in 1976 and was an immediate success. Later additions to the fleet allowed the East Coast main line and the North-East/South-West trunk route to benefit from this innovation. Typically HST services averaged over 80mph, but in 1985 one of the Leeds to London trains reached 145mph and ran 100 miles at an average of 120mph.

A tilting-train prototype, the Advanced Passenger Train (APT), was abandoned after prolonged teething troubles had outlasted the nervous fortitude of the British Rail administration. Designed for use on the electrified West Coast main line, a number of rakes of the APT were constructed, before problems in their operation led to their rapid withdrawal. A variant of the HST, however, was built

Above: **One of the high speed trains built for Japan's Tokaido Line in the 1960s.**

Left: **XPT, the Australian (New South Wales) version of the British HST.**

Right: **The solitary Soviet high speed train, which ran once weekly between Moscow and Leningrad.**

Main picture: **HST trains, soon after their introduction, stand in London's Paddington Station.**

Above left: **One of the second generation of Japan's high-speed trains arrives in Tokyo.**

Above: **One of the first French TGV trains. Similar trains were exported.**

Left: **Amtrak's first high-speed venture, the Washington-New York "Metroliner" service, which proved unable to meet the anticipated schedules.**

in Australia: the XPT. This was an eventual success in New South Wales, despite a public opinion that resented the initial practice of charging first- and second-class passengers exactly the same fare and which took a long time to grasp, that with their sharp curves, the lines in New South Wales could not permit the high speeds that were associated with the HST in Britain.

Other countries also adopted the high-speed concept. The USA had been among the first of these, with the "Metroliner" trains between New York and Washington, introduced on the eve of Amtrak's establishment. These had been a mild disappointment, for the envisaged high average speeds were not quite reached. But Amtrak, in the 1980s, was investing heavily in its North East Corridor route and faster schedules were promised. In Germany, a series of new high-speed railways was being built, connecting with existing main lines. South African Railways, never having had any high-speed pretensions, did half-heartedly introduce the "Metroblitz" train in 1984, which covered the 43-mile Johannesburg-Pretoria route in 44min. It was withdrawn a year later on the grounds of poor patronage, but the true lesson was that radically new services, if they were to attract enough passengers to justify them, needed long advance planning and really sustained publicity. The British and French railways, in particular, had succeeded very well because they understood these requirements.

Main picture: **A changeable-gauge "Talgo" train, providing a Spain-Switzerland service, arrives at Geneva behind a conventional French locomotive.**

Above: **One of the not-too-successful Canadian LRC tilting trains.**

Above right: **A British HST makes a quick turn-round at Leeds.**

Far right: **Conventional and TGV trains at the Gare de Lyon, Paris.**

36
PIGGYBACK, KANGAROOS AND MGR

Although the decline of "smokestack" industries gave railways an added incentive to compensate for diminishing traditional bulk traffics like ore and coal by competing hard for merchandise shipments, many railways still thrived on heavy low-value freight. For example, in its last years as an integrated state, the Soviet Union, whose railways carried as much freight as the railways of the rest of the world added together, had trains carrying block loads of coal, ore and timber following each other in endless succession at 10min intervals on the busier sections of line through the Urals.

The oil crises of the 1970s stimulated coal production in several parts of the world, with massive imports by some countries. Coal for Japan, for example, was shipped from Canada via the Canadian Pacific Railway and from Australia via the Queensland and New South Wales railway systems. In the USA, a few railroads benefited from the shift of coal production to the less sulphurous resources of the west. The Burlington Northern, among others, introduced unit coal trains typically consisting of 110 cars, with a total payload of 11,000 tons.

In the USA, long trains were traditionally operated as a means of reducing wage costs. As they became longer and heavier, the strain on couplings and braking systems was sometimes relieved by placing some of the diesel units at

Above: **US railroads increasingly turned to car-leasing companies for their freightcars, thereby avoiding capital investment.**

Main picture: **A Union Pacific transfer freight serving the docks at Oakland, California.**

Below left: **Single-commodity block trains are usually profitable. This is a French coal train in 1979.**

the middle or toward the rear of the trains, with radio control from the leading locomotive unit. This practice was imitated in the USSR, so as to reduce the number of trains on congested lines. In South Africa, too, double-length unit trains were run from the coalfields of the Transvaal and Natal down to Richards Bay. Such trains, over a mile long, carried a payload of 10,000 tons and had three electric locomotives at the head and five more in the middle.

In Western Europe, trains were much shorter. British Rail's heaviest regular train for many years was an iron-ore train of only 3,300 gross tons. BR, however; did develop a technique for moving coal from pithead to power station. What were known as "merry-go-round" trains were used. These were unit trains, which, with locomotives adapted for ultra-slow running, were loaded and unloaded while on the move. This eliminated terminal hold-ups and allowed the trains to attain high daily mileages, a prime requirement for low costs.

Britain did not adopt the "piggyback" system for high-value merchandise. Known in North America as TOFC (trailer on flatcar), this placed road semi-trailers on flatcars for the trunk component of their trip. The extra expense of carrying the trailers' running gear as well as their load-carrying body, plus height restrictions, excluded this technique from Britain. But in France and elsewhere in Europe, height restrictions were overcome by the "Kangaroo" flatcar, which had an underfloor pouch to carry the trailers' wheels.

193

When TOFC was introduced in the 1950s it did not meet with the approval of all American railroads, for some considered the container more viable. This could be carried on a flatcar and transferred to and from a road truck for pick-up and delivery, but needed expensive cranes at the railway terminals. The New York Central and a few other railroads adopted the "Flexivan" container system but, being in a minority, were eventually driven to use piggyback.

However, in the 1980s the container system, thanks to its adoption by shipping lines, was being accepted by many American railroads. Pacific shipping companies, led by the American President Lines, concluded that it was cheaper to trans-ship freight destined for the eastern USA at Pacific ports, rather than to take it by sea through the Panama Canal. The railroads could haul the lines' trains, with containers loaded two-deep, from, say, Los Angeles to Chicago, at an average speed of over 40mph, which was competitive with highway truck schedules. In the mid-1980s such "doublestack" trains typically carried 200 containers, were approximately a mile long, and were hauled by six diesel units.

Piggyback continued to be used, and a number of railroads introduced fast services to handle it. Sometimes it was possible, too, to negotiate reduced crews for such trains. However, although container and piggyback traffic grew, it was not without problems, not the least of which was that it was often unprofitable because of the competitive rates the railroads had to offer. Technical expedients in the form of novel rolling stock were sometimes adopted to improve matters. The Southern Pacific's "Ten-Pack," for example, used skeletal flatcars weighing 11 tons per trailer, as against the 23 tons of conventional flatcars. Then there was the "RoadRailer," which, after considerable travail, was becoming a plausible proposition in the mid-1980s; this was a highway trailer with a set of railroad wheels that could be lowered for movement over the rails, the trailers being close-coupled to form a train.

Above: **A Canadian Pacific mixed freight wends its way through the Rockies in 1957.**

Above right: **Britain's Royal Mail is conveyed through Kent.**

Below right: **Tri-level auto carriers of Canadian National Railways.**

Below: **A Santa Fe piggyback train in Arizona, heading for the Pacific.**

In Britain, container trains were known as Freightliners and won considerable new traffic. However, for the same reasons as in the USA, they had difficulty in making a profit. By the mid-1980s, after the government had allowed highway operators to introduce the so-called "juggernauts" (very large trailers), Freightliner services were regarded as viable propositions only when the length of haul was over 250 miles. Meanwhile, BR introduced a new fleet of air-braked freight cars with which it provided a network of regular "Speedlink" conventional freight trains. Helped, on occasions, by government grants to companies installing rail tracks on their premises, BR also entered into long-term contracts with major industries which often provided their own specialized freight cars for regular trains linking their establishments. The oil companies, for example, sent regular trains of refined products from refineries to distribution points, and there was a growing traffic in roadstone, with companies despatching heavy trainloads of stone in their own or leased freight cars from quarries to the distribution depots. Also common, and not only in Britain, was the carriage of new automobiles from factory to distribution

centers. Bilevel, and in the USA, trilevel, cars were provided for these services in which, paradoxically, the railroads had a marked cost advantage over any highway delivery.

In the postwar era, railway freight services were transformed just as radically as passenger services, and a clear indication of this was the increasing use of specialized freight cars. The traditional US boxcar, which could carry almost anything except perishables and liquids, although not very efficiently, began to lose its popularity, and the same phenomenon could be observed on other railways. Another advance was the introduction, first in the USA, then in Britain, of a nationwide electronic information system (known as TOPS in Britain). This enabled railways to tell their clients exactly where shipments were, and when they would arrive. It also facilitated planning of freight wagon movements so that, while fewer would be needed, they would be more speedily available for loading. In Britain, this contributed to the radical improvement of freight wagon utilization, expressed by the fact that whereas traffic fell by around 25% between 1938 and 1983, the freight-wagon stock was reduced by as much as 90%.

37
SUCCESS ON SHORTLINES

Almost all railroad traffic in the USA was handled by about two dozen Class 1 railroads, but there were hundreds of shortline companies in operation. They were hard to count, because openings, closures and mergers were almost a weekly occurrence, but in 1985 there were approximately 400 such lines. About 10% of these had more than 500 freight wagons in service and, taken collectively, they were important both as feeders of freight traffic to the big railroads and as suppliers of transportation services to their local communities.

In previous years, federal financial and technical assistance had been made available to selected shortlines. In 1980 the Staggers Rail Act, among other things, contained provisions for financial aid to independent feeder railroads and also relaxed the rate-making regulations for lines earning small revenues. After the Class 1 Rock Island and Milwaukee railroads became insolvent, fresh measures were taken to make it easier for local interests to take over selected lines from moribund companies.

Because of their freedom from national work-rules, their lack of long-term debt, their local knowledge and connections and, often, relief from local taxation, the shortlines could often achieve success where the original big railroads had failed. The states themselves sometimes took over lines, Vermont leading the way in 1963 by acquiring parts of the failing Rutland Railroad, which it converted into the short Vermont Central Railroad and Green Mountain Railroad. Others followed: for example, New York acquired the big commuter Long Island Railroad and Michigan the Ann Arbor Railroad, among others.

Although shortlines were not an exclusively American phenomenon, they are much less common elsewhere. In Britain, if the lines of industrial users are excluded on the grounds that they are not public railways, such lines barely exist, although there were a number of lines (such as the Easingwold Railway and the Derwent Valley) that managed to survive nationalization as independent concerns. Most of these lines, however, have closed or, if they do survive, no longer carry the traditional traffic, being retained primarily for leisure travel. In Germany, Switzerland, Austria and Japan, however, small railways are numerous,

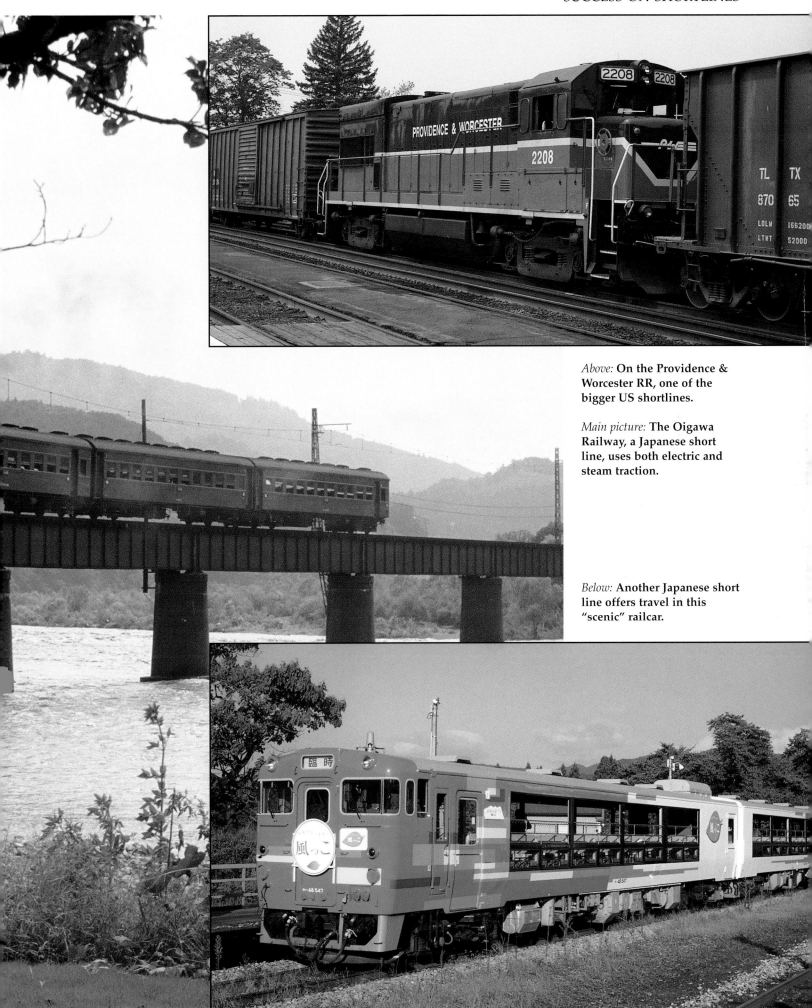

Above: On the Providence & Worcester RR, one of the bigger US shortlines.

Main picture: The Oigawa Railway, a Japanese short line, uses both electric and steam traction.

Below: Another Japanese short line offers travel in this "scenic" railcar.

and often more concerned with passengers than with freight. Topography had been a factor in these survivals, for in mountain regions a light or narrow-gauge railway could serve a particular valley without needing a physical connection to a main-line railway. Many of these lines were electrified and provided frequent services for rural localities which often had substantial populations as well as scenic attractions to provide a tourist traffic. Occasionally, and notably in Austria, local railways might belong to the state railway but be operated independently.

Historically, narrow-gauge railways were built after the main lines and were to provide cheap services for low-population areas. They should, therefore, have been early victims of rural truck and bus services. In many cases they were, especially in North America and western Europe, but some of them survived not only in central Europe but more or less throughout the world. In Portugal, where many meter-gauge lines were built to supplement the 5ft 6in (1,676mm) gauge network, the narrow gauge flourished, with new rolling stock and locomotives. In India, there was occasional regauging of track to 5ft 6in (1,676mm), but in general the meter and narrower gauges remained intact.

Germany was once a country of numerous narrow-gauge lines, and France and Belgium had meter-gauge systems alongside the standard gauge. Most of these have disappeared in France and Belgium, but narrow-gauge lines survived in both East and West Germany, especially in the former, where steam traction was still used. Some of the East German lines had a tourist potential, but they also provide freight and passenger services for their localities.

Above: **Japan rivals Switzerland in the number of its short lines. This is the Chichibu Railway, one of several that schedule steam trains in addition to their regular services.**

Left: **On the Austrian narrow gauge near Gmund. This short line now uses steam only on special occasions.**

Left: **Most Japanese short lines rely on diesel railcars or electric trains like this.**

Below: **On the electric Zugspitzbahn in mountainous Bavaria, a line which prospers from skiers and hikers.**

Two-foot gauge lines in Natal were closed, but the Port Shepstone-Harding line was resuscitated as the Alfred County Railway. Also active in South Africa was the lengthy 2ft (610mm) gauge Port Elizabeth-Avontuur line. Other South African narrow-gauge lines survived in industrial use, as they did in the cane fields of Australia, Cuba, Indonesia and elsewhere. The Cuban lines made seasonal use of numerous American-built steam locomotives, and these would survive into the next century.

In China, new narrow-gauge track was still being laid as an alternative to road-building. In 1986, there were about 2,250 miles of local railways, and about 1,500 miles of these were narrow gauge. Local railways of both gauges were being extended, and the Chinese claimed that the cost of building a 2ft 6in (762mm) gauge line was only about 15% that of a standard-gauge railway.

In Britain, where public narrow-gauge railways were rare, there existed a number of lines kept open by preservation societies but, in addition, two lines originally built for tourist traffic still flourished. One of these, the Vale of Rheidol line, once owned by the Cambrian Railways then by the Great Western, was now the only BR line operated by steam traction. The other was the Snowdon Mountain Railway, operating steam rack-and-pinion locomotives up the mountainside. This railway has the unusual 2ft 7½in (800mm) gauge, as do some lines in Switzerland. Both the Vale of Rheidol and the Snowdon still survive, although the former was sold by BR prior to the process of privatizing Britain's nationalized railway network.

38
PRESERVING THE RAILROAD

In the 1980s, each year, scores of special steam trains were operated over British Rail, most of them sponsored by BR but with a fair proportion organized by a consortium of private locomotive owners. With its numerous preservation schemes, tourist railways and museums, Britain clearly led the world in the railway preservation movement.

The involvement of BR in operating profitable vintage trains contrasted with its attitude of the 1960s, when it was determined to obliterate reminders of the steam age. By the mid-1980s, as well as accepting the operation by others of one-off steam excursions, it was running regular summer-only steam trains on several routes, with its "Shakespeare Limited," a Sunday dining car service from London to Stratford-on-Avon, attracting a high proportion of overseas tourists, and its York-Scarborough and Fort William-Mallaig services interesting a more domestic public. Other excursions were frequently operated with locomotives based on the privately-owned Carnforth locomotive depot in Cumbria.

Despite its initial reluctance to run preserved steam trains, the extent of BR's participation in steam excursions was quite unusual compared to other countries. In Germany the DB long resisted steam excursions, relenting only after the 150th anniversary celebrations of German railways showed that running steam trains did not lead the public to suppose that railways remained in the steam age. In the USA, some railroad managements (more often, their presidents) showed noticeable enthusiasm for such excursions; in the mid-1980s the Norfolk Southern Railroad was distinguishing itself with steam excursions over its very extensive network, using two former Norfolk & Western locomotives, the 4-8-4 No 611 and a resuscitated "Mallet," No 1218. Other frequent performers on US main-line railroads were a Union Pacific 4-8-4, No 8444, a Nickel Plate Railroad 2-8-4 of the "Superpower" generation, a "Superpower" 2-10-4 of the Texas & Pacific and a 4-6-2 of the Louisville & Nashville Railroad. One of the famous "K4" class 4-6-2s of the Pennsylvania Railroad, having stood on a plinth for many years, was returned to traffic in 1987. In Canada, the CNR was also hospitable to steam excursions, whereas the CPR was less so. A "Royal

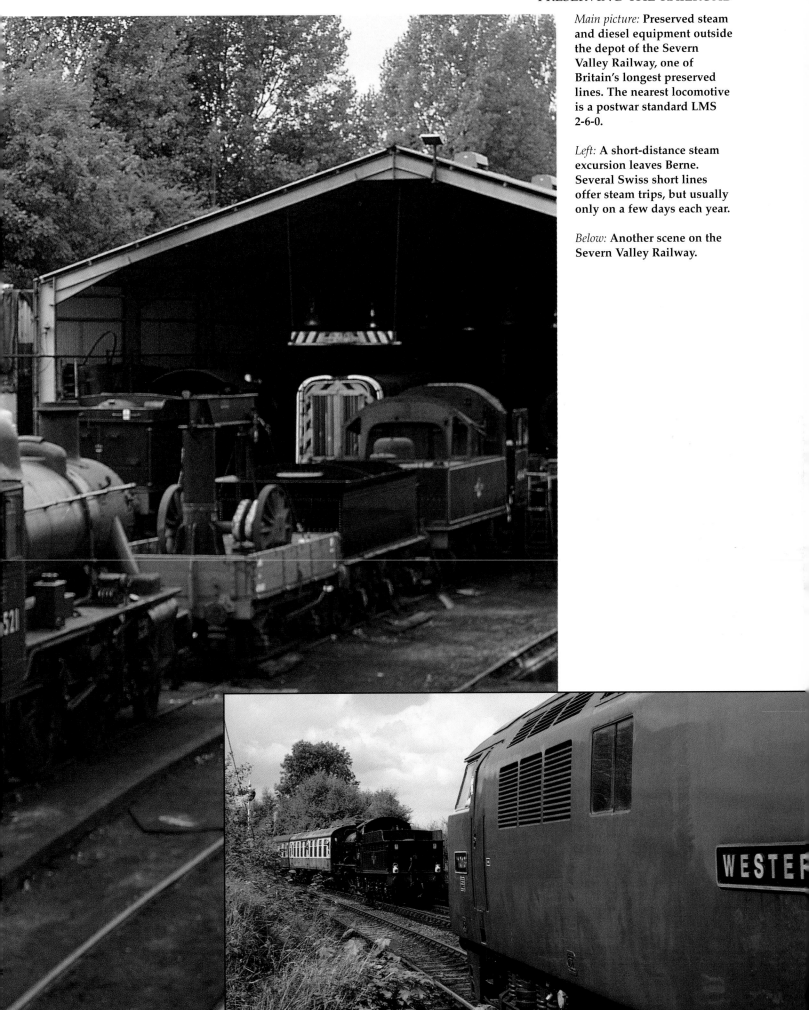

Main picture: Preserved steam and diesel equipment outside the depot of the Severn Valley Railway, one of Britain's longest preserved lines. The nearest locomotive is a postwar standard LMS 2-6-0.

Left: A short-distance steam excursion leaves Berne. Several Swiss short lines offer steam trips, but usually only on a few days each year.

Below: Another scene on the Severn Valley Railway.

Above: **One of Australia's oldest preserved lines, the Puffing Billy Railway near Melbourne. The locomotive is one of a class of 2-6-2 tank engines supplied by US builders to Victoria's narrow gauge lines.**

Main picture: **Turning the locomotive of a regular Japanese steam excursion offered by the Kyushu Railway.**

Top right: **On Britain's pioneer preserved line, the Bluebell Railway.**

Far right: **The Vivarais Railway, France's most successful preserved line, which uses metre-gauge "Mallet" type locomotives.**

Hudson" 4-6-4 of the latter company, however, hauled excursions out of Vancouver on the British Columbia Railway.

In Australia, it was enthusiast organizations which sponsored steam excursions, and the same situation existed in South Africa. Australian railways did, however, assemble "vintage trains" of old equipment, which they despatched under steam to various local celebrations, typically to towns celebrating their centenaries. In New Zealand, the "Kingston Flyer" was one of the earliest railway-sponsored regular steam excursions. Another regular steam excursion was in Malaysia, where there was a Kuala Lumpur-Batu Caves service, which was sponsored by the local Kentucky Fried Chicken organization.

The running of main-line steam excursions was only one facet of the railway preservation movement. The acquisition and rehabilitation of old abandoned railways, and the establishment of railway museums, were the two other main activities. The steam locomotive was usually the inspiration of these enterprises, but vintage rolling stock, signaling equipment and smaller items were also carefully preserved. As the years passed, old electric and diesel locomotives also began to feature.

The earliest of the enthusiast-preserved lines in Britain was the narrow gauge Talyllyn Railway in Wales, reopened as a preserved line in 1951. Other preserved railways were subsequently established in this area, including the Ffestiniog Railway with its unique "Fairlie" locomotives. Reopening of standard-gauge lines began with part of the Middleton Railway in 1959, to be followed by the first section of BR's network, the Bluebell Railway in Sussex, in 1960. The Bluebell prospered and amassed a wide range of locomotives, and has subsequently been extended northwards with the intention of linking up again with the national network at East Grinstead. Its success inspired many other preservation projects, and there was a long and growing list of such railways in Britain. Among the older established and larger projects were the Severn Valley (in

Shropshire), the Keighley & Worth Valley (in Yorkshire), the Torbay & Dartmouth (in Devon) and the North Yorkshire Moors railways. Most of these lines specialized, frequently reflecting the past railway age of their particular localities. For example, the Torbay & Dartmouth reconstructs the traditional Great Western branch line, while the Great Central runs its trains over a former main line of the old Great Central Railway. The Nene Valley Railway at Peterborough, however, possessed overseas locomotives and rolling stock, some of which operated in public service, alongside more traditional items.

The railroad preservation scene in the USA was a little more volatile, with quite a few lines ceasing operation after a few unprofitable years. Successful railway preservation schemes require either a wealthy sponsor or a willing band of volunteer labor. With the less-concentrated US population, it was sometimes difficult to assemble sizeable groups of railroad enthusiasts within easy reach of a project. Nor did the US lines enjoy the government-sponsored employment schemes that sometimes made a temporary workforce available to British lines. On the other hand, because of the tourist attractions they offered, some preservation schemes were initiated by state governments. West Virginia created a combined museum and active railroad from the remains of a logging enterprise at Cass, and Texas opened a state-preserved railway.

The National Parks system began to develop Steamtown, at Scranton in Pennsylvania. This came to fruition in the 1990s and provided both a steam excursion and a well-stocked roundhouse. The long-established and successful Strasburg Railroad in Pennsylvania had the advantage of the state's Pennsylvania Railroad Museum alongside. Another long-standing line was the 3ft (910mm) gauge Silverton Railroad, providing a scenic run in

Above: **A state-sponsored attraction, the Spencer locomotive workshops in North Carolina offer a short steam trip behind a 2-8-0.**

Main picture: **A line preserved to fulfil its original purpose, the Grand Canyon RR takes tourists to view the Canyon over a line originally built by the Santa Fe RR.**

Above left: **A former Canadian National yard locomotive of the Strasburg RR takes tourists through Amish country.**

Left: **On the Lakeside Railway in Britain's Lake District.**

Right: **Family entertainment on the Strasburg RR in Pennsylvania.**

Below right: **The Valley RR in Connecticut.**

Bottom right: **Russia's developing railroad museum at Shushari, near St Petersburg.**

Overleaf: **A "Shay" type locomotive hauls passengers on the Cass RR in West Virginia.**

mountainous Colorado. Not far away, the Cumbres & Toltec Scenic Railroad offered a similar attraction out of Chama, New Mexico. A notable success was the Grand Canyon Railroad, running daily over the long branch line built by the Santa Fe Railroad to develop the Grand Canyon as a tourist center. In Canada, the Prairie Dog Central Railroad for many years was offering trips out of Winnipeg behind a former CPR 4-4-0 locomotive. By the end of the 20th century, there were several other steam activities in that country.

French preservation schemes were handicapped by a shortage of surviving steam locomotives. Only a few steam preservation lines developed, of which the most successful was the meter-gauge Vivarais Railway, operating "Mallet" tank locomotives amid the mountains of the *Massif Central*. German and Swiss preservation schemes were characterized by a large number of lines, well-provided with locomotives, but each running only a few days each year.

Because of its strong railway enthusiast movement, helped by the slow rate of scrapping steam locomotives, there would be a very strong preservation movement in South Africa by the end of the 20th century. Among organizations arranging steam tours were the Transnet Heritage Foundation, which among other things operated a tourist-oriented steam service on the picturesque George-Knysna line. In Pretoria, there were Friends of the Rail and Rovos Rail and, at Germiston, Reefsteamers.

Australia and New Zealand were early operators of preserved steam lines, among the pioneers being the Puffing Billy 2ft (610mm) gauge line near Melbourne and the Hotham Valley Railway, near Perth. By the end of the 20th century, these had been joined by several more.

The main Japanese railway companies, which were created in 1987, made a point of providing steam trains, usually over scenic branch lines, on a regular basis. Some of these became so popular as family excursions that advance booking is now required. They developed just as there was a national policy of increasing Japanese exposure to the English language and were accordingly marketed with the English name of "Steam Locomotive" or "SL" trains. Thus, uniquely and paradoxically, Japanese steam trains became linked in the public mind with one aspect of modernity.

Large-scale railway museums preceded the end of steam. The present-day National Railway Museum at York, in Britain, has its origins in a more modest York Railway Museum of the interwar years and of the statutory duty imposed on the British Transport Commission established in 1948 to ensure the preservation of a representative selection of items of railway history, from locomotives and rolling stock to tickets and ephemera. Originally there were a number of locations housing parts of the National Collection, which remained under the control of the Commission until the opening of the new museum at York in 1975 when ownership was transferred to the Science Museum. Such is the scale of Britain's National Collection, that items may be on loan to other museums and even the privately-controlled preserved railways.

One of the best American museums, the Baltimore & Ohio Railroad Museum in Baltimore, also had a long history, as did the Transport Museum at Lucerne in Switzerland. More recent museums were the Railroad Museum at St Louis in the USA and the Canadian Railway Museum near Montreal. France had its Mulhouse Railway Museum, while exhibits in Germany were scattered through several museums. Even smaller nations possessed museums; the Danes, for example, created a museum at Odense, close to the home of the writer Hans Christian Andersen. In the USSR, a large collection of locomotives was being developed into a museum at Leningrad (now St Petersburg) and another museum was opened at Tashkent in Uzbekistan.

PART FIVE

RAILWAYS ENTER THE 21st CENTURY

Left: Union Pacific coal train pulled by two EMD "SD40-2" locomotives.

39
GENERAL

The 1990s witnessed something of a renaissance for the railway business in many of the developed countries. Travel patterns, clogging of highways and environmental concerns persuaded governments to encourage the refurbishment, renewal and restructuring of their railway systems. The question was, how best to achieve this upgrading and the answer, usually, was to break up the state railway systems into smaller units and then, in one way or another, attract private investment into them. There was also a belief that privatization would bring an element of competition, which might force the allegedly unenterprizing managements to show more initiative.

The USA was different because, apart from the national passenger carrier Amtrak, the railroads were already private. Here, in contrast to the fragmentation which occurred when British and some other railways were privatized, private ownership was at a different stage, with amalgamations creating very big companies. This, among other things, resulted in the reduction of transcontinental railroads to just two big companies.

Meanwhile, technical advances were making railways more desirable. The purpose-built high-speed railway, which had first appeared in Japan in the 1960s and in France in the 1980s, was copied by several other countries. Another high-speed venture was the introduction of tilting trains; on these the vehicle bodies were tilted to allow higher speeds over tight curves. Multiple-unit trains became faster, smoother and quieter, and this helped to popularize fast, frequent, trains to airports in Britain, to Frankfurt in Germany, Sydney in Australia and many elsewhere (including a highly innovative project in Malaysia, serving Kuala Lumpur Airport). At the same time, railway management was made cheaper and more effective by the use of computers.

The really radical innovation of dispensing with the wheel-on-rail combination by means of magnetic levitation (MAGLEV) was envisaged for a Berlin-Hamburg line, but then abandoned. The technology was developed originally in Britain and was exploited for a period with a short line serving Birmingham International Airport. However, an experimental MAGLEV line in Japan was claimed to be

producing hopeful results. Japan also operated urban overhead monorail lines, as did Seattle in the USA.

In the last part of the 20th century there was a move toward privatisation that left few state railways untouched either by full privatisation or the prospect of privatisation in the future. Change of ownership was preceded by change of structure, and in particular there was a worldwide interest in separating the ownership and management of the track and structures from that of the trains themselves. This was expected, among other things, to clarify the true cost of the track and make it easier to introduce "Open Access," the running of competing companies' trains over the same tracks, each paying a fee for using them.

When governments sold off their nationalized railways they did not necessarily reject offers from abroad so, for example, in Britain the majority of freight trains were operated by a consortium (called English, Welsh & Scottish [EWS] Railways) that was owned in part by an American railroad company — Wisconsin Central — which also handled railway operations in New Zealand. National Express, the British company that acquired the franchise to operate trains over the former Midland Railway main line between London and Sheffield, also operated trains in Victoria, Australia. National Express also held the franchise to operate all local services in Scotland. A French company acquired two of the franchises covering commuter services into London from Kent and Sussex. Even in China, where a communist government remained in power, the state railway was subjected to a degree of restructuring, with a continuing proliferation of local railways.

Trans-national railway integration was developing in Europe, with the encouragement of the European Union. However, national feeling, or parochialism, was still strong and the German and French railways, each in its own subtle way, resisted moves that would increase efficiency (that is, require less work for the same traffic). Meanwhile, ostensibly to increase their competitiveness against highway transport but sometimes to win traffic from other European railways, some railways combined with others in adjoining states to introduce trans-national freight companies. Thus the German, Dutch and Danish railways combined in this way to create the *Railion* freight company.

Railway equipment manufacture became strongly globalized as the more successful companies bought up smaller competitors in various parts of the world. These new acquisitions gave them greater strength in the various national markets while enabling orders placed in one country to be totally or partially fulfilled in another. The bigger companies introduced basic designs, which, with superficial differences, were marketed world-wide. This trend had appeared much earlier with the licensing of American diesel locomotive technology to various national companies, but, in the 1990s, was carried much further and extended to multiple-unit trains. Among the more successful companies was Alsthom (later known as Alstom), builder of the French high-speed trains, which merged with the British General Electric Co and bought up several other well-known companies. It was one of the first to see the advantage of "whole-life" train provision, not only supplying rolling stock but contracting to maintain it afterwards. The Adtranz concern, which had combined some long-lived Scandinavian, British, German and Swiss builders, was technically but not financially successful and, in 2000, was sold to an up-and-coming Canadian company, Bombardier. The latter, originally a small Quebec company manufacturing snow-sleds, had entered the transport market in the 1970s, bought up some notable British, German and Belgian concerns, and by the end of the century numbered Britain's Virgin Rail and America's Amtrak among its clients.

The problem was that, although the market for rail equipment was developing as countries began to reorganize railway transport, there were too many manufacturers. Many concerns, like Adtranz and Siemens, produced high-quality products but could not make much profit from them. In 2000, even Fiat, which was foremost in the booming tilt-train technology, sold its railway interests to Alstom. In the USA, GM, once the giant of the diesel locomotive industry, transferred locomotive construction to other countries, mainly to its manufacturing facility in London, Ontario, but also through licensing agreements with overseas makers including Clyde in Australia and Hyundai in Korea. But GM's competitor, the US GE, was an exception to the general trend; while maintaining alliances with foreign builders, it seemed happy with its situation in Erie, Pennsylvania, and in 1999 produced over 900 diesel locomotives there.

In China and Russia, existing locomotive works acquired modern technology, especially in the fields of electronic control and transmissions, by co-operation and licensing agreements with big western companies. In Japan there was, again, an excess of capacity, but no lack of bright ideas, and several improved versions of high-speed *Shinkansen* trains were introduced in the 1990s, as well as smart new trains for the ordinary 3ft 6in (1,065mm) gauge lines.

Below: **The elevated monorail is still rare, but can be used where an underground line is impractical. This example is in Tokyo.**

40 BRITISH RAILWAYS: BOOM AND CRASH

British Rail, the state corporation, relied on Treasury subsidies, and the Treasury as an institution was not enthusiastic about railway transport. With occasional exceptions like the West and East Coast electrification schemes, the Treasury was unwilling to sanction railway investment and the BR management was not permitted to raise capital from the private sector. This meant that any bright BR manager, seeing a promising commercial opportunity, was unable to raise the money to pursue it. That is, commercial initiative was repressed (critics tended to twist this situation, accusing BR management of lack of initiative).

In its last decade, BR had reorganized itself into "business sectors," each with its own management and balance sheet. This made it easier to see which parts were profitable and to spotlight those parts that were loss-making and in need of change. The "InterCity" sector, handling long-distance passengers, soon showed itself to be profitable and promising. The separation of London commuter services into one business sector, "Network SouthEast," was also successful and brought a general smartening-up, a traffic increase and reduction of the deficit. "Regional Railways" occupied another sector, covering many non-InterCity passenger services outside Greater London, although this situation was complicated by the involvement of a number of regional Passenger Transport Authorities that were involved in the funding of both investment and provision of subsidy locally. Freight services were also sectorized, with various commodity groups entrusted to a given sector. Sectors were allocated their own locomotives, distinguished by specific liveries or logos, although one sector could loan locomotives to another.

In the early 1990s, sectorization seemed to be breathing a new spirit into British Rail, but this was ended by privatization. The governing Conservative Party had always been suspicious of BR, partly because the latter was a socialist creation and partly because it believed that competition would produce a more efficient service. It had already privatized other state industries, usually with success, and BR with the Post Office were the last big national corporations to survive. Aware that its likelihood of re-election was slim, the government hurried railway privatization so that, by 1997, the election year, the process would become virtually irreversible by a succeeding government. This haste, and the quest for irreversibility, resulted in a privatization scheme that was ingenious but would later be studied by foreign governments as a case-study in how not to do it.

Below: **First and second-generation British diesels. The unit on the left is wearing its business sector livery.**

Above: The articulated air-cushion suspension of Eurostar trains used in Channel Tunnel services.

The process was indeed virtually complete when the government left office in 1997. Trains were run by Train Operating Companies (TOCs), which had bid for operating franchises. In order to win a franchise, which typically lasted for seven or 15 years, a would-be TOC had to promise service improvements, and there was also a requirement that train services should not fall below the existing level. TOCs accepted a subsidy that would decline with time and eventually be converted to payments to the Treasury when the company became profitable. There were limits on tariff increases; basic fares were to increase at less than the rate of inflation.

The government had chosen to fragment the system into two dozen TOCs, allegedly because it thought such fragmentation would hamper nationwide trade-union action. The main-line TOCs included Great North Eastern (GNER), First Great Western (FGW) and Midland Mainline (MML) operating respectively the old East Coast route, the London-Bristol/Cardiff/Penzance main lines and the former Midland Railway main line. The West Coast main line franchise was won by Virgin Rail, which also obtained the Cross-Country Trains franchise. Scottish services, apart from main line services into England, were entrusted to the Scotrail TOC. Northern Ireland Railways — never part of the nationalized BR network — were not part of this privatization process, remaining a state-owned corporation administered in Belfast. Other, smaller, companies took over regional and suburban services. Scotrail and Midland Main Line were franchises won by National Express, which also obtained the Gatwick Express, Silverlink, and Central Train operations, shared in the Eurostar services, and was soon bidding for overseas franchises.

The TOCs owned very little. They hired their rolling stock from three newly-created rolling stock companies and they paid another company, Railtrack, for the use of tracks, signaling and stations. If trains were delayed through the fault of Railtrack, the latter was required to pay the Train Operating Companies a fixed per-minute penalty.

These penalties could travel in the reverse direction, from TOC to Railtrack, if a train ran late and disrupted Railtrack's schedules for causes within the TOC's area of responsibility.

The government had originally intended Railtrack to be a state corporation, since it would dominate the rail industry. However, as such, it would have provided a future Labour government with an easy route to renationalize the system. Railtrack, therefore, emerged as a private company or, as its critics liked to describe it, a private monopoly.

The freight business was initially divided into several temporary corporations under BR management until they could be sold. Three (named Loadhaul, Mainline and Transrail) were conventional freight operators, each with its geographically defined territory, while Freightliner handled domestic container trains and Railfreight Distribution was entrusted with Channel Tunnel freight. These freight companies had their own rolling stock and liveries. In due course the three main freight operators were sold together to a consortium including Wisconsin Central, which reorganized them into the English, Welsh, and Scottish Railway or EWS. Wisconsin Central had earlier acquired BR's mail and parcels business — Rail Express Systems (Res). Railfreight Distribution, a serious loss-maker, was later taken over by EWS. Freightliner became private through a management buy-out.

Meanwhile, other branches of BR were sold off to private companies. These included workshops, regional track maintenance organizations, engineering and scientific research departments, health services, electrical departments and electronic communications organizations.

Some of the new companies justified the faith placed in privatization. GNER, which had the advantage of recent

Main picture: **One of the EMD (General Motors) locomotives used by the EWS Railway.**

Far left: **A GNER train leaves London for Scotland.**

Left: **A Railfreight Distribution international freight, hauled by a dual-voltage Class 92 locomotive.**

investment in track and rolling stock, soon earned a high reputation for its swift and well-organized trains to the northeast and Scotland. A smaller company, Chiltern Trains, began to operate a London-Birmingham service, which, though slower than the main operator, Virgin Trains, was cheaper. On the other hand, other companies had problems. Virgin services up the West Coast, which relied on quite elderly trains and infrastructure, soon acquired a bad and sometimes exaggerated reputation for lateness and train cancellations, giving rise to the jibe that Virgin trains were aptly named, since they tended not to go the whole way.

For decades, the railways had been subject to competition from road transport and, to some extent, the airlines. Nevertheless, the government felt that competition between various railway companies would produce better services. "Open Access" (more than one company using a rail line) was already established as an aim of the European Union, and, with the tracks managed by a specialized company, Railtrack, it seemed that the opportunity was there. However, so as not to discourage bidders for the various franchises, this other-company competition was largely ruled out for the first few years.

But the actual route configurations, and later a relaxation of restrictions, did enable some competing services to be established. Between London and Birmingham there were three routes and four possible operating companies. The prime operator was Virgin West Coast, more expensive but considerably faster. Silverlink operated over the same route with cheaper but slower, commuter-type, trains. Chiltern Railways operated its new trains over the former Great Western Railway route, while a fourth, roundabout, possibility was via Oxford with Virgin Cross-Country. In eastern England, there was competition between Ipswich and London. However, an attempt by the First North Western company to operate a competing service between Manchester and London encountered problems, largely connected with obtaining conveniently scheduled paths over the busy main line to London. "Open Access" has, more recently, allowed Hull Trains to launch a regular service between Hull and London over the East Coast main line in competition with the existing franchisee, GNER.

Fragmentation, the weakness of the new regime, had been the government's intention. In fact, through booking (the issue of tickets from any British station to any other British station in any part of the country) was abandoned in the original privatization proposals, a decision that was only reversed after protest by the public, more aware of the realities of travel than the ministers and civil servants who were planning the upheaval.

Fragmentation meant a huge number of interfaces between organizations, so few problems or opportunities could be dealt with by a single management. Decision-making therefore took longer and required an influx of legal specialists. The proliferation of lawyers, accountants and consultants was expensive, and additionally most observers believed that BR had been sold off at bargain-basement prices in the government's haste. Moreover, at least in the first years, the government subsidy exceeded that of BR times.

Nevertheless, partly because of general economic prosperity, the TOCs greatly increased their passenger carryings, and new services were introduced. Some of these were quite novel, especially when relatively small companies pursued new ideas. For example, there were some new cross-London services: Brighton-Rugby by Connex South Central and Chelmsford-Basingstoke by Anglia Railways. On some routes, the introduction of new services was limited because track capacity was so intensively used, and plans were made to eliminate some of the bottlenecks by quadrupling, improved signaling and even the construction of new lines. One of the biggest projects was for a reconstruction of the West Coast route, to enable Virgin Trains to introduce a fleet of high-speed, tilting, trains.

Elsewhere, construction of the new high-speed railway from the Channel Tunnel across Kent to London was well under way in 2000. A notable opening was the Heathrow Express line, largely financed by the British Airports Authority. Using existing track plus a spur to the airport, four trains operated each hour, with a maximum speed of 100mph (160kph). Elsewhere in Britain lines once closed were being studied for possible resuscitation.

The Heathrow Express trains were designed by Siemens in Germany but largely built by the CAF company in Spain. Between 1993 and 1996 BR had been prevented from ordering new rolling stock. This helped to ensure the demise of British rolling stock companies, which were closed or absorbed by the big global concerns, and left a huge backlog of fleet replacement, which was intensified by the subsequent traffic increase.

With privatization, and as part of their bids for franchises, the TOCs had undertaken to lease new rolling stock from the rolling stock companies, which in turn placed orders with the manufacturers. Delivery was slow, partly because manufacturers fell behind schedule but partly because Railtrack imposed severe safety conditions. To secure a "safety case" a manufacturer or TOC had to meet thick volumes of requirements. Those related to stray emissions of electro-magnetic radiation were especially troublesome. The possibility at some point of a traction motor or control equipment emitting impulses that would interfere with the currents used in signaling was quite real, and the testing programs were long. Railtrack did not seem to hurry, although in reality the delay was largely because the volume of testing was more than the handful of specialist staff could handle. Nevertheless, there were cases of batches of trains being built but not entering service for months, while the "safety case" was being negotiated.

In general, the new trains were well received. They looked modern, they were energy-saving thanks to new control and transmission innovations, and they promised an end to that long-standing British archaism, the slam-door. Locomotive-hauled passenger trains largely gave way to diesel or electric multiple-unit trains. The main routes using locomotive-hauled trains were the long-distance East and West Coast lines, a handful of cross-country routes and some trains in North Wales and East Anglia.

Locomotives were also used for freight services, although some locomotive-hauled postal trains were replaced by multiple-unit mail trains. EWS ordered as many as 250 new diesel locomotives from GM — similar to the locomotives delivered earlier to Foster Yeoman and designated Class 66 — to replace old and failure-prone units. A few higher-speed variants, Class 67, were imported for mail trains. GM units were also ordered by Freightliner, which additionally acquired re-engined rebuilds of the old Class 47, and by the ARC quarrying company (the latter chose the Class 59, as used by Foster Yeoman with which ARC subsequently amalgamated, the resultant Mendip Rail having nine of these units for haulage of stone trains).

In addition, 50 units of Class 92 were delivered for use in the Channel Tunnel service. Some of these went to SNCF, some to Railfreight Distribution and some to the ill-fated European Passenger Services (which was intending to use the locomotives to haul Channel Tunnel night sleeper trains, an abandoned project). These were electric locomotives suitable for use both on the 750V third-rail lines of southern England and on the 25kV ac lines beyond London. They were expected to haul most freight trains to and from the Channel Tunnel, but for a long period were little used, largely because of "safety case" problems. For the vehicle-carrying shuttle services through the Tunnel, a new class of locomotive was built, with the unusual Bo-Bo-Bo wheel arrangement.

In the first five years of privatization, passenger traffic increased by about one third. This was largely due to economic prosperity, but was assisted by the provision of more attractive trains and services by most of the companies. The American owners of the EWS freight company were fulfilling their pledge to increase rail-borne freight in Britain substantially. But there were already causes for anxiety. Although some of the companies had been formed by management buy-outs, the number and influence of professional railwaymen on the boards and in the top management of companies had generally declined. One TOC, owned by a bus company, soon after privatization was cancelling trains because of driver shortages; its management had thought that train drivers could be as easily fired, hired and trained as bus drivers. Railtrack, a dominating company whose directors owed their first duty to shareholders, farmed out track maintenance to contracting companies and employed too few engineers of its own.

At the end of the 1990s, opponents of privatization could claim that the downside of private ownership and fragmentation was already becoming evident. Shareholders of Wisconsin Central, owner of the EWS, were dissatisfied with their dividends and contrived a boardroom upheaval that ousted the company's President. A less ambitious policy for EWS gradually fell into place, and in 2000 Wisconsin Central offered its 42% holding in EWS for sale. Meanwhile, a series of well-publicized passenger train accidents concentrated many minds.

In 1997, on the Great Western main line out of London, a fast passenger train collided with a freight that had been

Left: **Virgin Trains Class 125 seen at Weston-super-Mare in July 2000.**

Right: **Class 153 single-unit railcar of Wales and West also at Weston-super-Mare in July 2000.**

crossing its approach. There were seven fatalities. The failure of the passenger train to respond to signals was the main cause of this accident and, in the subsequent enquiry, it became evident that driver instruction and observance of safety codes had been unsatisfactory. This line had been experimentally equipped with a new form of train protection device, but this had been switched out on the passenger train involved. In 1999, not far away, a commuter train ran into the path of another high-speed train at Ladbroke Grove, causing a violent collision and fire in which 29 passengers died. The resultant public outcry and enquiry raised a number of contributory causes; driver selection and instruction, placement of signals and inherently unsafe re-arrangement of tracks were among these. This was evidently a disaster in which Railtrack and the TOCs, as well as the communication between them, all emerged as unsatisfactory.

Then, in October 2000, a fast train of the GNER came to grief at Hatfield. Traveling at over 100mph, it was derailed by a badly-broken rail. The vehicles remained more or less intact, but four passengers were killed when the buffet car hit line-side structures. That death rate was remarkably and commendably small, but this was evidently one accident too many. It was almost immediately clear that a rail whose replacement had been too long postponed was the culprit. The type of defect was "gauge corner cracking," a fairly frequent though slow-developing phenomenon where train wheels bear heavily against the inner surface of a railhead, as they do when high speed and curves are involved.

What followed was an unprecedented collapse of collective wisdom. In a classic case of shutting the stable door too late and too fast, Railtrack decided to impose severe speed restrictions at points on the rail network where gauge corner cracking was detected. There were several hundred such points and Railtrack began a long rail-replacement process. Train Operating Companies were given little information about what was happening, and passengers still less. There were cases of whole trainloads of passengers marooned while quite minor defects were put right. Speed restrictions meant that trains could not reach their destinations in time to be turned round for their return journeys, so services were not only slower, but fewer. Conditions of travel somewhat resembled those of World War 2, except that in the war years passengers were better informed and more sympathetic toward the railway companies. This situation persisted for several months, resulting in a heavy loss of passenger traffic; passengers had lost faith in railway travel.

In BR times, railway engineers and managers descended on the scene of an accident post-haste, to clear the line as soon as possible (usually in less than a day). It was left to a subsequent enquiry and the findings of the government's Railway Inspectorate to ascertain causes and recommend

measures to avoid a repetition. But, by 2000, this process had changed. The accent was less on finding the cause of an accident, and more on attaching the blame. Police controlled access to what they regarded as the possible site of a crime. It took more than three weeks to clear the tracks after the Hatfield accident, during which the unfortunate Train Operating Companies were not able to use the line. Long after it was clear that a broken rail had caused this disaster, the police were looking for evidence of more sinister causes.

Many trains were re-routed in those weeks. In Scotland, one diverted train, proceeding slowly over track known to be of poor quality, crawled to a halt when the rails moved apart beneath it. The British Transport Police were first on the scene, and allegedly behaved in an over-authoritarian way with both railway staff and passengers. True or not, this allegation seemed further evidence that what was happenng was not simply a reflection of something wrong with the railways, but of something wrong with society as well.

Largely immune from the panic reactions of late 2000, the Eurostar services from London via the Channel Tunnel to Brussels and Paris were performing well in the first year of the new century. After these services began in 1994, traffic did not match predictions. But a recovery gradually set in, especially in the Brussels service, which initially had very light loadings. The operating franchise was awarded to the conglomerate that had won the build-and-operate contract to construct the purpose-built high-speed line from Folkestone to London, which, when finished, would enable the high-speed trains to achieve, in England, the same high speeds they achieved in France and Belgium. This was London & Continental Railways, but subsequently another consortium, including British Airways and the Belgian and French national railways, took over the operating rights. A government subsidy to cover the continuing operating deficit was expected to be only temporary. Meanwhile, the Eurotunnel company itself operated the drive-on drive-off trains conveying road vehicles through the Tunnel (the Euroshuttle).

Above: **A diesel locomotive in the livery of the short-lived Mainline freight company.**

Left: **A Eurostar high-speed train. In England, these cross-Channel trains use the existing tracks, but in the background of this scene land is being cleared for a new high-speed line to enable them to run at full power.**

41
CONTINENTAL EUROPE

German Railways (DB) were transformed in the 1990s. East and West Germany had been unified and the deficits of the new combined railway system were threateningly large, while critics claimed that the state organization was unwieldy and inefficient. A new organization emerged in which DB remained as a state-owned holding company while free-standing state subsidiary companies were formed for particular sectors. *DB Netz* was responsible for the infrastructure, applying a sliding scale of charges to railway operators wishing to use it. These operators consisted of *DB Cargo* for freight, *DB Reise & Touristik* for long-distance passenger, and *DB Regio* for local passenger service. There was also *DB Station & Service*, which did not operate trains. The principle of "Open Access" was introduced with new operators, provided they were technically competent, having the right to use *DB Netz* tracks. By 2000, about a hundred such new operators had emerged, including several industries that began to run their own trains for their own products. German locomotive manufacturers soon organized locomotive pools from which these new operators could lease traction power.

It was expected that locomotive-hauled passenger trains would disappear in the first decade of the new century. In the 1990s, long-distance services were equipped with the ICE-1 high-speed electric trains, powered by Siemens and consisting of 12 or 14 vehicles with a power car at each end. A half-length version, ICE-2, was also built, while the later ICE-3 was different in having its motors distributed down the train. The ICE-1 trains were fitted with resilient wheels and at Enschede in 1998 one of these broke at high speed. Derailed vehicles struck a bridge and disintegrated, causing 102 deaths.

For some lines, tilting trains were introduced. These were of several types, the Fiat technology being favored. With these new trains, schedules were cut and more comfort offered, especially in hilly regions.

Under the new organization DB was not obliged to operate loss-making trains. Local authorities paid its losses for operating local services, and new trains for such services began to appear in large numbers, frequently using more energy-efficient propulsion. The federal government

Above: **The power car, virtually a locomotive, of the German ICE-1 high speed train. In the 1990s all main lines were served by an interlocking pattern of these trains.**

Right: **By the end of the century, "Talent" lightweight diesel trains like this were appearing on short-haul German routes.**

helped to finance new lines, including new routes on which the ICE generation of trains could fully use their high-speed capabilities. Notable among new construction was the new and very expensive Köln-Frankfurt line being built at the close of the century.

French National Railways (SNCF) in the 1990s was still enlarging the TGV network. TGV-Atlantique, westward from Paris, was destined eventually to reach the Atlantic ports of Nantes and Bordeaux, but by 2000 extended only part of the way, the TGV trains continuing over conventional track to their final destination. TGV-Nord to Lille and Belgium was also used by the Eurostar international services. Some progress was made with the long-delayed Paris-Est TGV line which was to link Paris with Strasbourg, via Rheims. However, the expected low rate of return implied that this project would have low priority. On the TGV Sud-Est route, traffic was still growing, and a class of double-deck TGV trains was introduced. Experiments were

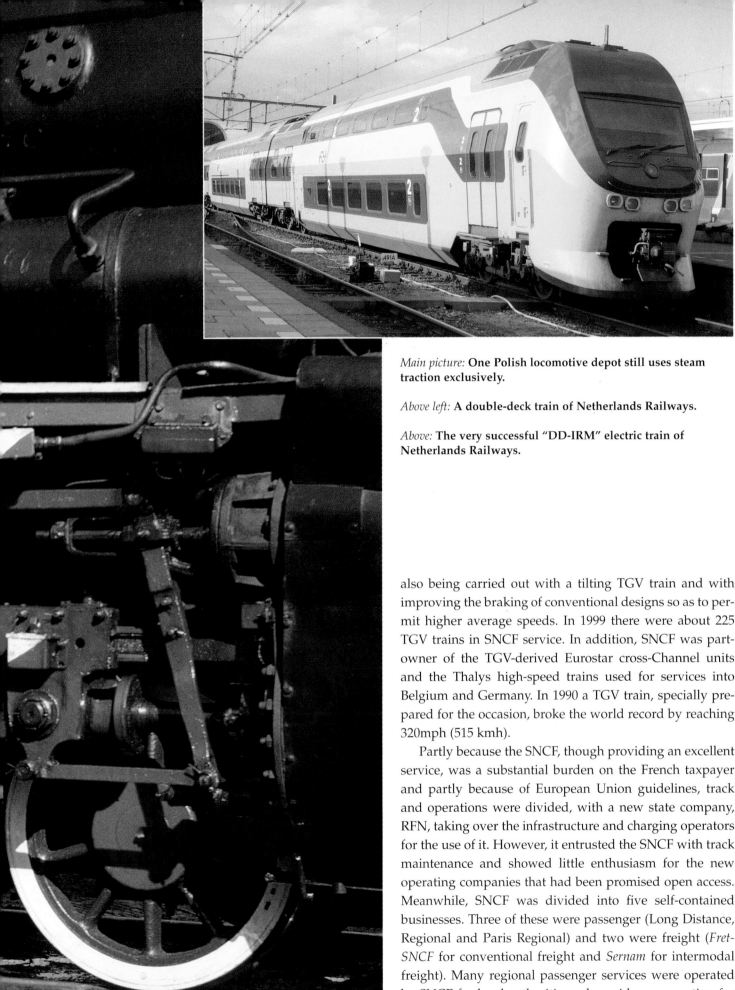

Main picture: **One Polish locomotive depot still uses steam traction exclusively.**

Above left: **A double-deck train of Netherlands Railways.**

Above: **The very successful "DD-IRM" electric train of Netherlands Railways.**

also being carried out with a tilting TGV train and with improving the braking of conventional designs so as to permit higher average speeds. In 1999 there were about 225 TGV trains in SNCF service. In addition, SNCF was part-owner of the TGV-derived Eurostar cross-Channel units and the Thalys high-speed trains used for services into Belgium and Germany. In 1990 a TGV train, specially prepared for the occasion, broke the world record by reaching 320mph (515 kmh).

Partly because the SNCF, though providing an excellent service, was a substantial burden on the French taxpayer and partly because of European Union guidelines, track and operations were divided, with a new state company, RFN, taking over the infrastructure and charging operators for the use of it. However, it entrusted the SNCF with track maintenance and showed little enthusiasm for the new operating companies that had been promised open access. Meanwhile, SNCF was divided into five self-contained businesses. Three of these were passenger (Long Distance, Regional and Paris Regional) and two were freight (*Fret-SNCF* for conventional freight and *Sernam* for intermodal freight). Many regional passenger services were operated by SNCF for local authorities, who paid compensation for financial losses. Some local authorities financed very good rail services and SNCF acquired new rolling stock for them.

Although freight traffic was hardly profitable, SNCF experienced a freight locomotive shortage and this,

Left: **The Thalys train, a French-built high-speed train used for international services inside western Europe.**

Below: **A Fiat tilting train in the "Cisalpino" service linking north Italy, Switzerland and south Germany.**

Right: **A French "Sybic" dual-voltage locomotive.**

combined with the high cost of operating old locomotives, led to the acquisition of a large class of new electric locomotives, the "Sybic" dual-voltage type with synchronous motors and capable of 125mph (200kph) when hauling passenger trains. However, existing classes of diesel locomotive were expected to soldier on, without replacement.

Italian Railways (FS) benefited from the pre-eminence of the Fiat company in tilting-train technology, and several series of tilting trains were acquired in the late 20th century, enabling quite fast trains to be operated before the new high-speed routes were ready. The latter, consisting of east-west (Turin-Milan-Venice) and north-south (Milan-Rome-Naples) lines, were expected progressively to come into service in the first decade of the new century. Restructuring of FS, following the general principles applied to other European Union railways, came relatively late with the appearance of *Trenitalia* in 2000. This, a subsidiary of the state railway, was an operating company divided into four divisions (long-distance passenger, regional services, freight and rolling stock). The matching infrastructure company appeared in 2001.

In Spain, the 1990s were a decade of railway development, with the opening of a high-speed railway on the one hand and considerable investment in the regional narrow-gauge lines on the other. Because high-speed routes were expected eventually to link up with the other European systems the Spanish gauge of 5ft 6in (1,676mm) was not used for them, standard gauge being chosen instead. The first high-speed (AVE) services operated in 1992 on the newly-built Madrid-Seville line and they secured a massive transfer of passengers from air and highway transport. At the end of the century, work was progressing on the

Madrid-Barcelona-French frontier route. Some early sections of this were built broad-gauge initially, so as to provide improved conventional services; the crossties allowed conversion to standard gauge later.

The AVE trains were built to the French TGV model. Meanwhile, on existing lines some accelerations were obtained by locally-built "Talgo" trains. Long a feature of the Spanish scene, "Talgo" trains were appearing in a tilting version that employed passive rather than active tilt (that is, the tilt was not powered, making it simpler but more moderate in its capabilities). "Talgo" trains capable of gauge-change had for some years been penetrating to Geneva and Paris, and a new generation of tilting "Talgo" trains appeared on international services.

Portugal, where the infrastructure was detached from Portuguese Railways (CP) in 1997, also saw the introduction of tilting trains. An example of the increasingly trans-national nature of the railway supply industry, these were of Fiat design, assembled in Portugal by Adtranz (which had taken over the Portuguese Sorefame company), and with electrical equipment by Siemens. The 10 six-car trains were put into service on Portugal's main line, Lisbon-Oporto.

Unlike Belgium, where restructuring was postponed, the Netherlands throughout the 1990s was engaged in a reappraisal of rail transport. The government launched a document titled *The Third Age of Rail*, which made clear that the intense services already offered by Netherlands Railways (NS) would be further developed, with regional services becoming the responsibility of regional governments. Track access charges, initially fixed at zero guilders per kilometer, were to be introduced so as to make easier the introduction of "Open Access" services; by 1999 22 train operators had been recognized. These included three of the new companies set up by NS (*NS Reizigers* for long-distance passenger trains, *NS Materieel* for construction trains and *NS Cargo* for freight). Among the new operators was Lovers Rail, which initially operated some passenger services in direct competition with NS but was then faced with obstructions placed by a government fearful that this new company would "cherry-pick" the most profitable services. Lovers Rail later concentrated on the Amsterdam-Haarlem route and among its several innovations were reduced-rate standing-only tickets, a bar in each vehicle and increased cycle stowage. Meanwhile, *NS Reizigers* was preparing to operate the new high-speed line being built from Schiphol Airport via Amsterdam to the Belgian frontier. On this high-speed line it was planned to operate fast inter-city double-deck trains. The "DD-IRM" class of double-deck trains already acquired in 1994 were the inspiration for these.

Swedish State Railways (SJ) had been among the earliest to be divested of their infrastructure. In 1988 the state National Railway Administration (BV) took over this function, and independent operators were given the right to tender for services formerly operated by SJ. After some years of trial and error, the situation at the end of the century was that SJ retained a monopoly of long-distance services, but other operators could compete for the supply of rail services to regional governments. Using the Swedish-designed "X2000" tilting trains, SJ improved services and increased its share of the business travel market. By 1999 there were 15 daily "X2000" services on the principal main line, Stockholm-Göteborg. However, in 2001, SJ was broken up into six operating companies.

Above: **A Belgian four-current locomotive for international services.**

Main picture: **The German Class 101 6,000kW locomotives were still being delivered at the start of the new century. They are suitable for both passenger and freight trains.**

Above left: **The German ICT tilting trains, delivered from 1998, have been used especially in mountainous southern Germany.**

The big event of 2000 was the opening of the fixed link between Sweden and Denmark, enabling trains to run via tunnel and viaduct between the two countries. Through services between Copenhagen, Stockholm and Oslo became possible without the use of the ferries , which had operated between Helsingør in Denmark and Hälsingborg in Sweden. Danish State Railways (DSB) became an operating company in 1997, when a separate infrastructure company was created.

Irish Railways (IE) remained a state corporation and in 1996, in conformity with European Union recommendation, its tracks were given "Open Access" status. European funds helped to improve the key Dublin-Belfast route. In the 1990s the locomotive fleet was renewed with Class 201 diesel locomotives supplied by GM.

In Switzerland, outside the European Union, EU trends were nevertheless noted and sometimes adopted. Thus infrastructure was separated from operations, and "Open Access" was introduced. The government supported further investment, especially in passenger services, and two big new projects for tunnels reflected the government's wish to carry heavy road vehicles by rail through the Alpine sections of their journey.

42
THE FORMER SOVIET BLOC

The dissolution of the USSR meant the division of Soviet Railways into 15 state railways. Simultaneously, the railways of the Soviet satellite states in Europe were untied from the Russian model. For the former German Democratic Republic, the obvious path of rejoining the German railway system was taken. Other countries faced the problem that, under communism, their railways had faced little competition and had been poorly financed; they had to face a new competitive world with their assets worn out and their personnel completely unaware of concepts such as user-friendliness. Each in its own different time

scale dealt with this problem, closing some under-used lines, and using western technology and western loans to begin the acquisition of modern traction and train-control technology.

The largest of these systems was Polish State Railways. This had an enormous mileage of little-used lines but under the new democracy their closure was resisted. Nevertheless, substantial reduction of unprofitable operations was achieved. In the late 1990s, restructuring into business groups leading to companies that could be privatized took shape. Much of the narrow-gauge mileage was being closed, and standard-gauge track was also to be further reduced. Meanwhile, tilting trains were ordered as a first step in making long-distance services look modern and attractive. At the other extreme, the earlier decision to maintain one locomotive depot (Wolsztyn) as a steam depot remained in force, largely in the hope of attracting western tourists. The purchase by Adtranz of a controlling share of the *Pafawag* locomotive works, and by Alstom of Poland's major rolling stock enterprise, promised eventual modernization of trains and locomotive stock.

The dissolution of the USSR meant the end of Soviet Railways, but a Railway Transport Council was set up to co-ordinate the work of the 15 state railways into which the

former system was divided. Some of the new independent railways in central Asia were very small, being simply the stub ends of what had once been main lines. What became known as Federal Russian Railways, however, was a very big undertaking, and Ukrainian Railways was also a substantial concern. Despite pressure from international banks, which at least on one occasion threatened to withdraw financial support from Russia if it failed to push Federal Russian Railways in a direction acceptable to the current western ideology of economic liberalization, the various components of the former Soviet railways held privatization at bay while restructuring their systems so as to make concepts of profit and loss more meaningful.

The creation of new states meant that former Soviet main lines were cut by new international frontiers. Many Moscow-Black Sea services were re-routed so as to evade time-consuming customs inspections on entering and exiting Ukrainian territory. Part of the Trans-Siberian Railway passed through the new republic of Kazakhstan, and, on one occasion, a track engineer, bringing components for track repair of the Kazakhstan sector, was arrested and charged with smuggling them.

All parts of former Soviet Railways suffered from under-investment, and as the years passed the proportion of time-worn equipment grew. Meanwhile, the economies faltered, but falling traffic helped the railways to cope despite their technical inadequacies. By 2000, the Federal Russian Railways, at least, were showing signs of a resurrection. Successive railway ministers had resisted fragmentation and preserved the system as a whole, and operations were being considerably improved by the introduction of electronic technologies. Laying of optical fibre cables along main lines, for example, enabled the railways to compete in the telecommunications market.

A private company was founded to build a Moscow-St Petersburg high-speed railway. The company obtained railway industrial plant and land at little cost and, although the construction of the line had not got under way, was capable of making a profit even without actually building the line. The train works which it owned was building the *Sokol* high-speed train, which was likely to be bought by the state railway, and its commuter trains were already in demand.

Below: **A scene on Russia's first preserved railway, the narrow-gauge Pereslavl Railway, north of Moscow.**

Main picture: **At Wolsztyn, in 21st century Poland, it is still possible to see steam traction regularly at work.**

Far left: **One of the newly-introduced Russian "Suburban Express" trains.**

Meanwhile the existing line between Moscow and St Petersburg was reconstructed so as to be capable of operating very fast trains. As a stop-gap, a new high-speed train, duplicating the single "ER200" train acquired in the 1970s, was built.

One of the problems of Russian passenger services was that so many passengers had a right to free or reduced-rate tickets, and some did not buy tickets at all. New supplementary fare trains were introduced, providing more comfort but not open to holders of concessionary tickets. Somewhat similar but shorter-distance were the "Suburban Express" multiple-unit trains. Sometimes called "Class Trains" because, unlike conventional Russian trains, they offered First, Second and Third class accommodation, they tended to cover trips of two to four hours out of major cities. They made a profit, despite their high complement of staff (which included three security guards). At city stations, automatic ticket-operated turnstiles were introduced, making possession of a ticket unavoidable if a train was to be boarded. Installation of these ticket barriers in Moscow immediately raised ticket sales by 50% or more.

By 2000, after years of discussion and foot-dragging, a restructuring of Federal Russian Railways was accepted by the government. It was not to be hurried and was likely to take more than a decade to achieve. Separation of infrastructure from operations was provided for. Separate passenger companies, some of which had already appeared, would be a step toward identifying passenger losses and ending the subsidization of unprofitable passenger trains by profitable freight services. The various companies that would be under the umbrella of the Federal Russian Railways holding company (a state corporation) would eventually be able to issue shares as a means of raising capital. "Open Access" already existed on a few limited services and was expected to expand. A crucial issue was who would own the general-use freight wagons, with the Railways Ministry insisting that it should be the owner, through the federal railways, thereby preserving the basics of an integrated countrywide system and not the fragmented structure seen in Britain and some other countries.

The 1990s also witnessed the beginnings of Russia's first steam tourist railway, a former narrow-gauge peat line near the historic town of Pereslavl. Russian conditions, in particular weaknesses in the legal framework of contract and property, together with the general economic situation, made the establishment of such lines very difficult.

43
THE AMERICAS

For US railroads, the 1990s were a period of merging and expansion. The most dramatic traffic increase was that of low-sulphur coal, especially from the Powder River Basin in Wyoming, but over the decade other forms of freight grew as well. With their traditional attention to Wall Street opinion, US railroads had been busily reducing their costs, so many of them were ill-prepared for traffic growth. There had to be a change of direction, with an increase of investment in improved track and new locomotives; in 1999 investment was almost double that of 1989. At the same time under-utilized track was closed or, frequently, sold to small local railroads that were better able to make profitable use of it.

Wall Street also favored railroad mergers, arguing that such amalgamations would make better use of existing assets and permit reductions in the labor force. In 1999 the Norfolk Southern Railroad, itself the result of an earlier merger, and CSX Transportation (again a company resulting from previous amalgamations) purchased Conrail, the NS acquiring mainly the part formerly belonging to the old Pennsylvania Railroad and CSX acquiring the bulk of former New York Central track. Despite careful preparation, neither NS nor CSX was able promptly to absorb the new traffic and new routings that these acquisitions brought, and many former clients of Conrail were disillusioned by the sudden, if temporary, decline of service standards.

But the Conrail debacle was a mere blip compared to the tangle that resulted from Union Pacific's acquisition of that other big western line, the Southern Pacific. Soon after this merger, there was such severe congestion that, for a long period, trains had to be cancelled, marshaling yards embargoed and traffic refused. Again, there was a drop in shipper confidence. The problem with this merger was that it had been born largely of a wish to reduce costs, and the disposal of assets and cuts in the workforce had been carried too far. Additionally, the imposition of the UP's working practices and attitudes on an SP workforce, which, until the merger, had its own ways of doing things, had a bad effect on morale.

The amalgamation of the Burlington Northern and the Santa Fe railroads into the Burlington Northern Santa Fe (BNSF) had gone much more smoothly. This merger, and the UP/SP merger, added to the previous mergers, meant

Left: **Virginia Railway Express is a locally funded commuter service operating from Washington DC.**

Above right: **One of many METRA commuter trains operated by the Chicago Regional Transportation Authority. This double-deck train is leaving the former Chicago & North Western terminal in Chicago.**

Right: **A "double-stack" transcontinental container train on former Santa Fe RR trackage in Arizona.**

Overleaf: **Amtrak "Genesis" locomotives await departure at New Orleans.**

Above: **Locomotives in their new company livery, soon after the formation of the BNSF Railroad.**

that the US transcontinental railroads had been reduced to two strong companies. However, the damage inflicted on shipper confidence by the Conrail and Southern Pacific dissolutions was probably a major factor in the federal government's non-approval of another big merger, between BNSF and Canadian National Railways.

CNR, formerly a Canadian government state corporation, was sold off in 1995, largely to US investors. It immediately began to act like the major railroad it was. It merged with Illinois Central, giving it a route down through the heart of the USA as far as the Gulf of Mexico. Its merger with BNSF would have created a really big railway (the suggested name was North American Railroad) and since — unlike other mergers — it was not between two railroads in the same region, there would have been few problems of redundancy of people and assets. Nevertheless, the federal government's Surface Transportation Board refused to approve this merger.

In both Canada and the USA, the main railroads continued to dispose of little-used lines to smaller companies. Some of those smaller companies like Wisconsin Central and Rail America — which took over a number of local lines — developed into prosperous companies that also operated railways outside North America. In Canada, the Canadian Pacific reorganized its lines east of Montreal into the St Lawrence & Hudson Railway which, one day, might stand alone. CPR also moved its headquarters from Montreal to Calgary, in line with its intention of concentrating on its profitable western lines. CNR shed most of its track in the Maritimes; the Cape Breton & Central Nova Scotia Railway, American-owned, took over CNR lines in Nova Scotia. Both CPR and CNR disposed of feeder lines on the prairies. In 2000, discussions were under way on the subject of pooling CPR and CNR track between Winnipeg and Toronto; both companies had single-track main lines through undeveloped terrain and there were advantages in sharing their use and thereby creating, in effect, one double-track route.

Both Canada and the USA developed dense-traffic commuter lines, subsidized by local governments and operated, sometimes, by the main-line railroads. Long-distance services continued to be provided by state-supported corporations, Amtrak in the USA and Via Rail in Canada. Both of these corporations were under sustained political pressure to cut their deficits or face dissolution, and Via Rail was forced to pare its services in the early 1990s. In 2001, however, it acquired a fleet of almost-new European rolling stock (vehicles built for intended night services through the Channel Tunnel, but never used), and a determined effort was being made to attract more passengers; but much would depend on politics.

Above: **An Amtrak express with Superliner double-deck carriages, pulled by a "Genesis" locomotive.**

Amtrak, though slowly reducing its deficit, was also under political pressure and was required to break even in 2002. This seemed an unrealisable goal unless it ended some of its longer-distance services outside the North East Corridor. Some of the medium-distance services attracted support from state governments; in the Pacific North-West, Amtrak imported "Talgo" tilting trains for regional services. Amtrak also added perishables, mail and express shipments to its traffic. Refrigerator and parcel vehicles, capable of passenger train speeds, were acquired and attached to its passenger trains. Early signs were that considerable traffic would be won from the highways by this service.

But Amtrak's main effort was devoted to a complete upgrading of services in the North East Corridor (Washington-New York-Boston) where it competed with the airlines for a large market. Its services here were already profitable, and Amtrak sought to develop this success by instituting what would be North America's first venture with true high-speed trains. Continuation of the existing electrification to Boston was undertaken, and a new fleet of tilting high-speed trains ordered from Bombardier, using Alstom technology. These 150mph (240kph) trains, providing the *Acela Express* service, would be supplemented by the *Acela Regional* trains. Appearance of these trains was delayed, but the first *Acela Regional* trains introduced in early 2000 seemed to promise an immediate one-third increase in traffic volume.

Other Amtrak innovations were to be a "Talgo Pendular" tilting train between Los Angeles and Las Vegas and more New York-Chicago services. There was an intention to run passenger trains from 2003 over the Florida East Coast Railroad, which had dropped such services following the prolonged strike of the 1960s. Chicago and Fort Worth were to be developed as hubs, with interconnecting trains radiating out from them.

Until 1993, Amtrak used passenger versions of standard US freight diesel locomotives, but, in that year, it put into service its "Genesis" design, built by GE. These, the first passenger locomotives built in America for several decades, were rated at 4,025hp, could run at 100mph (160kph) and were suited to indifferent track. They made extensive use of microprocessor control and fault-finding. Help with designing and building their lightweight frames came from Krupp in Germany.

A little later than in western Europe, US railroads began to use diesel locomotives with ac/dc transmissions. In 1993, GE was receiving bulk orders for its "AC4400" (4,400hp) design. CPR ordered over 200 of this type. The new transmission increased adhesion, so higher power outputs could be used without wheel slippage; one of these

Above: **In the new century, Amtrak aimed at carrying more time-sensitive and package freight, traditionally loaded in head-end cars.**

Right: **On the Illinois Central, "Main Line of Mid-America," which merged with Canadian National.**

units could replace two of the older conventional diesels. GM also produced ac/dc locomotives. Three were sent for trial on the Burlington Northern Railroad, which was greatly impressed by their ability to start heavy trains. The railroad promptly ordered 350 units of the "SD70MAC" production version. The invertor technology was acquired from Siemens in Germany but these units had a US-designed innovation in the form of "radial" trucks in which the axles moved to insinuate the wheels gently through curves, saving considerable energy and enabling six-axle trucks to negotiate track as comfortably as four-axle trucks. Later, the "SD70MAC" was developed into the more powerful (6,000hp) "SD90MAC."

In Latin America, the 1990s were a period of restructuring, but little improvement in services resulted, although the enhancement of Buenos Aires' commuter services was an exception. By the end of the century, all the major railways had been privatized, usually bringing a long-needed pruning of unprofitable services and unproductive labor. Typically, infrastructure remained under state control and operating rights were franchised out. Most passenger trains disappeared. There was little money for capital improvement, although some second-hand rolling stock was imported, notably from Spain. Mexican railroads, following the conclusion of the North American free trade agreement, were expected to flourish and US railroads (Kansas City Southern and Union Pacific) purchased part-ownership of two companies carved out of the former Mexican National Railways.

Above: **General Electric "Dash-9" locomotives, as supplied to the Burlington Northern RR in the late 1990s, haul a "double-stack" container train.**

Right: **Detail of the cab and front end of a "Dash 9-44CW" locomotive.**

44
AUSTRALASIA

Australian moves to railway restructuring were inspired by the success of privatization in New Zealand. There, high-cost and inefficient government railways were converted into a limited liability company in 1990. This was followed by a staff reduction from 21,000 to 5,000, and a 300% productivity gain. Thus slimmed, the system was sold to a consortium led by Wisconsin Central Railroad, which sought to gain traffic by offering improved services. The new company, named Tranz Rail, seemed to prosper, and second-hand locomotives were obtained from Australia, but by 2000 there were signs it had over-extended itself.

Australian railways had always been divided by state and gauge, but by the end of the century each of the mainland state capitals was connected to standard gauge track. In line with trends elsewhere, there was a restructuring, which differed from state to state but usually took the form of separating infrastructure from operations and permitting open access to the tracks by reputable companies. The railways owned by mining concerns remained outside these changes and continued as before in their single-traffic business. That part of the infrastructure that was standard-gauge and inter-state was managed by a new organization, Australian Rail Track Corporation (ARTC).

Some new lines were built — such as to Sydney Airport. The proposed high-speed line between Sydney and Canberra faced postponement, but the long-discussed and politically important 870-mile (1,400km) railway from Alice Springs to Darwin had good prospects of realization.

Australian National Railways, which had earlier taken over South Australian Railways, was privatized in 1997 and its freight operations were bought by Australia Southern Railroad, a consortium of US and Australian interests. Including three gauges, its main business was bulk haulage of grain and minerals. In New South Wales, the State Rail Authority (SRA), which had earlier taken over the New South Wales Government Railways, was restructured in 1996. Responsibility for its track was assumed by the Rail Access Corporation while FreightCorp, a state company, took over freight operations and Countrylink operated long-distance passenger services. The latter, like CityRail (which operated Sydney area short-distance passenger services), was part of

the SRA and received subsidies from the state government.

In Victoria V/Line Freight and V/Line Passenger became separate businesses in 1997, while Melbourne suburban services were divided into two companies and later auctioned off. V/Line Freight was sold to an Australian-US consortium and renamed Freight Victoria, while the passenger arm was acquired by a consortium that included the National Express coach company, which already operated rail franchises in Britain. Track in the state, apart from electrified routes, was transferred to Victorian Rail Track, a state corporation.

The former Western Australian Government Railways became known as Westrail and continued to operate passenger and freight services, but a separate track authority was provided. Among other things, this facilitated the principle of "Open Access." The freight sector was later sold to the owners of the Australian Southern Railway. The smallest of the state railways, on Tasmania, became Tasrail and was bought by a consortium that, again, included Wisconsin Central.

The former Queensland Government Railways, now Queensland Rail, operated Australia's biggest rail system and differed from other state railways in that it retained control of its infrastructure. "Open Access" took the form of inviting private companies into joint-venture enterprises. It was prosperous thanks largely to its long-distance mineral traffic. In the 1990s, it was trying to boost its passenger traffic by encouraging, among other things, tourism. On the 387-mile (622km) Brisbane-Rockhampton service, it provided a daily tilting train service, and its "Sunlander" train to Cairns (1,028 miles/1,654km) was noted for its comfort.

New rail transport companies operating under "Open Access" rules began to appear. Among them were National Rail, a freight carrier set up by the Commonwealth, Victoria and New South Wales governments and intended for privatization. There was also Great Southern Railway, which operates trains formerly managed by Australian National. These are the transcontinental "Indian Pacific," the "Ghan" to Alice Springs and the Adelaide-Melbourne "Overland."

Considerable investment in rolling stock accompanied the restructuring of Australia's railways, as new organizations pursued the ambition of gaining traffic through better services. Most of the new locomotives and trains, as before, were built by Australian builders under licence from outside companies. Thus, EMUs of Queensland Rail were supplied by the local Walkers company, using electrical gear supplied by ASEA and ABB (both later part of Adtranz). That railway's diesel orders in the 1990s were shared by the Australian Goninan, Clyde and Walker companies using US GE or GM technology. The pair of tilting trains were built by Walkers, using Japanese designs. National Railway's large, 120-unit Class NR 3,000kW diesels were built by Goninan using GE technology. FreightCorp's new diesels were GM types; these, Classes 82 and 90, were the subject of maintenance agreements with their supplier, Clyde Engineering (89 units supplied with, by contract, 84 always available).

45
AFRICA AND ASIA

The dire economic situation of most of Africa, combined with disorder and sometimes civil war in several states, meant that there was little railway development in the 1990s.

South African Railways remained the biggest system. In 1990, the state transport company *Transnet* was founded and the railways were entrusted to one of its divisions, *Spoornet*. With the withdrawal of most passenger services, *Spoornet* became primarily a state freight railway, with an attached main-line passenger division (it was expected that the operation of the luxury "Blue Train" would be handed to a private company). Commuter services, marketed as "Metro-Rail," were entrusted to another of *Transnet*'s divisions. In the 1990s, little investment was made in rolling stock, but planning for the De Aar-Kimberley electrification scheme continued. In nearby Zimbabwe, steam traction survived in the form of Beyer-Garratt locomotives used for yard work.

Nigerian Railways were worn-out and their traffic in steep decline. However, government funds were released in the later 1990s. Some track rehabilitation was achieved with Chinese help and new locomotives were acquired from Korea and China and second-hand ones from Newfoundland. A scheme to replace the 3ft 6in (1,065mm) gauge with standard gauge had been launched by the government in the 1960s and attracted some ridicule, since Nigeria had no links with other railways. In 2000, the proposal was revived and had a little more validity because a new line to link the steel industry with its port had since been built to standard gauge, for no apparent reason; critics saw this as one false step threatening to lead to another.

In the Far East, the economic downturn of the 1990s had its effect. A beginning had been made with the

Main Picture: **A current Series 700 Japanese *Shinkansen* train. Different nose contours have been tried in an attempt to reduce lineside noise at high speed.**

Above right: **The unorthodox contour of the Nankai Railway's trains to Japan's new Osaka Airport.**

privatization of Japanese National Railways (JNR) in 1987. This was a long and well thought-out process, owing little to political ideology but aimed at increasing efficiency, for the state's expenditure on subsidizing the railways was becoming unbearable. JNR was split into six passenger companies, one each for the smaller islands and three for the main island of Honshu. Thus, the network was divided on a territorial basis, there being little sympathy for the concept of competition between the main railways when air, highway, local railways and coastal shipping provided more than enough competition already. A sixth company was for freight, this operator paying the other companies for the use of their tracks. A separate organization looked after the repayment of what was left of the railways' debts and the high-speed *Shinkansen* network was entrusted to another entity, which leased the assets to the railways operating those services (later, the three Honshu railways took over this entity, but the leasing principle was continued).

Main picture: **Freight trains pass in northern China. Double-headed "QJ" type locomotives provide the traction.**

Above right: **South Korean DHC diesel trainsets receive attention at their maintenance depot.**

Below: **A low-profile Series E2 train used in the Tokyo-Nagano *Shinkansen* service.**

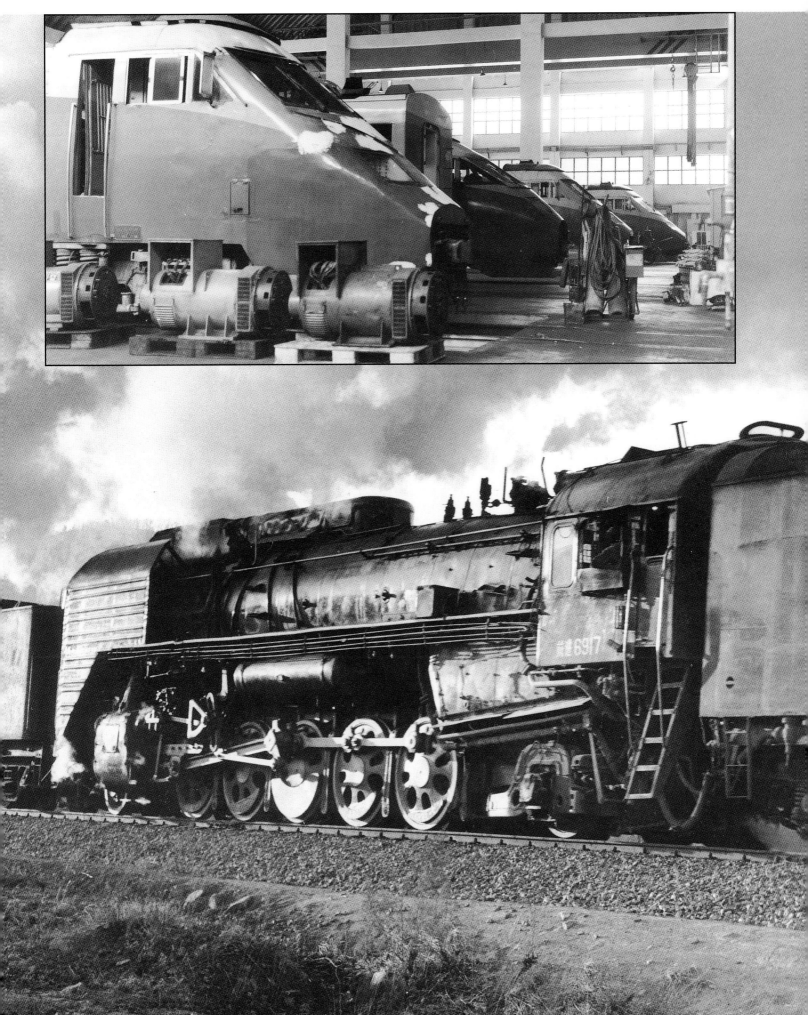

Above: **Modern Japanese architecture: the concourse of the new station at Kyoto.**

Main picture: **A Japanese tilting train, serving the mountainous line to Nagano, receives attention at Nagoya.**

The secondary local railways remained as they were but there gradually developed a "third sector" of railways, consisting mainly of low-traffic lines handed over by the main railways to local companies.

The new main-line companies were at first state-owned, but true privatization followed slowly when it became possible to buy their shares on the stock exchange. The advent of the new companies was followed by an intense effort to improve the railway image in Japan. There was a massive and apparently permanent clean-up of railway toilets, new smart trains were ordered, more women were employed, concerts were presented on station concourses and a few stations were rebuilt in striking architectural styles. Traffic increased notably, until the economic recession that struck Japan in 1991. After that, traffic tended to decline but a slow recovery followed. However, the intention of paying off long-term railway debt by the sale of railway land had to be abandoned for the time being. The Kobe earthquake caused further losses and 12 weeks of disruption to services. After it, *Shinkansen* lines were equipped with early-warning vibration detectors that could stop trains automatically at the first rumble of an earthquake.

New *Shinkansen* lines were opened. These were successful in increasing traffic but were less profitable than the first line. Complaints about the noise level of these trains from nearby residents increased, and part of the reason for the successive new designs of high-speed train was the need for a new streamlining form that would reduce noise and create less pressure disturbance when entering tunnels. The original "O" series trainsets were supplemented by the "100" series and the "300" series, with very different front ends, and in the late 1990s new forms of low-nose streamlining appeared on the "E-2," "700" and other series. Fairings were also introduced to block the noise of pantographs traveling at high speed. In 1996, JR Central Railway operated a test train at 275mph (443kph). In commercial service, JNR Central from 1992 was linking Tokyo and Osaka at an average speed, despite two intermediate stops, of 128mph (206kph). From 1997 JR West *Shinkansen* trains were scheduled at a maximum of 186mph (300kph) on the Osaka-Hakata line.

On the non-*Shinkansen* 3ft 6in (1,065mm) gauge lines, some smart trains were introduced, including the "787" series of the JR Kyushu Railway, noted for their luxurious interiors, and several classes of tilting train. All these reduced traveling time, making the railways stronger competitors of highway and air services.

At the end of the century, British railway managers were talking enviously of the "Japanese Method." This seemed to refer to the smooth and punctual operation of Japanese railways, where passenger train time-keeping was measured by the second rather than the minute. The faultless, fail-free, operation of Japanese railways was attributed partly to different attitudes but largely to the duplication of

any pieces of equipment that might conceivably develop faults. This smart, defect-free, operation was therefore attained at a price, but probably this was more than recouped by the advantages that come from predictability. A Japanese businessman having an appointment to keep did not have to travel on an early train to allow for possible delays; he could calmly await the train with the most convenient schedule, knowing that it would arrive punctually.

South Korea was another country hit by economic recession, one result of which was delay in completing the country's first high-speed railway, linking the two largest cities, Seoul and Pusan. Completion was not expected until 2004 and meanwhile the first prototype "Eurostar"-type trainset, supplied by Alstom, had little to do apart from figuring in publicity films. Meanwhile, fast-looking, but not especially fast, diesel trainsets of Class DHC with German mechanical transmission, handled the trains on the existing Seoul-Pusan line.

Almost all Korean National Railroad (KNR) revenue came from passengers. But the improvement of relations with North Korea and the subsequent reopening of the rail link between the two countries was expected to change that. Among other things, the concept of traffic from South Korea and Japan moving by rail through China and Russia to Europe came closer to realization.

An attempt was made to convert KNR into a company in 1996, but a strike by KNR staff and a realization that it

might be a costly process defeated this. Break-up of the state Indian Railways was also discussed in the 1990s, but was not adopted; the more-or-less self-contained railway regions were considered to offer adequate decentralization. India faced the problem of enormously expanding traffic and only limited capital resources for investment. This was a problem that would persist and many argued that the admission of private companies to the railway business might prove to be the best way forward. Meanwhile, modernization of the locomotive stock continued. Steam traction came to an end at the end of the century, while new designs of electric (Adtranz) and diesel (GM) locomotives were imported, followed by their construction in home workshops. To develop container traffic the railway-owned Container Corporation was established, running its scheduled "Contrac" trains over key routes.

Continuing economic development in China meant that the railways' capacity was badly strained, so double-tracking and electrification proceeded fast in the 1990s. The 9th Five Year Plan (1996-2000) prescribed in addition no less than 5,033 miles (8,100km) of new lines. Many of these were to provide access to coalfields, but some long lines were also being built in western China, which was virtually without railways. The once monolithic Chinese Railways was restructured in the 1990s. Autonomous regional railways were encouraged and non-trunk lines could be owned and operated by share companies.

Above: **Two "QJ" locomotives of Chinese Railways tackle a grade in Manchuria.**

Main picture: **A Chinese long-distance train makes an intermediate stop.**

Inset, top left: **By 2000 almost all Chinese long-distance non-electric passenger trains were hauled by home-built diesel locomotives.**

The target of ending Chinese steam traction in 2000 was not attained, and hundreds of 2-10-2 locomotives are still at work on freight trains, often double-headed. Nevertheless, the bulk of traffic is handled by diesel and electric locomotives. Technology-transfer deals have been made with western manufacturers, typically involving the import of a few technically-advanced units and their further manufacture in China. The Guangshen Railway, one of the first companies, borrowed a Swedish "X-2000" tilt-train for extensive trials in 1998, in the hope that high-speed services could be introduced on the Guangzhou-Kowloon line. The first true high-speed railway is being built between Beijing and Shanghai, and, by 2005, it is expected that all trunk routes will be capable of accepting speeds of 100mph (160kph), and some up to 124mph (200kph).

Thus, despite the different political and social circumstances in Asia, many of the trends paralleled those of western countries: restructuring of national railroads to give scope for smaller companies or operators, a realization that railway transport had a future that was worth developing, the need to keep separate accounts for train operations and provision of tracks. On the technical front, apart from the continuing development of container traffic, there was the introduction of advanced transmissions for both electric and diesel locomotives, the quest for purpose-built high-speed lines and the construction of tilting trains to obtain fast schedules on existing tracks. There may have been local differences, but rail transport followed a global pattern.

253

INDEX

Adtranz 213
Advanced Passenger Train (APT) 287
Alfred County Railway 199
Alstom 213
American Car & Foundry 89
American Civil War 11, 28
American Locomotive Company
  (Alco) 33, 121, 132, 144, 147,
  149, 151
American President Lines 194
Amtrak 143, 154, 157, 174, 177, 180,
  182, 189, 190, 212, 213, 234,
  238 - 240
Andersen, Hans Christian 206
Anglia Railways 218
Ann Arbour Railroad 196
Armstrong-Whitworth 134
Australian National Railways 87, 243
Australian Rail Track Corporation
  (ARTC) 243
Austrian Railways 128

Baldwin Locomotive Works 9, 31, 43,
  65, 67, 75, 77, 121, 144
Baldwin, Matthias 32, 33
Baltimore & Ohio Railroad 13, 14, 16,
  19, 23, 27, 78, 88, 113, 143, 206
Barsi Light Railway 64
Bear River Bridge 41
Beardmore 134
Beeching, Dr Richard 143
Belpaire, Alfred 32, 33
Benguela Railway 146
Birmingham & Gloucester Railway 22
Birmingham International Airport 212
Black Mesa & Lake Powell Railroad
  154
Blenkinsop, John 8
Bluebell Railway 202, 203
Boer War 82, 87
Bolivian State Railway 123
Boston & Maine Railroad 107
Brassey, Thomas 47
Brighton & South Coast Railway 19
Brighton Viaduct 115
British Airways 221
British Columbia Railway 203

British Expeditionary Force 83
British Rail 70, 72, 99, 143, 152, 156,
  173, 182, 184, 186, 187, 195,
  199, 200, 214, 218, 220
British Transport Commission 206
Brunel, Isambard Kingdom 13, 14, 16,
  20, 21
Buchanan, William 59
Budd Company 88, 97, 184
Buddicom, William 23
Buenos Aires Great Southern Railway
  123
Bugatti 135
Bull Run 29
Bullied, Oliver 106, 107
Burlington Railroads 55, 88, 91, 97,
  142, 143, 178, 180, 192, 234,
  240
Bury, Edward 22, 120

Caledonian Railway 18, 48, 59, 86
Calthrop, E 64
Cambrian Railways 199
Camden & Amboy Railroad 49
Canadian Government Railways 87
Canadian National Railways 87, 91,
  96 – 98, 115, 134, 161, 168, 185,
  194, 200, 238, 240
Canadian Northern 87
Canadian Pacific 36, 51, 63, 71, 75, 87,
  96 - 98, 99, 113, 117, 120, 142,
  184, 185, 192, 200, 238, 239
Canterbury and Whitstable Railway 10
Cass railroad 206
Central Pacific 36
Central South African Railways 87
Channel Tunnel 215, 218, 219, 221,
  238
Chapelon, Andre 107, 110, 115, 158
Chesapeake & Ohio Railroad 88, 117,
  143, 158
Chicago & North Western Railroad
  52, 58, 91
Chicago, Burlington & Quincy
  Railroad 62
Chichibu Railway 198
Chiltern Railways 217
Chinese Eastern Railway 63
Chinese Railways 251, 253
Chittaranjan Locomotive Works 160
Churchill, Winston 82
Churchward, George Jackson 120, 121
Cincinnati Union Terminal 87
Clyde Engineering 151
Colorado Central Railroad 67
Commonwealth Railways 87, 97
Connex South Central 218
Consolidated Rail Corporation
  (Conrail) 141, 143, 234, 238
Cooper, Peter 13
Cornish Riviera Limited 59
Cotton Belt Railroad 99
Crampton, Thomas 23

Daft, Leo 78
Danish State Railways (DSB) 229
Datong Works 158
Davis, Phineas 14
De Witt Clinton 1831 9, 17
Deceauville Portable Light Railway
  67, 68, 82
Delaware & Hudson Canal Company 9
Delaware & Hudson Railroad 117
Denver & Rio Grande Western
  Railroad 62, 67, 178
Derwent Valley Railroad 196
Deutsche Reichsbahn (DR) 86, 110,
  162, 200, 222
Diesel, Dr Rudolph 130
Du Bousquet 74, 77
Dunkirk 136

Easingwold Railway 196
Edward VII, King 57
Electro Motive Corporation 131, 134
Empire State Express 59
Ericsson, John 11
Erie Railroad 20, 77
Erie-Lakawanna Railroad 180
European Union 212, 226, 229
Eurostar 215, 221, 222, 225
Eurotunnel 221

Fairbanks Morse 144
Fairlie, Robert 30, 32, 33, 64
Feather River Valley 41
Federal Prussian Railways 231
Federal Russian Railways 233
Ffestiniog Railway, Wales 32, 33, 64, 203
Fiat 213, 222, 226
First Great Western (FGW) 186, 215
First North Western 217
Florida East Coast Railroad 142, 239
Flying Hamburger 93, 135
Flying Scotsman 26, 104
Forney tank 72
Forth Bridge 39
Fowler, Sir Henry 105, 107
Franco-Costi locomotive 117, 118
Franco-Prussian War 1870 – 71 29, 82
French National Railways (also
  Societe Nationale des
  Chemins de Francais – SNCF)
  86, 91, 154, 155, 168, 186, 219,
  222, 225
French Western Railway 116
Frichs 135
Frisco Railroad 180

Galena & Chicago Union Railroad 16
Gare du Nord, Paris 37, 166
Garrat Locomotives 71, 77, 116, 160,
  162, 166
Garratt, Herbert 77
Gatwick Express 215
Gauge Act 1846 21
Gauge Commission 42

General Electric Company 78, 129, 131, 132, 144, 146, 151, 152, 213, 239

General Motors 89, 134, 135, 144 – 147, 151, 152, 157, 213, 217, 219, 240, 251

George, Lloyd 47

German State Railway 115

Golden Arrow 97

Golsdorf, Karl 120

Gooch, Daniel 23

Goss, Professor 121

Gould, Jay 47

Grand Canyon Railroad 205, 206

Grand Central Terminal 78

Grand Junction Railway 16

Grand Trunk Railway 17, 41, 48, 62, 87, 91

Grand Trunk Western Railroad 103, 179

Granger Movement 37

Great Eastern Railway 19, 86

Great North Eastern (GNER) 215, 217

Great Northern Railroad 55, 62, 129, 143

Great Northern Railway 18, 46, 86

Great Southern Railway 243

Great Western Railway 16, 19, 20, 21, 23, 42, 43, 59, 60, 70, 75, 86, 89, 96, 100, 104, 106, 109, 120, 131, 137, 219

Green Arrows 104

Green Mountain Railroad 196

Gresley, Sir Nigel 93, 104, 105

Gulf Mobile & Ohio Railroad 145

Hackworth, Timothy 9, 11

Harrison, Joseph 22

Hartford & Connecticut Western Railroad 31

Hedley, William 8

Heilmann Locomotive 116

Highland Railway 84

Hill, James 62

Hitler, Adolph 139

Hotham Valley Railway 206

Hudson, George 46

Huskisson, William 12, 48

Illinois Central Railroad 42, 238, 240

Imperial Military Railways 87

Indian Peninsula Railway 126

Indian Railways 89, 147, 159

Intercity 185, 214

Intercolonial Railways 87

International Sleeping Car Company 26

Interstate Commerce Commission 86

Irish Mail 59

Italian Railways (FS) 226

Jackson, Stonewall 29

Japanese National Railways (JNR) 143, 246

Jervis, John 22

Kansas Pacific Railroad 47

Keleti Terminus, Budapest 38

Kentucky Fried Chicken 203

Kings Cross Station, London 94

Kirtley, Matthew 32, 33

Kitson-Still 117

Korean National Railroad 250, 251

Kylchap Exhaust 115

Kyushu Railway 202, 250

Lackawanna Railroad 71

Ladbroke Grove 220

Lake Superior 62

Lakeshore & Michigan Southern Railroad 27,

Lakeside Railway 206

Lancashire & Yorkshire Railway 78

Lapland Railway 124

Lenin 132

Lima Locomotive Works 77, 100, 144

Lincoln, President 19

Lipets, Alphonse 132

List, Frederick 18

Liverpool & Manchester Railway 11, 12, 14, 26, 28

Ljungstrom Turbine 116

LMSR Coronation Scot 93, 94

Lomonosov, Georgii 132

London & Continental Railways 221

London & North Eastern Railway 87, 91, 94, 96, 104, 108, 119, 128, 155

London & North Western Railway 18, 19, 26, 32, 50, 72, 86, 105

London & South Western Railway 16, 19, 58, 60, 61, 79

London Midland & Scottish Railway 86, 94, 101, 104, 105, 108, 110, 116, 128, 146

Long Island Railroad 196

Lord, President 20

Louisville & Nashville Railroad 143, 200

Ludwig, King of Bavaria 18

Mallard 88, 104, 105

Mallet locomotives 75, 77, 100, 101, 103, 105, 116, 118, 200, 206

Mallet, Anatole 75

Mann, William 26

Mason, William 30

Mendip Rail 219

Mexican National Railways 240

Michelin 88

Middleton Colliery Railway 8

Midland Railway 19, 25, 32, 41, 46, 72, 75, 79, 86, 212

Milwaukee & Mississippi Railroad 16, 62

Milwaukee Railroad 78, 96, 129, 143

Modernisation Plan 1955 152

Mohawk and Hudson Railroad 9, 17

Montreal Locomotive 147

Munich Crisis 136

Muskingum Electric Railroad 154

Nagelmackers 25, 26

Nankai Railway 244

National Express 212, 215, 243

National Railway Museum, York 206

National Transcontinental Railway 62

Nene Valley Railway 204

Netherlands Railways (also Nederlande Spoorwegen) 87, 225, 227

New Haven Railroad 31, 78, 132, 143, 154

New South Wales Government Railways 32, 60, 91, 97, 122, 243

New York & Erie Railroad 17

New York Central Railroad 19, 27, 58, 98, 132, 143, 151, 184, 194, 234

Nickel Plate Railroad 47

Nigerian Railways 244

Nord Express 97

Norfolk & Western Railroad 78, 103, 105, 117, 119, 129, 147, 159, 200

Norfolk Southern Railroad 143, 200, 234

Norris Brothers 8

Norris, William 18

North British Railways 86

North Eastern Railway 78, 79, 86

North Pacific Coast Railroad 37

Northern Pacific Railroad 55, 62, 143

Oerlikon 124

Oigawa Railway 197

Orange & Alexandria Railroad 29

Orient Express 97, 186

Panama Canal 62

Paris-Orleans Railway 79, 126

Passenger Transport Authorities 214

Peacock, Beyer 77

Pennsylvania Railroad 19, 32, 58, 70, 79, 116, 118 – 120, 126, 128, 129, 143, 154, 179, 200, 234

Philadelphia & Reading Railroad 22, 74

Philadelphia, Reading & New England Railroad 61

Pioneer 1836 9, 16

Polish State Railways 166, 230

Porta, L. 158

Portuguese Railways (CP) 227

Powder River Basin 234

Providence & Worcester Railroad 197

Prussian State Railways 74, 79, 86, 132

Puffing Billy 9, 202

Pullman trains 25, 52, 54, 60, 88, 96, 97, 178, 185

Pullman, George 24 - 26

Queensland Rail 243

Rail Access Corporation 243
Rail Diesel Car (RDC) 180
Rail Express Systems 215
Railfreight Distribution 219
Railroad Construction Corps 29
Railtrack 215, 217 – 220
Railway Clearing House 27
Railway Executive Committee 84
Railway Operating Division 83
Railways Act 1921 86
Ramsay-Macleod Turbine 116
Ramsbottom, John 30, 32
Reid-Ramsay Locomotives 116
Rhodes, Cecil 63
Rhodesian Railways 162
Ribblehead Viaduct, Yorkshire 41
Riga Terminal, Moscow 38
Rio Grande Southern Railroad 67
Rock Island Railroad 143
Rocket, The 11, 22, 48
Ross, John 17
Royal Mail 194
Russo-Japanese War 1904 82
Rutland Railroad 196

Santa Fe Railroad 145, 205, 234
Schipol Airport 227
Schlieffen Plan 82, 83
Schmidt, Wilhelm 74
Scotrail TOC 215
Seaboard Coast Line 143
Severn Tunnel 39
Severn Valley Railway 201, 203
Shay, Ephraim 77
Siemens 213, 218, 222, 227, 240
Silver Jubilee 93
Silver Purchase Act 1893 67
Silverlink 215, 217
Silverton Railroad 204
SNCF see French National Railways
Snowdon Mountain Railway 199
South African Railways 38, 97, 119,
        158, 190, 244
South Australian Railways 243
South Carolina Canal & Railroad Co
        16, 20
South Manchuria Railway 63
Southern Electric 128
Southern Pacific Railroad 19, 52, 101,
        113, 194, 206, 234
Southern Railway 86, 87, 93, 106, 115,
        127
Soviet Railways 117, 118, 123, 155,
        158, 230
Spanish National Railways 151
Sprague, Frank 78
St Hilaire, Quebec 48
Staggers Rail Act 143, 196
Stanier, William 101, 105, 106
State Rail Authority (SRA) 243
Stephenson Patentee 22, 23

Stephenson, George 8 – 11, 20, 22, 120
Stephenson, Robert 9, 16, 23
Stevens, John 9
Stockton & Darlington Railway 8, 12, 26
Stourbridge Lion 9
Strasburg Railroad 204, 205, 206
Suez Canal 36
Surface Transportation Board 238
Swedish State Railways 143, 227

Taff Vale Railway 26
Talgo Train 99, 174, 186, 190, 227, 239
Talyllyn Railway 203
Tangsham Works 158
Tay Bridge 48
Texas & Pacific Railroad 88, 200
Thompson, Edward 105
Thornton, Henry 87
Trail Operating Companies (TOC)
        215, 219
Train a Grande Vitesse (TGV) 187,
        189, 190, 222, 225, 227
Trans-Australian Railway 36, 44, 63,
        130
Trans-Europe Express (TEE) 186
Trans-Iran Railway 138
Transportation Act 1920 86
Trans-Siberian Railway 36, 60, 62, 63,
        82, 231
Trevithick, Richard 8

Ukrainian Railways 231
Union Pacific Railroad 19, 36, 47, 52,
        77, 88, 89, 91, 94, 100, 113, 117,
        145, 151, 193, 200, 211, 234
US Military Railroads
        Administrations 28
US Post Office 180
US Railroad Administration (USRA)
        85, 86
US Transportation Corps 85, 139

Valley Railroad 206
Van der Poele 78
Vanderbilt 47
Vauclain compound 74
Vermont Central Railroad 196
Via Rail 174, 184, 185, 238
Victoria Falls Bridge 63
Victoria Terminus, Bombay 34
Victoria, Queen 54, 57
Victorian Railways 60, 97, 243
Virgin Rail 213, 215, 217 - 219
Virginian Railway 77, 234
Vivaris Railway 202, 206
Volk's Railway 78
Von Siemens, Dr Ernst Werner 78

Wall Street 234
Wardale, P. 158
Welshpool & Llanfair Railway 65, 68
Western Pacific Railroad 178
Westinghouse Corporation 78, 129

Westinghouse, George 50
Westrail 243
Whistler, Col 20
Wilson, William 13
Winans, Ross 23
Windsplitter 88
Wisconsin Central Railroad 212, 219,
        238, 243
Woodward, William 100
World War I 41, 52, 59, 70, 78, 82, 83,
        86, 89, 96, 104, 122, 129 – 132,
        139
World War II 68, 72, 88, 89, 91, 110,
        117, 118, 121, 122, 125, 129,
        136, 139, 142, 166, 182, 220

Acknowledgments

The majority of the photographs in this book were taken or provided by the Author.
The Publisher wishes to thank the following for kindly supplying additional photographs:

© Joe McDonald/CORBIS: front cover

Chris Ellis: pages 6-7, 8, 9 (both), 10 (top), 11 (bottom), 12, 13 (all), 16, 17 (top), 18, 19, 22 (above and below left), 23 (all), 24, 25, 26 (both), 30, 30-31, 36, 37 (top), 39 (top), 40 (inset top and bottom), 41 (top), 48, 51 (right), 52 (center and bottom), 54 (all), 55 (bottom), 57 (bottom), 58 (left), 59 (right), 60 (both), 61 (top), 62, 63 (both), 70 (top), 71 (bottom), 80-81, 82, 83 (both), 84 (top and center), 85 (right), 90-91, 91 (top), 93 (below), 94 (top and bottom), 97, 98 (top), 101 (top), 102 (top), 106-107, 110-111, 118 (top), 130 (top and bottom), 130-131, 145 (bottom), 146-147 (all), 150 (top), 151 (top), 186, 210-211, 218, 219, 238, 239, 242.

Bison Picture Library: page 138 (both).

US National Archives: pages 28 and 29.